"*Awakening to Justice* is an account of a̲_____ holistic, complex, and sustained over time. It includes prominent and marginalized voices, celebrates progress and laments failure, and portrays a prolonged and countercultural struggle with the evil of human slavery. Because the narratives are honest, they are also hopeful. In moving deeply and truthfully into a past we are often tempted to avoid, the members of the dialogue model what it might mean to faithfully remember a past that is too much with us."

Ken Carter, bishop of the Western North Carolina Conference of the United Methodist Church

"*Awakening to Justice* offers profound insights and issues a compelling call to the church, urging active participation in the work of racial justice. This invitation encompasses the entirety of humanity, transcending White and Black perspectives, making it a relevant message for every church community. Together, your congregation will embark on a journey of meaningful engagement with all individuals, fostering unity and a love for neighbors that will radiate Christ's transformative power in our world today."

David Chang, lead pastor of Open Door Presbyterian Church

"Sometimes, God speaks to contemporary troubles with an answer given long ago. In an age when too many are afraid to tell the whole story of our history, this book invites the reader to understand that none of our contemporary issues of race are new. Indeed, in the example of Ingraham and his interracial circle, we can find a Christian model for moving forward toward racial justice and integrated congregational worship in our own time. Although Ingraham and his friends failed in their attempts to create an enduring community of racial equity, their efforts, their vision, and even their mistakes can be instructive to us. From one age of tragic polarization in the nineteenth century, Ingraham's story is one answer to our own partisan divisions today. This is a much-needed story of vision, of community, and of hope, and as usual, God has given it to us right on time!"

Valerie Cooper, associate professor of religion and society and Black Church studies, Duke Divinity School

"Every once in a while—if we are lucky—we come face-to-face with history. These encounters with the past anchor us, pushing us to re-imagine our present and re-vision our future. This volume is just such an encounter—vividly taking us to a long ago past that has, perhaps without us even knowing, set the course for our present, raising knotty and uncomfortable questions along the way. We come away enlightened, encouraged, and emboldened. And our faith is challenged as we are pushed to wrestle with the evergreen questions of how to live and do and be justice."

Bishop Leah D. Daughtry, The House of the Lord Churches

"In chronicling the discursive and relational space that nineteenth-century revivalist abolitionists provided for reckonings with race, contributors to this timely volume sternly but subtly suggest pathways to gospel-mandated advocacy and reconciliation to the contemporary Christian ecclesia."

Dennis C. Dickerson, Reverend James Lawson Chair in History at Vanderbilt University and retired general officer and historiographer for the African Methodist Episcopal Church

"Combating racism and strengthening the beloved community are urgent tasks for all Christians, especially those of us in the United States. The authors of *Awakening to Justice* have rendered us a great service by revisiting and analyzing key voices from our past. Working with the newly discovered journal of abolitionist David Ingraham and accounts written by his African American colleagues James Bradley and Nancy Prince, these scholars have provided us with a helpful resource for addressing issues of race and faith in our time. It is well worth reading."

Scott J. Jones, bishop in the Global Methodist Church

"The concept and praxis of abolition is all the rage in Black studies. Here a multiracial group of Christian scholars suggests this term of Black critical thought enacts a faithful form of Christianity among these mid-nineteenth-century, interracial disciples, aptly named revivalist abolitionists. Offering no easy or straightforward recovery of this moment of interruption, these scholars carefully articulate the promise of a critical history of antislavery social life as Christian practice—in anticipation of a world of racialization undone."

Marlon Millner, director of the Center for Black Studies at Northern Illinois University

"Brace yourself for discovery and prophetic hope! For those who think the fight for racial justice is a new one or those whose energy is flagging in the face of systemic racism, you will find solidarity in these courageous voices from the past. With surprising clarity, the witnesses in *Awakening to Justice* give us a through line to join the struggle for this holy work yet unrealized."

Amy Oden, church historian and seminary professor

"*Awakening to Justice* is a powerful, collaborative effort from a diverse group of scholars who call God's people to honestly learn from the past so we can address our complex, systemic inequities today. I highly recommend this book that gives hope to all people who want to build a future of racial justice together."

Brenda Salter McNeil, author of *Becoming Brave: Finding the Courage to Pursue Racial Justice Now and Roadmap to Reconciliation 2.0: Moving Communities into Unity, Wholeness and Justice*

"In the tumultuous present of race in America, these distinguished scholars provide a welcome window on the past stories of known and little-known abolitionists. These riveting accounts showing the deep connection of Christian faith and racial justice are sure to find a wide audience."

Ronald C. White, author of *A. Lincoln: A Biography* and *American Ulysses: A Life of Ulysses S. Grant*

THE DIALOGUE ON RACE
AND FAITH PROJECT

AWAKENING TO JUSTICE

FAITHFUL VOICES FROM
THE ABOLITIONIST PAST

Jemar Tisby
Douglas M. Strong
Christopher P. Momany
Sègbégnon Mathieu Gnonhossou
David D. Daniels III
R. Matthew Sigler
Diane Leclerc
Esther Chung-Kim
Albert G. Miller
Estrelda Y. Alexander

iVp
Academic
An imprint of InterVarsity Press
Downers Grove, Illinois

InterVarsity Press
P.O. Box 1400 | Downers Grove, IL 60515-1426
ivpress.com | email@ivpress.com

InterVarsity Press® is the publishing division of InterVarsity Christian Fellowship/USA®. For more information, visit intervarsity.org.

Scripture quotations, unless otherwise noted, are from the New Revised Standard Version Bible, copyright © 1989 National Council of the Churches of Christ in the United States of America. Used by permission. All rights reserved worldwide.

The publisher cannot verify the accuracy or functionality of website URLs used in this book beyond the date of publication.

Cover design: Cindy Kiple
Interior design: Daniel van Loon

Old photo of people: Oberlin class of 1855, Public Domain, available from Oberlin College archives here:
https://npgallery.nps.gov/AssetDetail/63fde8a0-786f-4d83-9252-ce3d35a76f6f

ISBN 978-1-5140-0918-5 (print) | ISBN 978-1-5140-0919-2 (digital)

Printed in the United States of America ♾

Library of Congress Cataloging-in-Publication Data
A catalog record for this book is available from the Library of Congress.

31   30   29   28   27   26   25   24 | 13   12   11   10   9   8   7   6   5   4   3   2   1

CONTENTS

ACKNOWLEDGMENTS

THE AUTHORS OF THIS BOOK are all team members of the Dialogue on Race and Faith, a project graciously funded by the M. J. Murdock Charitable Trust, the Maclellan Foundation, the Pinetops Foundation, Seattle Pacific University, and a number of generous individual donors. In addition to the authors, other Dialogue on Race and Faith team members include Tiona Cage, Joy Moore, Stephen Newby, and Stephen Rankin. The editors would like to extend particular appreciation to Jon Bentall, Laurie Collins, John Harrell, Noelle Keller, Heather McDaniel, Steve Moore, and Erin Morrow, without whom the completion of this book would not have been possible, and to Adrian College for their permission to use the David Ingraham journal.

Prologue

Jemar Tisby

"Is Christianity the White man's religion?"

As a Black man and a new Christian in predominantly White, evangelical spaces, I asked that question in different ways, as do many Christians of color in America. Is this space for me? Can I be my fully embodied self and still be accepted here? Will I ever find a place where I can be both Black *and* Christian at the same time?

The exact phrasing may vary a little from person to person, but the query, the doubt, the wondering is always there.

The pessimism many people hold toward Christianity when it comes to race is well-earned. I wrote an entire book, *The Color of Compromise*, about how throughout US history White Christians more often compromised with racism than confronted it. The system of perpetual enslavement of people of African descent and their status as property was undergirded by proslavery theologians who used the Bible as the basis for subjugating their fellow human beings who were created in the image of God. Prosegregation preachers likewise looked to Scripture to sustain racial inequality and injustice. Even today some Christians use the symbols of Christianity to promote withholding civil rights and diminishing democracy for people of color.[1]

This question—"Is Christianity the White man's religion?"—haunts us. It causes Christians to wonder whether there is any hope or possibility that the faith we adhere to can overcome the racism that has been threaded

---

[1]Jemar Tisby, *The Color of Compromise: The Truth About the American Church's Complicity in Racism* (Grand Rapids, MI: Zondervan, 2019).

throughout our history and institutions. For people who are not Christians, the question by itself might lead to turning away from a faith whose adherents have been responsible for so much racial injustice.

But the story of Christianity is not solely one of racism and White supremacy. It is not completely a tale of compromise and complicity with slavery, Jim Crow, and the denial of basic human rights.

There is another witness from our history—a Christian witness to racial justice, a prophetic past.

This book emerges from reflections on the journal entries of a nineteenth-century Christian abolitionist. Such individuals were all too rare in the days of race-based chattel slavery, but this man was of an even rarer sort. He was White.

David Ingraham's journal extends from 1839 to 1841 and details his efforts as a Christian missionary in Jamaica and his travels throughout the Northern United States. From his accounts as well as those of his contemporaries, we see that he treated the Black people he encountered and served with dignity and fairness. He believed, because of the God in whom he professed faith, that all people should be free and that slavery was a sin that should be immediately eradicated.

The book you're holding also incorporates the reflections of his colleagues James Bradley and Nancy Prince, each of whom was Black and worked with Ingraham for a time. Their work offers the perspective of the oppressed and demonstrates that interracial abolitionism not only was possible but is also a historical fact.

The struggle for racial justice continues to this day. We are confronted by racial profiling that too frequently leads to the brutalization and even the murder of unarmed Black people by police officers. We saw a White supremacist slaughter nine Black Christians at Emanuel AME Church as they concluded a Bible study meeting. We see a mounting spate of violent attacks on people of Asian descent simply because a pandemic reignited long-standing prejudices. Certain kinds of immigrants—those from poorer nations and whose skin is Black or Brown—get vilified by a political faction that insists that they must be kept out of the United States with literal walls.

What will the witness of the Christian church be in this time of racial upheaval? In this next iteration of the civil rights movement, will Christians demonstrate compromise in the face of racial injustice, or courage?

The longer I engage in the work of racial justice advocacy, the more persuaded I become that many answers to the most pressing problems of the present can be found by studying the past. What would it take to form modern-day benevolent societies dedicated to eradicating racial injustice? How can we engage in truly equitable interracial cooperation without replicating the power imbalances of the broader society? What distinct message does Christianity offer in this racial context?

As has been true throughout US history, the most visible racial divide cuts through the relations between Black and White Americans, but analyzing that rift informs the efforts of people of all races and ethnicities. Addressing questions about the contours of the current racial justice movement is work that also belongs to all people of faith. Congregations, study groups, college and seminary students, and individual Christians can all draw from stories of faithfulness, like those you will encounter in this book, to help shape their approach to contemporary justice issues. We do not have to labor for change as though we were the first to do so. We can pursue social action in the present even as we stay in conversation with those who did similar work in the past.

From Ingraham, Bradley, and Prince, we learn that racial justice is never a popular practice. We can glean lessons in resilience and perseverance from their example. We can also discover how they imperfectly pursued righteous ends. Sometimes people compromise their values, reveal their blind spots, and fail those whom they profess to serve. These figures teach us that the road toward justice is full of rocks and uneven ground and can often be shrouded in darkness to make us stumble in our walk.

But history can offer us hope. Even as the historical record proves the dismal pattern of racism among so many Christians, it also reveals that some resisted the status quo. It shows that there were people of faith who understood religion in an alternative way, viewing what they believed as a source of liberation rather than oppression. It is because of their work, their faith, and their hope that much progress in society has been made.

We are heirs to that hope as well if we allow ourselves to be. If an interracial group of Christians gathered almost two hundred years ago in opposition to their nation's most heinous atrocities and in promotion of the dignity of all people, then the same can be true now. That's especially true given that we are living in a renaissance of popular interest in the academic study of

history, calling many voices back to the surface of our conversations or ele-
vating forgotten ones for the first time. Public-facing explorations of history,
including the 1619 Project journalistic endeavor, bestselling books such as
Jesus and John Wayne, and documentaries such as *13th*, whether or not we
agree with their conclusions, have reminded the broader populace of the
tremendous force that the past exerts on the present. The these and other influences have come to the fore at the same time that conversations about racism
have been roaring once again to the forefront of the national dialogue. The
Black Lives Matter movement (especially in the historic uprisings in 2020), a
turbulent political climate, and the rise of White Christian nationalism have
all compelled the nation and the church to reassess our racial landscape.[2]

Figure P.1. Dialogue on Race and Faith team discussing Christian racial justice advocacy,
December 2022

The time is ripe for change. But we dare not go forth without a foundation.
History provides the historical base for the present-day work of justice. It
cautions us, tempers us, and inspires us. We can learn from people like Ingraham how to put faith into action, and what may await us in the endeavor.

This book is a work by scholars who are Christians. As academics, they
bring a fine-grained knowledge of their fields of study to their analyses of

---

[2]The 1619 Project, www.nytimes.com/interactive/2019/08/14/magazine/1619-america-slavery.html;
Kristin Kobes Du Mez, *Jesus and John Wayne: How White Evangelicals Corrupted a Faith and
Fractured a Nation* (New York: Liveright, 2020); *13th*, directed by Ava DuVernay (Los Gatos, CA:
Netflix, 2016).

Ingraham's journal and the nineteenth-century antebellum context in which it was written. As Christians, they understand their faith as leading to the expansion of the free exercise of rights and toward respect for all people as equal in dignity and significance. What drew me to participate in the project was the embodied nature of the experience. As scholars from various backgrounds gathered to analyze, discuss, debate, and synthesize these historical events, we found ourselves benefiting from the type of community and cooperation that the historical actors in our study tried to create.

I am certain that even if one is not fully convinced or inspired by the presentation of the past in this book, then observing the way that we as scholars, practitioners, and Christ followers interacted with each other in pursuit of the truth and a more just world will function as a real-time demonstration of the good news of Jesus.

Christians across the nation and the world can mobilize for the good work of honoring the image and likeness of God in their neighbors. In the twenty-first century, we who call on the name of Christ can be witnesses for racial justice in our day if we learn from those who were witnesses to racial justice in theirs.

WAKING A SLEEPING CHURCH

Douglas M. Strong and Christopher P. Momany

O it seems as if the church were asleep, and
Satan has the world following him.

DAVID INGRAHAM, 1839

WHAT IF YOU COULD DISCOVER an artifact that would change your life? That's exactly what happened to Chris Momany in the fall of 2015.

It was an otherwise uneventful workday in late October when Noelle Keller, the archivist at Adrian College in Michigan, received a large box. Staff members in the alumni office had found the dust-filled container high up in a supply closet during a remodeling project and sent it to the library. Opening the box, Keller extracted a miscellaneous hodgepodge of twentieth-century objects haphazardly stuffed inside: yellowed newspaper clippings, headshots of a former college president, assorted photos, even a freshman beanie from the 1950s. But resting at the bottom of the stack, she found something else—an aged notebook with a marbled cover, filled with page after page of handwriting. Keller noted the dates on the pages and made a startling, unexpectedly breathtaking deduction: this item had come from much further in the past.

But what was it? Keller phoned Chris Momany, the college's chaplain and resident religious historian, to ask whether he could identify the origin of the notebook. Momany instantly recognized the significance of the find. Not waiting for a moment, he rushed over to the library. When he arrived at Keller's workroom and peered down at the first page of the opened tablet, he

Figure I.1. David Ingraham's personal journal, 1839–1841, held in the archive of Adrian College, Michigan

saw a date: July 14, 1839. That was twenty years before the establishment of the college. How did they possess a text that predated the institution?

Momany puzzled for a moment, and then an idea struck. The Reverend Asa Mahan, a holiness theologian and abolitionist, founded Adrian College in 1859. Could this be one of Mahan's early notebooks? If so, it would have been a treasure that he brought with him to Michigan from Ohio, where he had previously served as president of Oberlin College. But Momany wasn't convinced that Mahan really was the source of the discovery. For one, the handwriting in the notebook was too readable, and Mahan had earned a reputation for having incomprehensible scrawl. This script seemed different—almost, well, *legible*—and the document was organized like a personal diary. So who was the author?

In a moment of recklessness, Momany asked Keller if he could put the artifact in his briefcase and take it home over the weekend. He offered a promise not to drink coffee while searching the notebook for clues and that he would only keep a pencil (not a pen!) close by. Keller consented: after all, the relic had been knocking about in containers or various cabinets for almost two centuries by then.

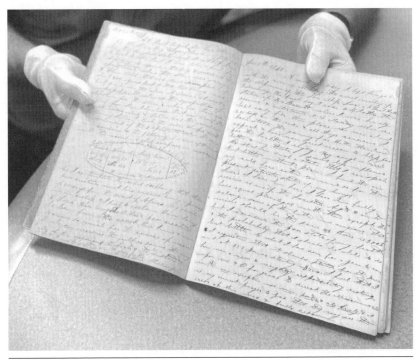

Figure I.2. Page from David Ingraham's journal, December 25, 1839, showing his diagram of the slave ship *Ulysses*

The next day, Momany began to read, handling the old notebook very carefully as he examined its fragile pages. Slowly, very slowly, the author's identity unfolded before him. The notebook contained references to educational and pastoral work in Jamaica, where emancipation had taken place in 1838, just a year before the starting date of the journal. There's a well-established link between Oberlin and missions on behalf of recently freed enslaved people.

But about a quarter of the way through the manuscript, Momany's eyes fell on something unique on a certain page. Unlike all the other pages, which were filled only with handwriting, this one included a drawing of some kind. Momany stared for a moment at the weathered text, then gasped. He was scrutinizing a rough sketch of a ship that had been used to transport enslaved people. On the table in front of him was a bird's-eye diagram of a Portuguese vessel that the British Royal Navy had impounded for illegally trafficking hundreds of West African men, women, and children.

Through much sleuthing, Momany eventually uncovered the journal's provenance: it belonged not to Mahan after all, but to David S. Ingraham, a

White, Oberlin-educated abolitionist missionary who ministered to emancipated communities in Jamaica. Ingraham had started schools and churches among his congregants on the island, teaching people to read and preaching a message of love for God and humanity.

Ingraham's diary measures 7 ¾ × 11 inches. It contains about one hundred brown-tinted leaves of faded cursive. The entries begin in the summer of 1839 and end nearly two years later, in March 1841, just four months before the author's untimely death from lung disease. The artifact, Momany determined, had previously been unknown to scholars, or to anyone, for that matter, before the day it was discovered in a storage closet in 2015.

Ingraham drew his layout sketch of the "slave brig *Ulysses*" in his journal after having boarded the seized ship at Port Royal, Jamaica. By interviewing the crew of the Navy schooner that intercepted the brig, Ingraham found out that 556 abducted people, before being unshackled by British authorities, had suffered incomprehensible misery and humiliation aboard. In his journal (and later in a letter sent to the editors of several US newspapers, reprinted in this book's appendix), Ingraham documented the abuse that the West Africans had endured during a fifty-day voyage.

His journal, lost and forgotten for so long, imparts detailed accounts of current events, expressions of devotion to God, profound theological insights, and tender commentary about his family and congregants, all of which are important things for us to recount and interpret for the present day. But Ingraham wrote his most impassioned remarks immediately following his inspection of the ship. "It seems as if the church were asleep," he lamented. "O where are the sympathies of Christians for the slave and where are their exertions for their liberation? . . . Who can measure the guilt or sound the iniquity of this nefarious traffic?"[1]

So just who was David Ingraham? And what was it that motivated him to fight for freedom? Ingraham was one of the student "rebels" at Lane Theological Seminary in Cincinnati who took an unqualified stand against slavery during a historic series of debates in 1834, to the great consternation of seminary administrators, who meted out harsh discipline against students who took that position. The punitive action prompted Ingraham and thirty-one other rebels to leave Lane and transfer to Oberlin, a revivalist abolitionist

---

[1]David Ingraham, manuscript journal, Adrian College Archives, 24.

college farther north in Ohio. Students were not the only ones to leave. Asa Mahan, one of the few Lane trustees to support the students, moved to Oberlin too, as did the famous evangelist Charles G. Finney, who joined the Oberlin faculty. Mahan himself would become Oberlin's president. Years later, he wrote fondly about Ingraham, referring to him as the "first fruit" of his ministry, a mentorship that may explain how Ingraham's journal ended up at a college, Adrian, at which Mahan would also become president.[2]

MORE THAN JUST AN OLD MANUSCRIPT

Historians relish the chance to get their hands on archival material that has been mislaid. But Chris Momany wondered how he should disseminate the information that was contained in the discovery. He reached out to Doug Strong, a fellow historian of Christianity, to share the news and to strategize about what to do. Strong and Momany determined that Ingraham's faith-filled manuscript merited far more than just a transcription.

The journal's reappearance coincided with the 2010s' increased visibility of anti-Black violence in the United States. The gruesome deaths of Trayvon Martin, Michael Brown, Breonna Taylor, George Floyd, and others, as well as hate crimes directed toward Asian Americans, spotlighted the ongoing reality of race-based discrimination at individual and systemic levels. At the time of this writing in the 2020s, Americans of all ethnicities have found themselves navigating through the turbulent waters of an overdue racial reckoning. Christians, whose discipleship demands that they engage in that process of cultural self-examination, also have a particular obligation to provide upcoming generations with clear-eyed historical retrospectives and biblically based ethical guidance. What was taking place in the era in which Ingraham lived, during which he encountered the *Ulysses*? And what is God calling us to do here and now as practitioners of repentance and agents of justice?

Poring over Ingraham's nineteenth-century diary, Momany and Strong realized that studying the artifact could be a means through which twenty-first-century Christians might address the reality of racism in society today. Why not allow the journal, the scholars wondered, to be a vehicle for people of various backgrounds to study the past for the sake of the present? Perhaps the stories of David Ingraham and other justice-seeking revivalist abolitionists of his day

---

[2] Asa Mahan, *Out of Darkness into Light* (London: Wesleyan Conference Office, 1877), 241.

can inspire contemporary dialogue and activism for racial equity. Was there an abolitionist legacy that bore witness to a hopeful, more faithful tomorrow? A fuller and more nuanced historical narrative may offer relevant resources for reflection and action in faith communities. Could Christian abolitionists of the past provide us with a new history on which to build a new future?

With the support of several charitable foundations, Momany and Strong invited a multiracial team of fourteen scholars to join hands on a common project known as the Dialogue on Race and Faith. The group, consisting of theologically educated scholars manifesting a richness of disciplinary diversity in complementary fields, represented a broad range of ethnicities, institutions, and areas of expertise. They met remotely for a time and gathered in person on several occasions, traveling together to historic sites in the antislavery hubs

Figure I.3. Dialogue on Race and Faith team meeting in Washington, DC, December 2021

of Cincinnati and Oberlin, Ohio, to museums in Washington, DC, and to Benin, where so many people were kidnapped and carried off to slavery on American shores, including those who were abducted aboard the *Ulysses*. The group read common texts and discussed them in light of the places they visited and the local scholars they encountered along the way. The team's collaboration helped members to appreciate the camaraderie that interracial abolitionists from two centuries ago experienced with each other in their day.

Everyone in the group agreed that because of the significant, previously unknown nature of Ingraham's manuscript, it made sense to keep his journal at the center of the project. It also seemed important to call attention to Ingraham's melding of personal piety with thoroughgoing racial justice advocacy, something unusual in the historical record for an antebellum White person. But the group also knew that the project would be much more authentic and powerful by incorporating the voices of other abolitionists, particularly African Americans.

In order to round out the story, the team chose also to examine the lives of men and women who were linked to Ingraham, including his wife, his daughter, fellow Black and White students at Lane Seminary and Oberlin College, his Afro-Caribbean congregants in Jamaica, and the previously enslaved people from West Africa who had traveled on the impounded ship that he examined at Port Royal.

More specifically, the scholars identified two autobiographies of African Americans who interacted with Ingraham: a "Brief Account" (1834) of the life of James Bradley, a formerly enslaved person who became Ingraham's fellow Lane Rebel and Oberlin classmate; and a *Narrative* (1853) penned by Nancy Prince, an African American from Boston whom Ingraham recruited to teach with him in Jamaica. Both Bradley and Prince wrote spellbinding recollections of their experiences.[3]

The combined narrative of this cadre of revivalist abolitionists weaves a tapestry of devotion to God and advocacy for social reform. The nineteenth-century activists described in this book demonstrated simultaneous commitments to vital piety and racial justice. During an era when almost all White Americans believed in White superiority, a few people advocated for racial equity—African Americans, of course, but also a small number of White revivalists, almost the only Whites in their era to act with such rigorous pursuit of holiness in the social arena. The unusual assemblage of antebellum Christians testified to the love of God through words and actions. "O that we may all be encouraged," wrote David Ingraham in his journal, "to walk nearer to God and do more for the salvation of the oppressed." James Bradley echoed similar sentiments: "God will help those

---

[3]James Bradley, "Brief Account of an Emancipated Slave Written by Himself, at the Request of the Editor," in *The Oasis*, ed. Lydia Maria Child (Boston: Benjamin C. Bacon, 1834); Nancy Prince, *A Narrative of the Life and Travels of Mrs. Nancy Prince, Written by Herself*, 2nd ed. (Boston: published by the author, 1853), Internet Archive, https://archive.org/details/narrativeoflifet1853prin /page/8/mode/2up. We also consulted an earlier edition of Prince's autobiography, from 1850, as we will show later in this book.

who take part with the oppressed . . . in this holy cause, until the walls of prejudice are broken down [and] the chains burst in pieces."[4]

THE REVIVALIST, HOLINESS, AND
ABOLITIONIST CONTEXT

To grasp the fullness of the story of these incredible sojourners, one needs to understand a few aspects of their historical context. The cultural setting of nineteenth-century religion and social reform furnished the stage on which our biographical figures played their roles.

It's essential, for instance, to understand that religious participation and the influence of religious thought expanded dramatically during the early national period of the United States. Building on the energy exuded by the Christian renewal movements and awakenings of the eighteenth and nineteenth centuries, church membership doubled between the Revolution and the Civil War in proportion to the population. And renewal wasn't just happening in America: it extended throughout the transatlantic world, especially as missionaries, both White and Black, carried the gospel message abroad.

Revivalism provided the main engine of the expansion. That term, *revivalism*, signified both an evangelistic method and a religious style. Its innovative methods (which Finney called "new measures") included multiday worship services, men and women praying together, and pointed appeals by ministers. Revivalism's style emphasized biblical preaching that resulted in life-changing experiences with God. Whether it was at an evangelistic service in a church building or at an outdoor camp meeting, people came to faith by the tens of thousands at first and eventually by the hundreds of thousands.[5]

In the United States, revivalism arose first in college communities and then spread across a broad spectrum of the population. People from many ethnicities welcomed God's awakening move in their lives and expressed the joy of their spiritual transformation through fervent worship. Believers felt an assurance of God's love and pardon, received by grace through a "new birth" conversion.

---

[4]Bradley, "Brief Account," 111-12; Ingraham, journal, 3.
[5]For more information on early nineteenth-century revivalism, see Timothy L. Smith, *Revivalism and Social Reform* (1957; repr., Eugene, OR: Wipf and Stock, 2004); and Keith J. Hardman, *Seasons of Refreshing: Evangelism and Revivalism in America* (Eugene, OR: Wipf and Stock, 2006).

Figure I.4. Charles G. Finney's "Big Tent," with a capacity of 3,000 people, was used to hold revival and antislavery meetings that included an emphasis on holiness. Oberlin College's Tappan Hall (named for benefactor Lewis Tappan) is depicted behind the tent.

While the spiritual transformation was deeply personal, it also had social implications. Black preachers, for instance, stressed the "liberty" implied by the new birth. For African Americans, the freedom of feeling forgiven by God had the potential to contain multiple emancipatory meanings, what W. E. B. Du Bois later termed a "double consciousness."[6]

The revivalists proclaimed that new believers should express their faith through devotional piety to God and concrete acts of charity for other people. Some of the revivalists also taught that the Holy Spirit empowered men and women to live a holy or "sanctified" life, in which the most essential trait consisted of loving God and one's neighbors. Finney, Mahan, and Ingraham eagerly accepted and preached a holiness emphasis. Those who hoped to receive God's spiritual gift of "entire sanctification" were expected to renounce sinful (evil or harmful) deeds, including unjust actions toward anyone.

Some White revivalists in the 1830s, especially those associated with Finney, began to stress a perspective that African American Christians had always held: that slaveholding and "caste" discrimination (racialized prejudice) were sinful. By identifying such practices as sins (offenses against

[6]W. E. Burghardt Du Bois, *The Souls of Black Folk: Essays and Sketches* (Chicago: McClurg, 1903), 5.

God) and not merely as bad behavior, preachers highlighted the seriousness of the transgressions. Slavery, stated the revivalists in Oberlin, violates a person's God-given free will, "turns hope to despair, and kills the soul." And since everyone is "created in God's image," no one should be treated as inferior, as "objects of scorn and persecution." Once the revivalists labeled slavery and discrimination ("the oppression of public sentiment") as sin, they expected all Christians who were seeking to be sanctified to pursue "an immediate repentance of the sin," which would be shown by taking concrete actions against slavery and racism.

During the same decade (the 1830s) when new-birth revivalism expanded and the theological move toward holiness increased in the United States, abolitionists organized themselves, establishing voluntary benevolent societies, a type of parachurch organization. The leaders of the societies started with a bold and definitive goal: to end slavery without delay. "Abolitionism," as it came to be defined in those years, presumed that enslaved people should be freed immediately and unconditionally, with no compensation to slaveowners. Since abolitionists defined slavery as sin against God, it had to be eradicated right away.

Abolitionism was not the only social reform option that addressed the slavery issue. During the antebellum period, quite a few White people, especially in the North, claimed to be against slavery. But the broad category known as *antislavery* included anyone who believed that slavery was a problem, no matter the reason and without regard to the fervency with which they held that conviction. Many so-called antislavery supporters didn't measure up to abolitionist standards. Some antislavery advocates, for example, thought that slavery could be ended gradually or incrementally, perhaps by paying planters to release enslaved people. Some simply wished to limit the expansion of slavery into new regions of the country. Others, called colonizationists, wanted to coax or force free Blacks to move to Africa. Even self-professed abolitionists often held less-than-stellar opinions regarding African Americans. Many wanted to end slavery but still harbored racist endorsements of White superiority. Theodore Parker, for instance, who was heralded at the time as an exemplary White abolitionist, depicted

---

[7]"Constitution of the Oberlin Anti-Slavery Society" (June 1835), manuscript copy, Oberlin College Archives.

African Americans with disparaging, racist descriptions in his private correspondence. But some revivalist abolitionists did champion both antislavery principles and a commitment to racial equality, publicly and privately. A number of these revivalists established evangelistic training schools that embraced social reforms, sought to demonstrate God's love through admission practices that paid no regard to race or gender, and endeavored to model communities in which interracial relationships could flourish. At least a dozen such revivalist abolitionist schools launched before the Civil War, including Oberlin, Adrian College, Berea College, Illinois Institute (later Wheaton College), Knox College, New York Central College, and Oneida Institute (see map 5.1 in chapter five). Their founders sought to form communities that stressed devotion, worship, character development, evangelism, social activism, mission, and racial inclusion.

LABOR AND PRAYER FOR FREEDOM

Lane Seminary, though it was a revivalist school, was not uniformly abolitionist. Most of the students at Lane worked actively for social justice, though not the school's administrators; hence the exodus of the Lane Rebels for Oberlin in 1835. But Oberlin, by many accounts, did cultivate an environment of interracial social acceptance. A number of African American students, such as John Langston, attested to the warmth and companionship they experienced at the college. Whites likewise wrote about their affection for their African American peers.

In 1837, David and Elizabeth (Betsey) Ingraham, recently married and graduated from Oberlin, determined to put racially inclusive principles into practice at their new mission station at Cotton Tree near Kingston, Jamaica. David and Betsey attempted to re-create the type of Christian fellowship they had known while studying at Lane and Oberlin. Reading through Ingraham's journal, it becomes evident that he treated Afro-Caribbeans and White Americans alike, with similar kindness and tenderness. He wrote about his Black congregants as though they were his family. His congregants reciprocated his expressions of "affection"—so much so that twenty years after his death, Black members of the church still remembered him as "one they so much loved."[8]

---

[8]Ingraham, journal, 35, 36, 41, 86, 94, 96-97; Sarah Ingraham Penfield, letter, January 3, 1859, in Thornton Bigelow Penfield and Sarah Ingraham Penfield, *Letters from Jamaica 1858–1866*, ed.

Witnesses including James Bradley, David Ingraham, Ingraham's Jamaican congregants, and Nancy Prince described the intentional efforts by some revivalists to develop proximate, crosscultural relationships as having the potential to create communities of equity. Interactions between Blacks and Whites did result in opportunities for interracial inclusion—fragile and short-lived, perhaps, but still real.

But what about the unequal power dynamics between Blacks and Whites? African Americans historically have not been viewed or treated the same way as Whites when interacting in interracial common spaces, such as classrooms and church sanctuaries. Generations of socialization, even when it has been unconscious, have typically reproduced conditions of inequality over time. Could true cooperation have existed in such relationships?

The fellowship at Lane (at least among students), at Oberlin, and at the Jamaica mission station did illustrate the beginnings of racially equitable communities. Ingraham, Bradley, Prince, and some other revivalist abolitionists testified to the possibility of spiritual mutuality. Yet while interracial relationships are a great first step, they do not create racial justice. A love ethic based on proximate connections is not a panacea for dealing with discrimination. Personal fellowship or even community-wide racial inclusion efforts (like what emerged in Oberlin and other abolitionist towns) are not sufficient. Such relationships only move the needle on justice when they are coupled with strategies for raising awareness of the problem of racism and for taking concrete steps toward social transformation. There must be an agenda for structural change that includes systemic action, such as civil rights legislation or reparations for past injustice.

David Ingraham knew these things to be true. For him, cultivating interpersonal relationships became an onramp for justice advocacy. He insisted that love for one's neighbor had to result in observable, concrete actions on behalf of the disinherited. He contended that he, along with all Christians, ought to give "time, talents, property, influence, health and life to the cause of the poor and oppressed."[9]

It's a sad fact of history that Ingraham was an outlier on these things, since many White abolitionists did not push for racial equity as he did.

Charles G. Gosselink (Silver Bay, NY: Boat House, 2005), 26, Penfield Family Web Site, www .penfield.fm/jamaica/jamaica.pdf.
[9]Ingraham, journal, 76.

Nonrevivalist White abolitionists contended for immediate emancipation, but often they nonetheless held views of racial inferiority. Even Charles Finney and some of the other White revivalist abolitionists who believed in racial equity frequently compromised on these things. Finney, for instance, feared that Christians' engagement in justice work might overshadow the church's evangelistic preaching. He and some of his fellow revivalists hesitated when they perceived too much social activism in the mix.[10]

But Ingraham, Bradley, Prince, and a few others advocated seamlessly for spiritual fervor, evangelism, *and* social reform, all at once. Writing in his journal, Ingraham implored God to bring about "the freedom of the world. For this let me labor—for this let me pray."[11] A small faction of revivalist abolitionists—African Americans and their White colleagues—stand out as examples of those who labored and prayed for racial justice. They were not numerically dominant in the United States, but this group of devout Christian activists still represented a leading edge of social change in nineteenth-century America for the church and the larger culture.

A RETELLING OF NINETEENTH-CENTURY RELIGIOUS HISTORY

As Christian theologians and historians, the authors of this book are heirs to an inspiring legacy of camp meetings, great awakenings, revivals, and spiritual outpourings, in which God converted millions of people of all races and ethnicities to Christ and empowered them with the Holy Spirit. And yet, as *American* Christian theologians and historians, we find ourselves lamenting our culture's four-hundred-year history of racially motivated violence—slavery, Jim Crow, intimidation, prejudice—during which the church has mostly been complicit, failing to live up to the ethic of Jesus. The same holds for places outside the United States too; we observe a similar disparity when we study the intersection of Christianity and race relations throughout the churches of West Africa, the Caribbean, and elsewhere.

Pastor and theologian Howard Thurman noted the terrible disjunction between Christianity's professed commitments and the stark historical reality of its partnership with racism. "This is the question," he wrote in 1949,

---

[10]Jemar Tisby, *The Color of Compromise: The Truth About the American Church's Complicity in Racism* (Grand Rapids, MI: Zondervan, 2019), 68-69.
[11]Ingraham, journal, 4.

"which individuals and groups who live in our land always under the threat of profound social and psychological displacement face: Why is it that Christianity seems impotent to deal radically, and therefore effectively, with the issues of discrimination and injustice on the basis of race? Is this impotence due to a betrayal of the genius of the religion, or is it due to a basic weakness in the religion itself?"[12]

In answer to Thurman's searing question, the authors of this book, scholars who profess faith in Jesus Christ, believe that the church's lack of an adequate response to injustice is *not* a basic weakness in Christianity but is indeed a betrayal of the heart of the gospel message. Throughout the Scriptures, God desires to form a people who love God with all their hearts and minds and who love all their neighbors as God loves them. God the Holy Spirit enables believers to participate in the work and mission of God by living holy lives. If these claims are true, then all Christ followers have work to do to retell the story of Christianity, whether in the United States or elsewhere. In light of the good news of God's salvation, holiness, and liberation, Christians are called to speak the truth about the church.

First, we need to be ruthlessly honest about the racial views that prevailed during most of modern church history in the transatlantic world. The historical record frequently displays a dismal picture of the church as the handmaiden of Western racism and colonialism. The authors of this book don't contradict the prevalent scholarly framework that bears witness to that truth; in fact, we add to it with chapters on the African slave trade and the lives of Northern free Blacks. Along with other recent writers, our team of scholars tells a piece of the history of the church's failure to live up to the standards of its confessions.

But our team perceives a second task in the retelling too: to approach our work with an empathetic interpretive lens, one that doesn't count the church or its doctrine as morally bankrupt simply because so many Christians got things so egregiously wrong for such a long time. We believe that there were exceptions, Christians who did understand how God's love ought to impact the social world in which they found themselves—in other words, persons of faith in Jesus Christ who did not buy into the lies of racism and White cultural supremacy or the idea that the oppression of Blacks by Whites was

---

[12]Howard Thurman, *Jesus and the Disinherited* (1949; repr., Boston: Beacon, 1976), xix.

an unalterable fact of life. The historical figures we study in this book are such persons, prophets who stood up tall and brave amid the suffocating racial climate in which they lived, and it's our conviction that they deserve to be trusted in the ways they depicted themselves. Consequently, we try to "think with" these individuals, rather than just "think about" them. Our goal is to allow the voices of revivalist abolitionists to speak for themselves as they speak to us and to you.

We intend our project, including this book, to portray a version of events different from the popular narrative and truer, one that shows that the American segment of the body of Christ was not unequivocally corrupt when it came to racial matters—that there were faithful within its ranks who did speak for justice, and not in spite of what they believed about Jesus but because of it. The alternative storyline gives an account of a minority of Christians who rejected oppressive structures and racist prejudices. This story, one of Black and White coworkers standing up for a sanctified gospel message, is little known today, buried beneath a monolithic, reductionist portrayal of nineteenth-century American Christianity. We think that these people, and other disciples of Jesus like them, understood what really was vicious (there was plenty) and spoke against it, living as agents of holiness and justice in a corrupt world, just like their Lord had been before them.

Our book introduces readers to the courageous saga of James Bradley, David Ingraham, and Nancy Prince, a trio of activist Christians who interacted with one another in the 1830s and who serve as examples of the revivalist abolitionism that was exhibited in Oberlin and a few other communities. Each chapter presents a distinct angle of vision into the lives and vocations of these people. The different frames of reference offer readers multiple avenues along which they can travel with our featured figures, exploring the faith journeys of these extraordinary people. Each chapter also contains connections to our current context, thereby inviting readers to envision how to live out God's call for themselves.

Chapter one provides profiles of the three figures, resulting in a kind of composite biography. Chapter two delves into the background of the 556 people kidnapped from their homes in West Africa and forcibly loaded aboard the *Ulysses*, the slave ship that David Ingraham examined. By understanding more about the backstory to their captivity, we honor the lives and acknowledge the suffering of unnamed enslaved men and women. Chapter three explores the experiences of nineteenth-century African Americans such as Nancy Prince and James Bradley. That inquiry shows how, even for Blacks who lived north of the slave states, daily existence was precarious and often subject to the capricious whims of those in power—and yet how Prince and Bradley also found spaces of faith-based inclusion. Chapter four portrays the central role played by abolitionists' worship and devotional practices, and chapter five describes the theological grounding for abolitionist activism. Chapter six looks at the lives of Black and White women during the pre–Civil War era and how they interpreted their hardships. Chapter seven recounts how Christian activists who had power and influence used their privilege to support social justice projects, especially looking at their philanthropy. Finally, chapter eight depicts the role of Black Americans in the formation of biracial Christian communities such as Oberlin and the struggle to sustain such ventures.

Altogether, the book shines a spotlight on the lives of several remarkable but commonplace people who put their faith into action. They chose to trust God and act righteously when they were faced with challenges, confronting injustice, standing up for what was right, relying on God for help when they suffered, and living with love and purpose. Their faithfulness encourages us to act with determination when dealing with the moral issues of our own time.

JESUS AND JUSTICE

In the middle decades of the nineteenth century, Christians associated with Charles Finney's style of revivalism (at its best) formed intentional communities such as Oberlin to be examples of interracial cooperation and equality. In the deeply racialized culture of antebellum America, these faith-based experiments held out hope for a different, more inclusive future, one in which love for Jesus and the pursuit of his justice would prevail in people's hearts, minds, and actions. An alignment of fervent revivalist spirituality, holiness theology, and social activism among some Christians, both White and African American, resulted in a new vision for God's good reign and significant progress in defeating the evil practices of human trafficking and discrimination.

What can we learn from this period of social experimentation and theological vitality? How might we benefit from the experiences of our forebears in the faith? Can we retrieve a redemptive message of God's purpose for our own day? In these times when the history of Christianity is castigated (often rightly) for its complacency in the face of racial injustice, can we find any tangible examples of faithfulness? What can we learn and whom can we honor as we advance the work of antiracism? And even though the overtly Christian abolitionism of Oberlin and other communities did not always last very long, people today are intrigued by accounts of cross-racial inclusion. If such places existed, how did they come about, and can we foster new ones now?

African Americans like James Bradley and Nancy Prince detected glimmers of hope through their participation in interracial communities. They believed that the potential for freedom from discrimination was historically attainable. They thought it reasonable, from their own experience, to visualize seasons of life free from prejudice. Inclusive locales like Oberlin and Ingraham's Jamaican congregation at Cotton Tree painted a picture of possibility that could not be erased and whose importance was immediately understood by people who were struggling for equality.

The study of revivalist social justice efforts in the nineteenth century can provide a fresh approach to today's conversations about race and faith in the church. That's what we've attempted to do in this book. Maybe finding a dusty artifact in a box somewhere really can change our lives. May the witness of how some of our mothers and fathers in faith challenged racism through their commitment to love God and others help us find our way through the struggles we face now.

CHAPTER ONE

"How Long, O Lord?"

A NARRATIVE OF THREE CHRISTIAN ABOLITIONISTS

Christopher P. Momany

"How long, O Lord, how long" shall this nefarious traffic continue?
DAVID INGRAHAM, 1840

My heart ached to feel within me the life of liberty.
JAMES BRADLEY, 1834

*God speaks very loud, and while his judgments are on
the earth, may the inhabitants learn righteousness!*
NANCY PRINCE, 1850

THE GLORIOUS FIRST OF AUGUST

On August 1, 1841, David Stedman Ingraham, an abolitionist missionary to Jamaica, died in Belleville, New Jersey, exactly seven years after slavery was abolished among British-dominated lands. He and others had struggled for a day when complete justice would roll down like waters, but the day had not yet come, particularly in his native United States, where slavery was still legal. His body ravaged by tuberculosis, Ingraham drew his last, labored breaths on the anniversary day of emancipation in the British Caribbean, keenly aware that the fight for racial equity was far from over. "Brother Ingraham has put on immortality!" wrote his friend Theodore Weld. "He died last night at half past twelve Oclock. He will celebrate the glorious first of

On the Friends of NEGRO EMANCIPATION, this Print is Inscribed

Figure 1.1. Jamaicans celebrating West Indian emancipation, August 1, 1834

August with his brother Angels in his own Father's house!" While the timing of his death symbolized arrival at a destiny, from our earthly perspective so much was left undone. Almost two hundred years later, we still ache at the incompleteness of the task.[1]

I remember listening to my fourth-grade teacher tell stories of her days in the civil rights movement. Geneva Isom was a unique educator and Sterne Brunson School in Benton Harbor, Michigan, was a unique place. Our community struggled with economic injustice and discrimination, and as a White student in a predominantly Black school, I had to learn a lot about my own privilege. But I remember being treated well by a diverse group of young friends. We thought we were the generation who would teach the world to thrive together. But that was fifty years ago. Here we are, a quarter of the way through a new century, and we continue to live with persistent racism. I can hear Psalm 13:1 ringing in my ears: "How long, O LORD?" When will things change? When will God's intended reign of dignity appear?

THE BEGINNING OF A MOVEMENT

David Ingraham descended from a long line of New Englanders. His mother, Elizabeth Stedman, was born in Ashburnham, Massachusetts, and his father, John, was most likely born in New Hampshire. They were married in Chester, Vermont, on January 19, 1808. Eliza, their eldest child, was born in Vermont in 1810, and David was born two years later, probably after the family had moved to western New York State.

John Ingraham served in a New York militia company during the War of 1812, and the family lived near the town of Lima, directly south of Rochester. That region was alive with spiritual revival at the time, and David Ingraham's journal records a homecoming of sorts when he traveled through Lima in the late summer of 1840 to see his "old friends once more." At some point, his parents moved to Michigan Territory, but much of his heart remained in western New York.[2]

Ingraham entered a profound period of his life in 1830. In January he joined the Second Congregational Church of Pittsford, New York, located

---

[1]Gilbert H. Barnes and Dwight L. Dumond, eds., *Letters of Theodore Dwight Weld, Angelina Grimké Weld and Sarah Grimké, 1822–1844*, 2 vols. (New York and London: D. Appleton-Century, 1934), 2:871-72.

[2]David Ingraham, manuscript journal, Adrian College Archives, 67.

between Rochester and Lima. Records show that he was received as a
member upon "examination," and it may have been his first formal affiliation
with a church. The pastor of the Pittsford congregation, a preacher named
Asa Mahan, possessed a razor-sharp mind and a love for justice. Born in
central New York State, he had studied at Hamilton College in Clinton, New
York, and then at Andover Theological Seminary in Massachusetts. Barely
thirty years old when he served the Pittsford church, Mahan became Ingraham's mentor, writing much later that Ingraham had been "the first fruit" of
his ministry. Their bond was strong and continued after Mahan accepted a
call to Cincinnati's Sixth Presbyterian Church in late 1831. Within a year,
Ingraham moved to Cincinnati as well and joined Mahan's congregation.
Neither of them had any idea of the battle that was to come.[3]

Cincinnati was a borderland, situated on a series of hills that sloped down
to the Ohio River, a body of water symbolic of the divide between a nominally free North and the machinery of Southern slavery. Cincinnati was also
home to a new venture in higher education, Lane Theological Seminary,
which opened in 1829. Perched northeast of the city in an area known as
Walnut Hills, it aimed to be an incubator for pastors who would lead revival
up and down the Ohio Valley. Lane's first president was none other than
Lyman Beecher, a Yale-educated pastor and head of a family that would
make its name in abolitionist circles. With Beecher at the helm and a bright
student body of committed young people, the Protestant establishment
hoped to ward off other religious traditions and claim the region for ener-
getic, conversion-focused ministry.

The venture showed great promise. A competent faculty, a strong board
of trustees, and most of all, a talented student group, took shape. When
Mahan began his duties at Sixth Presbyterian Church, he found himself
asked to serve as a trustee of Lane Seminary. Before long, David Ingraham
began studies at Lane. The seminary catalog lists David S. Ingraham as a
student for the year 1833–1834.

Yet there was more to the growth of Lane than the arrival of Mahan and
Ingraham. In 1832 a cadre of students with abolitionist convictions had
come to Lane from Oneida Institute in Whitesboro, New York. Leading

---

[3]Asa Mahan, *Out of Darkness into Light; or the Hidden Life Made Manifest Through Facts of Observation and Experience* (Boston: Willard Tract Repository, 1876), 241.

Lane Seminary.

Figure 1.2. Lane Theological Seminary, Cincinnati, Ohio

the group was Theodore Weld, a convert from the preaching of Charles Finney, the legendary revivalist who had set much of New York State ablaze around the time that the Erie Canal opened. In Utica, New York, in 1826, Weld had come to Christ through Finney's direct and rapid-fire oratory. Six years later, Weld found himself as the organizational catalyst of the Lane student body. The institution was heading for an honest confrontation with slavery.

JAMES BRADLEY AND DAVID INGRAHAM MEET AT LANE SEMINARY

Among a host of notable young people who gathered at Lane was an extraordinary student named James Bradley. Born about 1810 in West Africa, he had been enslaved and forced to the United States at a very young age. Later he recalled that the "soul-destroyers" tore him from his mother's arms and forced him aboard a ship. That floating hell eventually arrived at Charleston, South Carolina, where Bradley was sold to a man and taken to Pendleton County, Kentucky. Soon he was sold again. When Bradley was a teenager, he was taken to Arkansas Territory. The brutality of his childhood and youth was severe, but as Bradley later noted, it was also not particularly unusual.[4]

In 1834 he recalled how his heart had ached for freedom during his enslavement. "I was never told anything about God, or my own soul," he wrote. When the man who claimed to be his master died, Bradley took on the management of the family's business. He also sacrificed hours of sleep each night, working side jobs, hoping to buy his freedom. In 1833 he accomplished his goal and headed to Ohio, a state where at least officially there was no slavery. While in Cincinnati, he heard of Lane Theological Seminary and hungered for "the light of knowledge." Bradley became the only Black student at Lane and later spoke of having been treated with respect there.[5]

Therefore, as 1833 closed, Asa Mahan's trusteeship, James Bradley's hunger for learning, Theodore Weld's leadership, and David Ingraham's love for God and others were coalescing in the hills northeast of Cincinnati. Lane Theological Seminary could boast a student community of disciplined and convicted young adults, and they were not about to conduct themselves without purpose. Something profound was stirring in their hearts and minds, and the year 1834 promised to be momentous.

THE GREAT LANE DEBATES

During the bleak winter of February 1834, the students at Lane Seminary organized a series of debates. The gatherings, scheduled over eighteen evenings, were more like extended conversations, intended to consider the issue of slavery from many angles. They addressed two major questions, one concerning immediate abolition and the other concerning methods to end slavery in America. Each evening session lasted two and a half hours.

Seventeen people spoke during those events, arguing in favor of emancipation even though almost half of them had come from families that benefited from slavery. Weld spoke first, issuing a series of lectures that argued for immediate emancipation. His impact was substantial, but the most convincing speech was probably the one that Bradley gave.

Bradley narrated the injustice of slavery from personal experience, but he also did more than that. Not content merely to recite a harrowing tale, he

---

[4]James Bradley, "Brief Account of an Emancipated Slave Written by Himself, at the Request of the Editor," in *The Oasis*, ed. Lydia Maria Child (Boston: Benjamin C. Bacon, 1834), 106.
[5]Bradley, "Brief Account," 108, 109.

applied relentless and sometimes sarcastic logic to the evil. Opponents of immediate abolition were known to make self-serving arguments. First, they held that it would be somehow dangerous for society to free enslaved people, and second, they asserted that those freed would not be able to care for themselves. Bradley blasted such nonsense with his personal example and unyielding reason.

Freed persons, he asserted, would seek honorable work and education, contributing to the betterment of all. Moreover, the enslaved were already skilled at providing for themselves and had shown that they could do so while also compensating for inept abusers. Bradley could point not only to his own narrative of thriving as a free person but to his record of having run the business affairs of his Arkansas oppressors while simultaneously improving his own prospects.

Those eighteen animated evenings led to overwhelming student support for immediate abolition. The students also roundly refuted so-called colonization, a term that was being used to describe a movement that sought to end slavery but force freed persons to settle in Africa. The young people at Lane were not buying that approach. They denounced colonization as an insult to those who had as much claim upon America as anyone else.

Following the debates, several students drafted a constitution for an antislavery society. The document echoed American revolutionary principles and stated that enslaved people possessed a God-given right to "liberty, and the pursuit of happiness." Writing two years later, Weld summed up the guiding philosophy of the Lane students: "Persons are to be treated according to their intrinsic worth *irrespective of Color, shape, condition* or what not." The reference to "intrinsic worth" was no accident. It described a value endowed by God for all people. In 1848 Asa Mahan would write a textbook on ethics, *Science of Moral Philosophy*, that made the intrinsic worth of people a starting point for thought and action. But the language of intrinsic worth was far from being some irrelevant terminology used by privileged thinkers. It grounded a whole movement against slavery, not least the student advocacy at Lane.[6]

---

[6]Weld was apparently quoting from another source, now obscured, that served as a defining principle for him and his Lane contemporaries; emphasis included in the Weld source. "Preamble and Constitution of the Anti-slavery Society of Lane Seminary," *The Standard*, n.d., Library of Congress, www.loc.gov/resource/rbpe.24800600; Barnes and Dumond, *Letters*, 1:270; Asa Mahan, *Science of Moral Philosophy* (Oberlin, OH: James M. Fitch, 1848).

Abolition. Geo. Clark.

THE STANDARD.---Extra.

PREAMBLE AND CONSTITUTION
OF THE ANTI-SLAVERY SOCIETY OF LANE SEMINARY.

Believing it incumbent upon all, who associate for the advancement of the general good, to state explicitly their object, their reasons for seeking it, the means proposed for its accomplishment, and the *principles* which are to control their action; we make the following exposition.

1st. *Object.* Our object is the immediate emancipation of the whole colored race within the United States: The emancipation of the slave from the oppression of the master, the emancipation of the free colored man from the oppression of public sentiment, and the elevation of both to an intellectual, moral, and political equality with the whites.

2d. *Reasons.* We advocate the immediate emancipation of the slave for the following reasons.
1st. He is constituted by God a moral agent, the keeper of his own happiness, the executive of his own powers, the accountable arbiter of his own choice; personal ownership his birth right, unforfeited and inalienable; liberty, and the pursuit of happiness, his chartered rights, inherited from his Maker and guaranteed by all the laws of his being.

[The remaining newspaper columns consist of dense small print continuing the reasons, principles, mode of operation, and the text of the Constitution, followed by a list of OFFICERS including WILLIAM T. ALLAN, Ala., President; MARIUS R. ROBINSON, Tenn., Vice Pres.; ANDREW BENTON, Mo., Rec. Sec.; JAMES A. THOME, Ky., Cor. Sec.; COLEMAN S. HODGES, Va., Treasurer; HENRY P. THOMPSON, Ky., Auditor; JAMES BRADLEY, Ar. Ter.; HENRY B. STANTON, N. Y.; ABNER S. ROSS, N. J.; JAMES STEELE, N. Y.; SERENO W. STREETER, Mass.; GEORGE CLARKE, Conn.; GEORGE WHIPPLE, N. Y.; JAMES MORRISON, Ohio; JAMES M. ALLAN, Ala.; THEODORE D. WELD, N. Y.; JOHN T. PIERCE, Mass.; HUNTINGTON LYMAN, La. — Board of Managers.]

Figure 1.3. "Preamble and Constitution of the Anti-slavery Society of Lane Seminary," 1834 (note the names of James Bradley and Theodore Weld, among others)

The elders at Lane were alarmed by the student debates. The trustees feared a backlash. Tensions mounted over the spring and summer of 1834 until formal action by the trustees created a real crisis: they approved a policy that called for the dissolution of the student antislavery society and the exercise of arbitrary power to dismiss student agitators. Mahan remembered those critical times with a mix of disgust for his trustee colleagues and admiration for the students. He made his opposition to these heavy-handed measures known and was one of very few leaders on campus to support the students. His children were attacked in the street and he found himself shunned by most of Cincinnati's civic leaders.

After the trustee crackdown was published, Weld, Bradley, and Ingraham (along with most of the student body) left Lane in protest. On December 15, 1834, the students released a document called "A Statement of the Reasons Which Induced the Students of Lane Seminary, to Dissolve Their Connection with That Institution." Weld, Bradley, and Ingraham, along with forty-eight others, attached their names to the eloquent defense of the student position.

At this moment of uncertainty, a complex set of forces intervened that would eventually bring many Lane students north to Oberlin Collegiate Institute (later renamed Oberlin College). The college in Oberlin, about thirty-five miles southwest of Cleveland, had been founded in 1833 by John J. Shipherd and Philo P. Stewart. Financial challenges and low enrollment plagued its first years of operation, but late in 1834, Shipherd got wind of the Lane situation and visited Mahan's home in Cincinnati. Conversation ensued between Shipherd and the former students, who by then had become known as the Lane Rebels.

While many of the expatriates were willing to go to Oberlin and inject the school with much-needed vitality, they would only commit under certain conditions. Mahan would have to be appointed Oberlin's president, and their own professor, John Morgan (formerly of Lane Seminary), had to be added to the faculty. Most of all, African American students would have to be admitted to Oberlin, and the trustees had to promise not to interfere with academic matters. The Rebels also wanted their gifted colleague Weld appointed to Oberlin as a professor of theology, but he declined, later becoming an agent of the American Anti-slavery Society in Ohio. Weld did, however, recommend his mentor, Charles Finney, for the professorship.

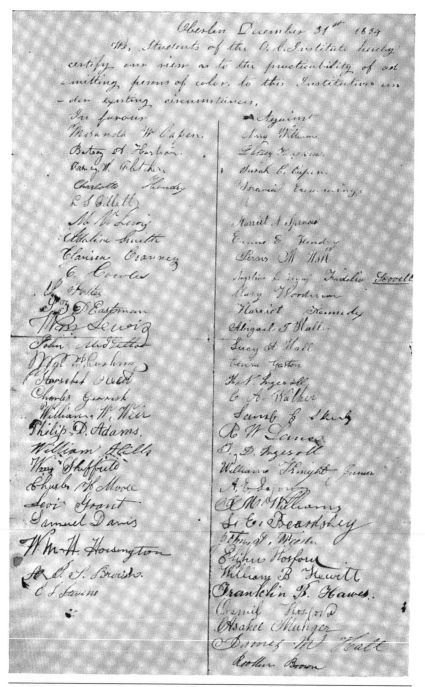

Figure 1.4. Survey on the "practicality of admitting persons of color" to Oberlin Collegiate Institute, December 31, 1834 (note Betsey A. Hartson's name, second in the left-hand "in favour" column)

The Lane Rebels possessed a great deal of bargaining power, but their proposal was not accepted outright by Oberlin's board of trustees. Oberlin College came to be regarded as a leader in equal-opportunity education, and several women had been enrolled that same year, in 1834. But would the trustees open Oberlin to African Americans? In December a document appeared, drafted by students who were already attending the college, speaking directly to the admissions policy. The student statement read: "We, Students of the O. C. Institute hereby certify our view as to the practicability of admitting persons of color to this Institution under existing circumstances." Beneath this introductory sentence were two columns, one listing those students who supported the admission of African Americans and one listing those who opposed the proposal. Twenty-six students were in favor, and thirty-two were opposed.[7]

The second person listed in favor of admitting African American students was a young woman from Elyria, Ohio, named Betsey A. Hartson (1815– 1845). Hartson would eventually marry David Ingraham. Before the Lane expatriates stepped foot in Oberlin, Hartson and others were advocating for equal opportunity and an open admissions policy.

Finally, on February 9, 1835, the board of trustees agreed to receive students of color. Mahan felt he was now able to accept the presidency in good conscience. Arthur and Lewis Tappan of New York City were prepared to offer generous financial support for the reorganized college, and by the spring of 1835 Oberlin Collegiate Institute was a new place.

James Bradley traveled to Oberlin in March 1836. On the way he was threatened by racists, later recalling that bigotry was so thick in some places that he could "stir it with a stick." Bradley enrolled at Sheffield Institute, a satellite preparatory school of Oberlin Collegiate Institute some fifteen miles northeast. Ingraham attended the main campus in Oberlin.[8]

At some point following the spring of 1835, Betsey Hartson and David Ingraham developed an interest in each other, and they were married on August 10, 1837, not far from Oberlin. Fittingly, Mahan performed the service and blessed the young couple as coequal partners in ministry. They had no

---

[7]Petition of Oberlin students regarding admission of students of color, December 31, 1834, Oberlin College Archives, miscellaneous file; see also http://www2.oberlin.edu/external/EOG/Lane Debates/StudentsPetition.htm.

[8]James R. Wright to Elizur Wright, Jr., April 4, 1836, James Bradley file, Oberlin College Archives.

idea that their marriage would be cut short by terminal illness, but over the next four years, they crowded a lifetime of love and justice into their union.

THE CALL TO PERFECTED LOVE

Oberlin College quickly developed a reputation for spiritual renewal and social justice advocacy. In September 1836 a revival took place on campus. President Mahan had been preaching that God's grace was able not only to forgive sin but to empower right living. Mahan concluded that through God's grace it is possible to live a life of perfected love. This second work of God was known as entire sanctification.

It is one thing to contemplate God's mighty love in the act of forgiveness. It is quite another to consider how God might make one upright, loving, and just. What kind of completeness or maturity can Christians expect in this life? That fall, a recent graduate of the Oberlin theology department, Sereno Wright Streeter (one of the Lane Rebels), wanted an answer to this question. Mahan could not offer a clear response at the time but promised to give it thorough study and prayer.

During the winter of 1836–1837, Mahan joined his colleague Charles Finney in New York City, where Finney had an established ministry. As it happened, David Ingraham determined to visit the Caribbean that year, hoping a change in climate would improve his health. He also desired to be of some sacred service while he had breath. Suffering from tuberculosis, Ingraham stopped in New York to visit Mahan and Finney before leaving the country. The three engaged in profound conversation, and Mahan remembered Ingraham's words: "I am as ready to die here as anywhere else, and now as at any other time, if such is the will of my God." Ingraham found passage on a ship to Cuba and began a kind of exploratory trip for subsequent work in Jamaica.[9]

By the summer of 1837 Ingraham was back in Ohio, where he received ordination and he and Hartson married. In December of that year, the newlywed couple journeyed to Jamaica and began their pivotal mission with formerly enslaved people. The Ingrahams were some of the earliest American abolitionists to go to Jamaica. They desired to encourage Afro-Caribbeans in their quest for economic independence. By engaging in this mission of

---

[9]Mahan, *Out of Darkness into Light*, 242.

education and evangelism, Christian abolitionists like the Ingrahams hoped to repudiate the racist objection to emancipation promoted by proslavery Whites that freed people of color could not advance or govern themselves. Much like James Bradley's blistering critique at Lane, the Ingrahams believed that emancipated people were a blessing to the public good.

The journal that Ingraham kept during much of his Jamaican ministry began more than a year after he arrived on the island. The first entry came on July 14, 1839, and the last was on March 14, 1841. The journal is a marvelous window, sometimes mundane, often moving, to the experience of the Ingrahams and to the social dynamics in post-emancipation Jamaica.

The very first statement within the document exudes gratitude for God's grace: "This has been one of my best Sabbaths. O how unworthy am I of such blessed privileges." Ingraham strove for a more just community, but he always grounded his commitment in a deep spiritual experience. The journal records the challenges of travel across mountainous country, the hard work of crosscultural communication, the universal grind of local-church politics, and more, all in addition to confrontation with the continuing effects of slavery. Ingraham was not without his flaws and could not entirely escape his perspective as a privileged actor among those he served. But during a time that was gripped by dehumanizing forces, David and Betsey Ingraham joined others in efforts to make at least one corner of the world a better place.[10]

Among the many themes within Ingraham's journal, a certain fondness for language having to do with vision or sight appears again and again. This filter even haunts Ingraham's identification with Oberlin teaching on sanctification. On May 23, 1840, while beginning a return visit to the United States, he noted his poor health, then wrote about Charles Finney's landmark lectures that had appeared in the *Oberlin Evangelist*: "But have had some joy in reading and meditating on the word of God, Have also read one of Prof Finneys lectures on Sanctification. I see the subject plainer and plainer and see that nothing, but unbelief hinders me from the enjoyment of this great and glorious privilege."[11]

At times, Ingraham used vision language in counterpoint to the cloud of ill health that hung over him. "I have been thinking much of death lately," he

---

[10]Ingraham, journal, 3, emphasis original.
[11]Ingraham, journal, 46, emphasis original.

confessed in June of 1840, "and have endeavored to look it in the face." A bit further in the journal his concern for seeing focused on intimacy with Christ. He spoke of wanting to see Jesus as He is. O how lovely, inexpressibly lovely He appears." But Ingraham's otherworldly awareness did not in the least diminish his compassion for others. He lived as one who wished for fulfillment of the heavenly vision on earth.[12]

DOCUMENTING THE INIQUITY OF THE SLAVE TRADE

Ingraham's poignant yearning had also been evident in the journal some months earlier. On Christmas Day in 1839, Ingraham visited Port Royal, Jamaica (near Kingston), and stepped aboard a ship that had recently been used to imprison and transport enslaved people from the western coast of Africa. The vessel was identified as the Portuguese brig (two-masted ship) *Ulysses*. It had been intercepted by the British war schooner *Skipjack* south of Cuba on November 30. Newspaper accounts tell of a chase that lasted twelve hours before the Portuguese craft was overtaken.

The people held captive on the *Ulysses* had come from the ports of Ouidah and Popo in Dahomey (now Benin), Badagry (now Nigeria), and the River Nunez (now Guinea). Ingraham's journal entry for December 25, 1839, is arresting. It is also the only page of his manuscript to include a diagram or sketch (see appendix C). His chilling description of the ship indicates inhumanely tight quarters. The ceiling height is listed as having been two feet, five inches. The stern of the vessel included an area that measured sixteen feet by fourteen feet and held 117 girls. The next compartment was twenty feet by twenty feet and held 107 women. The third was thirty-two feet by eighteen feet and held 216 men. The fourth, at the bow, was fifteen feet by twelve feet and held 93 boys. In all, 533 people survived the ordeal, while 556 had boarded at the beginning of the voyage. Ingraham could record the dimensions of the *Ulysses*, but he also cried, "Who can measure the guilt or sound the iniquity" of such abusive trade?[13]

The end of the trip did not signal the end of injustice for those who had been held captive aboard the *Ulysses*. After landing at Montego Bay, Jamaica, seven

---

[12]Ingraham, journal, 48, 54, emphasis original.

[13]Ingraham, journal, 24. The dimensions given by Ingraham for the internal compartments of the *Ulysses*, recorded in his journal on December 25, 1839, differ slightly from those dimensions given in his published letter of January 15, 1840 (see appendix D).

died within a month. Most of the remaining 526 people were forced to work on various plantations, primarily in St. James, Westmoreland, and Hanover. Seventy young men were coerced to join one of the British West India regiments as soldiers. Many went to work for a man named Thomas MacNeill of Westmoreland and were treated little better than those in a formal state of slavery. Within the year, several people quit MacNeill, charging him with terrible working conditions. Those who left were pursued by police, who attempted to force them back to MacNeill's property, but an uprising among locals defended them.

Ingraham contrasted conditions on the *Ulysses* with God's intended justice. "How long, O Lord?" he lamented. "How long shall these poor creatures be torn from their homes and made to endure so much for the avarice of men?" On January 15, 1840, he followed his personal examination of the ship with a detailed letter to abolitionist newspapers (see appendix D).[14]

The terror aboard the *Ulysses* leaves us with a horrible challenge. The forced anonymity of those who were captive in its hold makes it extremely difficult to give them proper honor. We can acknowledge their suffering: the violent separation from their families, the constant hunger from barely being fed, the stench of their surroundings in the ship's hold on a fifty-day voyage. But we can also listen very carefully for their individual life stories, their courage and genius, their agency the unique power they possessed as persons.

My own participation in this research arises from a sense of obligation that I have accepted to hear the voices of the people who were forced aboard the *Ulysses*. To learn history and to write books are fine, as far as they go. But this project is different, perhaps deeper. We are engaging the very *meaning* of history here, and I freely admit that I bring my standing convictions regarding the sacred nature of people to this effort. This is a story about personhood denied—and then, hopefully, about personhood reaffirmed.

Some might consider the term *obligation* misapplied to this project. After all, there are interesting discoveries involved, moments of insight, even some inspiring witnesses of old. But living into an obligation is one way to find godly purpose. We are, indeed, obligated as human beings and followers of Christ to listen to those who have been ignored, to respect them. If vocation entails receiving a call, then this is vocation writ large. Among the many thousands of people who were brutalized and then forgotten during

---

[14]Ingraham, journal, 24.

the shameful reign of Atlantic slavery, the men, women, and children of the *Ulysses* give us an opportunity to hear, to change, and to work toward something better in the world.

DAVID INGRAHAM RECRUITS NANCY PRINCE

When Ingraham visited the United States during the summer and fall of 1840, he gave a lecture about the Jamaican mission at Boston's Marlboro Chapel. It was the same site where Mahan had delivered an influential series of lectures on sanctification a few years earlier.

While in Boston, Ingraham called on a woman named Nancy Prince, who was living at the home of J. W. Holman, a Free Will Baptist pastor and abolitionist. Having already known of Prince's interest in Jamaica, Ingraham encouraged her to join the mission there. In August 1839 he had written his friend Amos Phelps that should Prince journey to Jamaica, "our arms and doors shall be open for her." A year later the invitation was formally issued in person, and she sailed for Jamaica aboard a ship called the *Scion* on November 16, 1840.[15]

Prince had already lived a full, challenging, and impressive life when Ingraham recruited her for mission work. She was born in Newburyport, Massachusetts, in 1799. Her mother was the daughter of Tobias Wornton, a man who had been taken captive in Africa and brought to the American colonies. Wornton had been enslaved, but he fought for liberty in the American Revolution and is remembered today for his military service at the Battle of Bunker Hill. He later gained his freedom. Prince's maternal grandmother was Native American. Her father, Thomas Gardner, worked in the whaling industry on Nantucket and was a free person. Prince made sure that others knew her ancestry. It demonstrated her family's investment in the blessings of liberty and her right to the same freedom as any other American.

Prince moved to Boston as a young person and was baptized at the African Meeting House in 1817. She then joined the free Black community on the north side of Beacon Hill and married a man named Nero Prince in 1824. Her husband secured a post among Russian royalty, and before long, Nancy and Nero Prince found themselves in St. Petersburg. Illness would eventually force Prince to

---

[15]D. S. Ingraham to Amos Augustus Phelps, August 6, 1839, Anti-slavery Collection, Boston Public Library.

return to Boston, and in a twist of tragedy, her husband would die before they could be reunited. But during her days in Russia, she observed a world that was built upon social hierarchy but did not order such distinctions according to race. The experience informed her later analysis of North American injustice.

In going to Jamaica, Prince hoped "to raise up and encourage the emancipated inhabitants, and teach the young children to read and work, to fear God, and put their trust in the Saviour." She made great contributions but also witnessed serious inequities. At one point she confronted racist propaganda from the United States claiming that emancipation had not helped the Jamaican people. She also indicted some missionaries when they demanded that Jamaicans pay for Bibles and the instruction of children. Prince observed that a common wage in Jamaica was but thirty-three cents per day, hardly enough to sustain a home and underwrite mission initiatives. Still, she believed in the possibility of authentic advocacy for recently emancipated people and labored on their behalf for some time, even after Ingraham's death in 1841.[16]

Prince and Ingraham toiled in different locales at first but reconnected during the summer of 1841. In July of that year, Prince encountered Ingraham as he came down from his work in the mountains, his health failing. Ingraham determined to sail for America again, knowing that his days were numbered. David and Betsey Ingraham, along with their daughters Sarah and Jane, set sail for Baltimore, continuing onward to the home of Theodore Weld, Angelina Grimké, and Sarah Grimké in Belleville, New Jersey. David succumbed to his tuberculosis while at the Weld-Grimké home on August 1, 1841. The revered abolitionist Theodore Sedgwick Wright, founding member of the American Anti-slavery Society and the first African American graduate of Princeton Theological Seminary, was sent for to preach his funeral sermon. While Betsey never returned to Jamaica after David's death, Sarah Penfield and her new husband, Thornton Bigelow Penfield (known to his family as "Bigelow"), went back to the island twenty years later in the 1860s. They served under the auspices of the American Missionary Association and worked at a place known as the Oberlin Mission Station. Today the legacy of the Ingraham family lives in the Oberlin Complex: a high school, medical clinic, and church, north of Kingston.

---

[16]Nancy Prince, *A Narrative of the Life and Travels of Mrs. Nancy Prince*, 2nd ed. (Boston: published by the author, 1853), 45.

The terrible incompleteness of the legacy left by Ingraham, Bradley, and Prince challenges us to continue the fight. "How long, O Lord?" When will God's justice reign? We have spiritual ancestors in these three who in their own courageous ways pointed toward God's future. How will we respond to the call they answered?

To confront this question requires us to act, and we would leave matters incomplete if we were merely to document past abuse and historical attempts to rise above injustice, though such aims are worthy. An exploration of this kind would fail miserably were it to lead to no action at all. Yet there is an equal danger, one that is often neglected in a rush to action. Before we can act justly, we must hear. White activists, in particular, are prone to overlook their privilege, take matters in hand, and force a change, often with plenty of self-congratulation along the way. The reprehensible irony of such behavior is that it turns others into instruments for the accomplishment of an agenda driven by well-meaning White people. But if the intrinsic worth of persons is critical for this kind of work, then hearing is as important as doing. Those of us with privilege must listen first and *then* act *with* others. All of us must understand our power or past lack of power in the conversation. Many of us are indeed called to speak and be heard, perhaps for the first time. Others, also perhaps for the first time, are called to listen and hear.

If we are to listen well, we must be willing to hear the whole story. Most of us know something about slavery and abolitionism in nineteenth-century America. But how well-versed are we in the lives of the African persons who were captured, enslaved, and transported in inhuman conditions across the Atlantic in the middle passage? Who were they? Where did they come from? What was the political, social, and economic context that would lead to the bondage of the 556 men, women, and children who were aboard the *Ulysses*, the slave brig that David Ingraham examined? Chapter two will describe West Africa around the time that the *Ulysses* set sail, offering a glimpse into the lives of the persons whose existences were shattered by the coming of the European slaving industry, and how it came to be that they were taken away from the places they called home.

"Soul-Destroyers Tore Me from My Mother's Arms"

WEST AFRICAN RESISTANCE TO THE SLAVE TRADE

Sègbégnon Mathieu Gnonhossou

I think I was between two and three years old when the soul-destroyers tore me from my mother's arms, somewhere in Africa, far back from the sea. They carried me a long distance to a ship; all the way I looked back, and cried. The ship was full of men and women loaded with chains; but I was so small, they let me run about on deck.

JAMES BRADLEY, 1834

The Ulysses . . . took her cargo of 556 slaves from the River Nuna [Nunez], from Popo, Sargos [perhaps Lagos], Whydar [Whydah/ Ouidah], and Bodgerry [Badagry]. . . . Let us think of the awful suffering occasioned in enslaving so many: the fathers robbed of their wives and children—children torn from the embrace of their mothers, and every relation and feeling dear to the human heart, severed and mangled—and who that has heart to pray, can refrain from exclaiming, "How long, O Lord, how long" shall this nefarious traffic continue?

DAVID INGRAHAM, 1840

I COME FROM AKPRO-MISSERETE, a town made up predominantly of Gun people, in the north of Porto-Novo, the capital city of Benin. My family's roots go back to Abeokuta, a city of refuge for those who left the disintegrating kingdom of Oyo—torn, as it was, by wars of control over the slave trade routes. Abeokuta was located in the Egba kingdom, which was part of what is now Nigeria. I remember becoming aware of the legacy of enslavement that had taken place along the West Coast of Africa when I took my first history class in middle school.

I had mixed feelings about what I learned, and for two reasons. For one, the class caused frustration in me toward White people, but that frustration was also tempered and complicated by my own experience. When I was younger, in grade school, I had lived in a house with a White American, a Peace Corps volunteer, whose service involved school construction in our villages, and I remember him being a very nice person. (When I came to the United States as an adult, I found him through a Google search and we were happily reconnected.) Second, I was perplexed about the role that Christianity played in the story, as it was told to us—as a part of the so-called three Cs of colonialism (Christianity, commerce, and civilization). I was born into a Methodist family, so I had a generally favorable view of Christianity, yet given my ancestors' background as refugees in Abeokuta, my ancestors almost certainly knew persons who were taken captive in slave raids and trafficked across the Atlantic to the New World by Europeans who claimed to be Christians.

Many generations later, my family continues to own land in what is now Benin. I have found it important for understanding my homeland, and for understanding the abolitionist revivalist response to African enslavement, to examine just how it came to be that so many multitudes of my ancestral people were enslaved and what resistance meant for those who stayed behind. This chapter examines how enslavement gripped that part of the world and plunged so many human beings into bondage.

THE CAPTURED SLAVE SHIP *ULYSSES* REVEALS GRAVE INJUSTICE

More than three centuries after it began, the European practice of enslaving Africans, usually called slave trading, had been outlawed by Great Britain (in 1807), the United States (1808), and France (1815). Yet the institution of slavery, the actual use of slave labor, would not become illegal in Britain and France (and their territories) and the United States until 1834, 1848, and 1865, respectively. Clandestine slave trading by smugglers continued relatively unabated until the late 1860s, feeding the slave markets of the Americas.[1]

On November 30, 1839, the Portuguese slave ship *Ulysses*, illegally carrying enslaved Africans, was captured near Cuba by the British vessel *Skipjack*. By the time of its capture, the *Ulysses* was on its eighth voyage, having previously eluded numerous attempts by the Royal Navy to seize its brig and rescue its captives. Records left by *Skipjack* crew members indicated that on that one voyage alone, 556 enslaved people had been forced onto the *Ulysses*, abducted, as Ingraham noted, "from the River Nuna [Nunez], from Popo, Sargos [perhaps Lagos], Whydar [Whydah/Ouidah], and Bodgerry [Badagry]," ports located in the contemporary nations of Guinea, Benin, and Nigeria.

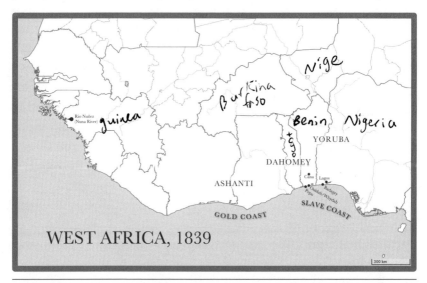

Figure 2.1. West African ports named as the embarkation points for enslaved people onboard the ship *Ulysses* (in David Ingraham's 1840 letter to *The Colored American* and other papers)

The ship was taken to Jamaica, a British territory at the time, where the captives were freed. David Ingraham, an Oberlin-trained American missionary in Jamaica, bore witness to the atrocities that happened aboard the *Ulysses*, diagramming the ship's dimensions in his journal, speaking of the dreadful conditions, and imploring the church to remain silent no longer to the injustice of human trafficking. "Let us consider," he wrote, "the suffocation they must have

---

[1] Roger Botte, "L'Esclavage Africain Après l'Abolition de 1848: Servitude et Droit du Sol," *Annales: Histoire, Sciences Sociales* 55, no. 5 (September–October 2000): 1009-37, 1011.

endured, from the little air they could get, and their consequent burning thirst, and small allowance of water; and who can but weep at the thought? And who can think of this and not see and feel through all his soul, the abomination and horror of that foul system which is commenced and generally continued at such an expense of human woe and cruelty?"[2]

THE SLAVE TRADE IN WEST AFRICA

Enslavement in West Africa was facilitated in large part through the kingdom of Dahomey, located in what is now Benin. King Guezo, who ruled from 1818 to 1858, was the monarch of Dahomey during the time that the *Ulysses* made its infamous voyages. He rose to power through bitter royal rivalries that resulted in a coup d'état against his brother, King Adandozan. The main sponsor of the coup was the wealthy Portuguese-Brazilian slave merchant, Francisco Félix de Souza (1754–1849), who had previously been imprisoned by Adandozan. Guezo freed De Souza and appointed him as a special representative for commercial matters, to be based in the port city of Ouidah (Whydah). Enslavement had flourished under Adandozan, who went so far as to negotiate a privileged commercial position for Dahomey through European diplomatic channels. But the business of enslavement became even stronger under Guezo's rule and included the practice, albeit rare, of enslaving people from Guezo's own kingdom in addition to those from Dahomey's hostile neighbors.[3]

British officials repeatedly tried to persuade Guezo to end enslavement. In 1849, Viscount Palmerston, Britain's foreign secretary, wrote a *Letter to be Delivered to African Chiefs*, meant to convince King Guezo to shift away from enslavement and to focus instead on commercializing natural resources. "In this manner," wrote Palmerston, "the great natural resources of your country will be developed; your wealth and your comforts will be increased; and the detestable practice of stealing, buying, and selling men,

---

[2]This paragraph and the preceding one: D. S. Ingraham, "Capture of the *Ulysses*—the Suffering of the Slaves," in *The Colored American*, April 4, 1840. River Nuna (Nunez) is in Guinea. "Popo" could be both located either in contemporary Togo (Little Popo) or Benin (Grand Popo). These two regions are nearby one another, though they now belong to two different countries. Ingraham's record only mentions Popo without specifying which one. We have not been able to locate Sargos in contemporary West Africa, though perhaps it referred to Lagos in today's Nigeria; we do know that Bodgerry (Badagry) is in present-day Nigeria, just over the border from Benin. Whydar (Whydah/Ouidah) was part of the kingdom of Dahomey, now Benin.
[3]Ana Lucia Araujo, "Dahomey, Portugal and Bahia: King Adandozan and the Atlantic Slave Trade," *Slavery and Abolition: A Journal of Slave and Post-Slave Studies* 33, no. 1 (2012): 1-19.

Figure 2.2. A mother in West Africa courageously resists a "soul-destroyer" (James Bradley's term for men involved in the slave trade)

women, and children, which is now the bane and the disgrace of Africa, will be put an end to."[4]

Palmerston's description of the "detestable practice" corroborates James Bradley's description of how he had left Africa as a child of two to three years, captured with other people to be sold. It also echoes David Ingraham's emotional plea for Americans to recognize the human costs associated with slavery. Bradley's and Ingraham's expressions, such as "I looked back, and cried," "The ship was full of men and women loaded with chains," "The awful suffering," "Fathers robbed," and "Children torn from," all reflect the woes associated with enslavement. When the *Ulysses* finally arrived at its destination of Montego Bay, Jamaica, twenty-three enslaved Africans had died. Seven more would die within a month from aftereffects of the journey. Indeed, the Portuguese captain of the slave brig had torn down a partition from his cabin so that he could stack 115 more people into a "dismal den" (Ingraham's term) and thereby make a greater profit for himself.[5]

---

[4]Tim Coates, ed., *King Guezo of Dahomey: 1850–52: The Abolition of the Slave Trade on the West Coast of Africa* (London: The Stationery Office, 2001), 3-4.

[5]James Bradley, "Brief Account of an Emancipated Slave Written by Himself, at the Request of the Editor," in *The Oasis*, ed. Lydia Maria Child (Boston: Benjamin C. Bacon, 1834), 106; *British and Foreign Anti-slavery Reporter*, October 7, 1840, 262; Ingraham, "Capture of the *Ulysses*."

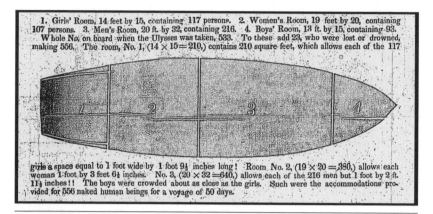

1. Girls' Room, 14 feet by 15, containing 117 persons.   2. Women's Room, 19 feet by 20, containing 107 persons.   3. Men's Room, 20 ft. by 32, containing 216.   4. Boys' Room, 13 ft. by 15, containing 93. Whole No. on board when the Ulysses was taken, 533.   To these add 23, who were lost or drowned, making 556.   The room, No. 1, (14 × 15 = 210,) contains 210 square feet, which allows each of the 117

girls a space equal to 1 foot wide by 1 foot 9½ inches long!   Room No. 2, (19 × 20 = 380,) allows each woman 1 foot by 3 feet 6¼ inches.   No. 3, (20 × 32 = 640,) allows each of the 216 men but 1 foot by 2 ft. 11½ inches!!   The boys were crowded about as close as the girls.   Such were the accommodations provided for 556 naked human beings for a voyage of 50 days.

Figure 2.3. Diagram of the slave ship *Ulysses,* from David Ingraham's letter to *The Colored American,* 1840

HOW NEGATIVE PORTRAYALS OF AFRICANS PROVIDED SUPPORT FOR THE SLAVE TRADE

How was such a grave injustice possible? What could make someone like King Guezo willing to supply slave ships with captives, even from one's own country? The popular storytelling is that a preexisting slaving system was used by Africans who were ready to sell other Africans to gain wealth for themselves and their kingdoms. Enslavement has often been described as having been initiated by African chiefs and middlemen. "The trade on the coast," reads one such accounting, "was for gold or humanity, it was a trade that passed from African to European hands." Some historians emphasize African villainy; European slave traders, they have said, rarely traveled into Africa's interior to capture their human cargo, instead depending on indigenous rulers to provide enslaved Africans and fuel the trade. "From the beginning of the external slave trade," one such historian has written, "African rulers attempted to control the trade by limiting slave markets to commercial centers. Because local African governments obtained slaves through wars, raids, kidnapping, and tribute collection, these same African rulers would also supply slaves to the coast for sale to the European slavers." Some historians go so far as to say that Africans persisted in the practice of enslaving each other even after all of Europe came to want its abolition.[6]

---

[6]James Walvin, *Atlas of Slavery* (Harlow, UK: Pearson Education, 2006), 58; Wayne Ackerson, "African Institution," in *Encyclopedia of the Middle Passage*, ed. Toyin Falola and Amanda Warnock (Westport, CT: Greenwood, 2007), 23.

But to what extent is that narrative true? Such an unnuanced perspective does not fully account for how the slave trade evolved or the stories of the many Africans who did not support it, including West Africans' nonviolent resistance to the slave trade. Just as the motives of various Europeans were mixed, with some endorsing enslavement for personal gain while others called for its abolition, so too were the motives of West Africans. But while it is true that a few of them became part of the European-initiated slave trading system, a greater number of Africans resisted enslavement in various ways.

Since the motive of many Europeans was to acquire enslaved Africans to feed the booming industrial capitalism of Europe and the Americas with free labor, many European portrayals of the slave trade vilified Africans, African governments, and African kings and chiefs as the culprits responsible for the genesis of the slave trade in the first place. "Africans sold their own people" was a common saying at the time, one that was used as a basis for increasing enslavement and has since become useful in opposing appeals for reparation. But it is a caricature, one that was and is still centered on a Eurocentric narrative of Africa as a dark, uncivilized, and barbarous land, and that was used for normalizing the enslavement of Africans and the colonization of the continent for hundreds of years.[7]

A Christianized version of this negative portrayal of Africans was based on a misreading of the Genesis passage in which a drunken Noah curses Canaan, one of his grandsons. Ham, Canaan's father, has offended Noah, who responds by declaring that the descendants of Canaan will forever be slaves. A bizarre interpretation of that biblical story was used for justifying portrayals of Africans as the cursed descendants of Ham. Black and White abolitionists discredited this flawed reading of the Bible passage and its implicit depiction of Africans as the inferior part of the whole of humankind. In the same African American newspaper (*The Colored American*) that contained David Ingraham's horrendous description of the *Ulysses* slave brig, an article in the very next issue—the piece was addressed to "My Colored Friends"—tried to correct the faulty interpretation of Scripture. Speaking to Christians of African descent who might have come to accept such a pejorative line of thought, the author wanted African people instead to "hold up

---

[7] Henri Louis Gates Jr., "Ending the Slavery Blame-Game," *New York Times*, April 22, 2010, accessed April 24, 2022, www.nytimes.com/2010/04/23/opinion/23gates.html.

[their] head" and "be not cast down" in response to commonplace racist statements, such as this example: "What can this poor, neglected, down-trodden people accomplish? What can these feeble and condemned children of Ham do, whose touch is contamination, whose breath is poison, whose society is pollution, whose perspiration is death?"[8]

The denigration of Africa and Africans is noticeable from documents as early as Phillis Wheatley's 1773 poetry, which described Africa as pagan, "the land of errors, and Egyptian gloom," from which God mercifully took her through enslavement. The belittling description has persisted throughout the centuries and is traceable even among notable antislavery icons such as Frederick Douglass, whose attitude toward African civilization was a mixture of positive and negative. More recently, comedian Richard Pryor claimed that he thanked God for slavery since it took him out of Africa. Descriptions like these have served to emphasize the so-called natural bar-barism of Africa by linking the growth of enslavement to intentionally pro-voked wars and slave raids as a means of procuring enslaved Africans, either for sacrifice or for sale. Nineteenth-century press reports and some mis-sionary documents served to paint enslavement in West Africa by Euro-peans as a "civilizing" work, a lesser evil compared with that of leaving Af-ricans in the hands even of their own brutal and heartless monarchs.

The real purpose of the Europeans' negative portrayals of Dahomey, however, was not to civilize or transform Africans but to mobilize Western public support for existing imperialist interests and military interventions.

---

[8]See J. D. Gardiner, "Address Delivered at the Laying of the Cornerstone of a New Church Belonging to the Colored People of Sag Harbor," *The Colored American*, April 11, 1840; Stephen R. Haynes, *Noah's Curse: The Biblical Justification of American Slavery* (New York: Oxford University Press, 2002), 68-76, 97-102; David M. Goldenberg, *Black and Slave: The Origins and History of the Curse of Ham*, Studies of the Bible and Its Reception 10 (Berlin: De Gruyter, 2017), 40-42, 153-55, 238-49. An earlier Genesis passage, the story of Cain's murder of Abel, also came up in common accounts of African racial infe-riority or villainy, using a misappropriation of Cain's "mark"; see Genesis 4:1-16 NRSV. Ruth W. Mel-linkoff, *The Mark of Cain* (Berkeley: University of California Press, 1981), 76-80; J. D. Gardiner.
[9]Phillis Wheatley, *To the University of Cambridge, in New-England*, in *Religious and Moral Poems*, also titled *Poems on Various Subjects, Religious and Moral* (1771; Project Gutenberg, 2019), www .gutenberg.org/files/409/409-h/409-h.htm#link2H_4_0007; Daniel Kilbride, "What Did Africa Mean to Frederick Douglass?," in *Slavery and Abolition: A Journal of Slave and Post-slave Studies* 36, no. 1 (2014): 23, doi.org/10.1080/0144039X.2014.916516; Marion Berghahn, *Images of Africa in Black American Literature* (New York: Macmillan, 1977), 40-41; Henry Louis Gates Jr., *Wonders of the African World* (New York: Knopf, 1999), 7; Véronique Campion-Vincent, "L'Image du Dahomey dans la Presse Française (1890–1895): Les Sacrifices Humains," *Cahiers d'Études Africaines* 7, no. 25 (1967), 27-58.

Those interventions served to create the barbarous conditions in the first place, which then led to further interventions—an ongoing loop of injustice that was used to rationalize and perpetuate profit-motivated oppression.[10]

Partly due to some scholarly grounding that has backed up the popular perspective, these negative portrayals have clung tightly to Africa. Throughout the nineteenth century, the kingdom of Dahomey had a reputation across Europe, especially in France and England, as a hub of barbarism and enslavement. By the time of the 1839 capture of the enslaved West Africans aboard the *Ulysses*, King Guezo was the ruling monarch in the area, and indeed, Guezo's leadership lent credibility to the narrative. Paul Merruau (1812–1882), a contemporary French explorer and novelist, wrote about Guezo's personal involvement in slave raids and his association with the main European slave captains. According to Merruau enslavement took place in a three-stage process: warfare, led by an African chief; then the purchase of prisoners by European traders; and finally, the forced shipment of slaves by European captains. Dahomey earned a reputation not only as the "Slave Coast" but also as a bloody kingdom of unimaginable cruelties, in which human sacrifices by decapitation were carried out annually.[11]

THE INTRODUCTION OF EUROPEAN ENSLAVEMENT

But what was the larger context of King Guezo and the Dahomean kingdom? The continuous European interventions had profoundly transformed several smaller West African kingdoms that had existed prior to the introduction of slavery. Those kingdoms, which Dahomey eventually conquered, had been kin-based communities with values of solidarity so strong that European visitors who first encountered them interpreted their lack of private land ownership as the erasure of the individual. But that reading of the landscape was incorrect; it was simply that joint families, rather than individuals, were the basic social and political units in these independent kingdoms. The characteristics of these earlier kingdoms were so starkly different from those of the latter kingdom of Dahomey that it is right to see Dahomey as an amassment of political power constructed by European slave traders. The slavers' influence transformed the entire region from that

---

[10]Campion-Vincent, "L'Image du Dahomey," 57-58.

[11]Paul Merruau, "Le Dahomaey et le Roi Guezo," *Revue des Deux Mondes, Nouvelle Période* 12 (December 15, 1851; repr., Las Vegas: Histoire, 2021, as a standalone book), 8.

kin-based society into an abstract civil governance, with similarity to what
we may recognize in a Western monarchy.[12]

The transition required Dahomey to intentionally undermine the preexisting kin-based bonds, solidarity, and communal life that had defined the
kingdoms it conquered. Africans such as Guezo and his predecessors, who
led the kingdom of Dahomey from the civil law perspective, created political
conflicts with other Africans who still lived with the native African sense of
solidarity. Dahomey, for instance, purposefully separated families and communities, mixing groups of people together in ways that created mistrust
and constant strife.[13]

Between 1724 and 1727, in just one example, the Dahomey monarch sub-
jugated Ouidah (Whydah) for control of its international trade. To do so
required conquering neighboring communities as well, creating severe rivalries between people groups and destroying the kin-based relationships
that held the region together. Those neighboring communities mounted a
strong resistance that initially caused the Dahomean monarch to retreat, but
he later returned with strategies foreign to Africa at the time, such as formal
economic agreements and the corruption of native rulers, mixing the whole
enterprise with military power. The new tactics, largely European in origin,
achieved a conquest by which he henceforth controlled both Ouidah and its
neighboring community.[14]

Once Ouidah fell to Dahomey, it grew to become the infamously largest
center of slave trading in the region. Over a million people were forcibly
shipped from its slave ports. Francisco Félix de Souza, the notorious Bra-
zilian slave trader, lived a life of luxury in Ouidah. Since many of the enslaved people on the *Ulysses* were taken from Ouidah, it is highly probable
that the Portuguese captain of the *Ulysses* worked directly with De Souza.

Although a climate of abolitionism as expressed by British officials such as
Palmerston had developed during the time in which Guezo ruled, the anti-
slavery mindset was compromised by prior dealmaking among European

---

[12]Stanley Diamond, "Dahomey: A Proto-state in West Africa" (PhD diss., Columbia University,
1951), 20-22.

[13]Diamond, "Dahomey," 26-31.

[14]Léonard Wantchékon, H. W. Serge Ouitona, and Valère Sogbossi, *De Gléxwé à Ouidah: Histoire
d'une Ville Multi-séculaire (XIVe–XXIe siècle)* (Tampere, Finland: Atramenta, 2021), 25-28; David
Ross, "Robert Norris, Agaja, and the Dahomean Conquest of Allada and Whydah," *History in
Africa: A Journal of Method* 16 (1989): 312-13.

SHIPPING SLAVES THROUGH THE SURF, WEST-AFRICAN COAST. A CRUISER SIGNALLED IN SIGHT.
(From a Sketch by a merchant on the Coast.)

Figure 2.4. Abducted West Africans are transported through the surf to a waiting slave ship, 1856

powers. These deals facilitated the persistence of African enslavement, particularly from the port of Ouidah. Just prior to Guezo's rise to power, the 1817 Anglo-Portuguese Anti-slave Trade Treaty made enslavement illegal north of the equator but legal to the south. Though Dahomey was located just north of the equator, Ouidah-bound Portuguese traders invented an excuse: legal enslavement areas, they said, were *nearby* the equator—close enough to justify their enslaving activities everywhere in West Africa.[15]

From 1835 until 1839, Cuba-bound vessels registered as Portuguese often evaded the law, continuing their enslaving in Ouidah. The practice went on for a few years before the British took drastic unilateral measures to increase enforcement and arrest suspected Portuguese slave ships, one of which was the *Ulysses*. Ship captains took note, inventing elaborate ploys to elude the Royal Navy's patrols. Crews, for example, would notify conspirators on land that the empty vessel was approaching to retrieve new slaves for an Atlantic passage; those on land would then hurry the slave cargoes to isolated places to be brought aboard as quickly as possible.[16]

---

[15]Robin Law, *Ouidah: The Social History of a West Africa Slaving "Port," 1727–1892*, Western African Studies (Athens: Ohio University Press, 2004), 156-57.

[16]Law, *Ouidah*, 157; Patrick Manning, *Slavery, Colonialism and Economic Growth in Dahomey, 1640–1960*, African Studies (New York: Cambridge University Press, 1982), 47.

HOW EUROPEANS INTRODUCED AND
EXPANDED ENSLAVEMENT

The European slave trade made this era a chaotic, violent one. The never-ending barrage of invasions, slave raids, and territorial expansions in the region gave rise to massive movements of population and the emergence of refugee communities. Indications are that most of the people who were abducted from Ouidah during 1831–1840, the period in which the *Ulysses* was captured, originated from predominantly Yoruba lands (the present-day cities of Save, Ketou, Nago, Porto-Novo, and Wèmè) and were largely Yoruba by ethnicity, captured through Dahomean slave raids. Yet despite the decline that was characteristic of most kingdoms on the Bight of Benin as the slave trade ripped men, women, and children from their shores, scholars agree that the kingdom of Dahomey was a different story. It not only survived the period of transatlantic enslavement but emerged as an even more powerful kingdom than it had been before.[17]

How did such an anomaly take place? It seems that Dahomey's power and influence arose because of a deliberate strategy by European slave traders to set up the kingdom as their intermediary for slave trading purposes, transforming (as we have noted) the semi-autonomous kingdoms of the area into a centralized, bureaucratic kingdom exactly suitable for the commerce of transatlantic enslavement. The rise of Dahomey in the eighteenth and nineteenth centuries as an economic and military force in the region would not have been possible without a European presence to assist its metamorphosis for enslavement purposes.[18]

Contrary to the dominant thesis that enslavement was first and foremost an African practice, I submit that it was foreign to the region from which the captives aboard the *Ulysses* originated. There was no word for the slavery introduced by foreigners among the Gbe people (eastern Ghana through western Nigeria). As a result, their languages (Ewe, Gen, Fon, Adja, Phla) had to adapt to the new practice. When the practice came to Africa and had to be named, the Gun people (one of the Fon varieties in Benin and Nigeria)

---

[17]Manning, *Slavery,* 30-45; see also the delimitation on the map of the Bight of Benin in Manning, *Slavery*, 23.

[18]Robin Law, "Dahomey and the Slave Trade: Reflections on the Historiography of the Rise of Dahomey," *Journal of African History* 27, no. 2 (1986): 237-67; J. Cameron Monroe, "Dahomey and the Atlantic Slave Trade: Archaeology and Political Order on the Bight of Benin," in *Archaeology of Atlantic Africa and the African Diaspora*, ed. Akinwumi Ogundiran and Toyin Falola (Bloomington: Indiana University Press, 2007), 114-15.

referred to slavery as *kanlinmon*, the components of which mean "beast" or "animal" and "seeing." Thus, the newly coined word indicated that a slave (*kanlinmon-non*) was a human who was "perceived as an animal," an apt term given the unsanitary conditions, physical restraints, iron shackles, and other forms of violent repression that were used during enslavement and throughout the history of the middle passage of slaves across the Atlantic. Another word used to describe the practice is *kannumon*, the components of which mean "cord, net," "tail end," and "trap." Thus the newly coined word indicated that the enslaved person (*kannumon-non*) is a person trapped using a net, a deceptive method invented for slaving raids. But it's important to note that such a perception of human beings was absent from the African linguistic experience before such foreign contact took place.[19]

Before Dahomey emerged as a slaving kingdom, Allada and Hueda, two communities that later became part of it, emerged as major trading ports. Allada's trade was typical of African kingdoms, developing at first through intra-African commercial relationships. Archaeological findings suggest that both Allada and Hueda grew by cultivating international trade long before they became a major enslaving area in the seventeenth century. None of the earliest Europeans who traveled to the area reported seeing the trade of human beings. When European slave trading did emerge in these communities, it was only on a small scale at first. But when Europeans later threw their support behind Dahomey, including by supplying arms, the result was that other kingdoms and cities in the region turned into major enslavement allies. Such was the case with the city of Popo, just outside of Dahomey. Popo became a major slave port and was home to some of the enslaved people who were forced aboard the *Ulysses*. The first European commercial overture to Popo came from the Portuguese (1641–1650), followed quickly by the Dutch and English. The British got the upper hand, eventually raising the flag for the Royal African Company in Popo to secure "this new trade."[20]

---

[19]The words *kanlinmon-non* and *kannumon-non* are so offensive in Gungbe that early Bible translations in that language do not use them to translate Hebrew and Greek words for *slave*. Such translations used other words instead—*afànumẹ* or *mẹmẹsi*—which communicate a temporary (and sometimes voluntary) dependency. It's also worth noting that Arabs had preceded Europeans by several centuries in engaging in slavery in the region. See John Hunwick, *West Africa, Islam, and the Arab World: Studies in Honor of Basil Davidson* (Princeton, NJ: Markus Wiener, 2006), 75-90.

[20]J. Cameron Monroe, "Urbanism on West Africa's Slave Coast: Archaeology Sheds New Light on Cities in the Era of the Atlantic Slave Trade," *American Scientist*, September–October 2011, 402;

There are additional examples of the extent of eventual European influence and power in the region. For instance, the kingdoms that used European guns against one another in utterly destructive warfare left only European slave traders' lodges intact, such as De Souza's villa. Meanwhile, native lackeys, who helped increase the volume of enslavement, built European-style houses for themselves.[21]

What happened in Dahomey mirrored the larger European enslaving presence in the rest of West Africa during the same era. Categories like *master* and *slave* had not been apparent in indigenous social structures. Yet, given the wealth accumulation and the increasing classism in urban areas that took on European characteristics, Dahomean politicians developed practices that hid those newly introduced class distinctions from the people's view. The goal was to make the new, foreign-style Dahomean social order appear to be native. That way the African elites who cooperated with European slave traders and accumulated wealth and power might do so unnoticed. But the wealth garnered from transatlantic commerce was funneled into a circle of royal palace elites, resulting in a clearly visible dichotomy between the culture of indigenous rural communities and that of urban areas, which were starting to function more and more like those of Europe.[22]

Cana, one of the communities that Dahomey had conquered, is a good example of this tension. It emerged from the eighteenth century "as a major city involved in the transshipment of human captives to coastal slave traders."

Kenneth G. Kelly, "The Archaeology of African-European Interaction: Investigating the Social Roles of Trade, Traders, and the Use of Space in the Seventeenth- and Eighteenth-Century Hueda Kingdom, Republic of Bénin," *World Archaeology* 28, no. 3 (February 1997): 351-69; Neil L. Norman, "Hueda (Whydah) Country and Town: Archaeological Perspectives on the Rise and Collapse of an African Atlantic Kingdom," *International Journal of African Historical Studies* 42, no. 3 (2009): 387-410; I. A. Akinjogbin, *Dahomey and Its Neighbours, 1708–1818* (Cambridge: Cambridge University Press, 1967); Patrick Manning, "The Slave Trade in the Bight of Benin, 1640–1890," in *The Uncommon Market: Essays in the Economic History of the Atlantic Slave Trade*, ed. Henry A. Gemery and Jan S. Hogendorn (New York: Academic, 1979), 115-17, 135; Law, "Dahomey and the Slave Trade," 239-42; Robin Law, ed., *The English in West Africa 1681–1683: The Local Correspondence of the Royal African Company of England, 1681–1699*, pt. 1 (Oxford: Oxford University Press, 1997), 256.
[21]Silke Strickrodt, "The Atlantic Slave Trade and a Very Small Place in Africa: Global Processes and Local Factors in the History of Little Popo, 1680s to 1860s," in *The End of Slavery in Africa and the Americas: A Comparative Approach*, ed. Ulrike Schmieder, Katja Füllberg-Stolberg, and Michael Zeuske (Münster, Germany: Lit Verlag, 2011), 15-26.
[22]J. Cameron Monroe, "Cities, Slavery, and Rural Ambivalence in Precolonial Dahomey," in *The Archaeology of Slavery: A Comparative Approach to Captivity and Coercion*, ed. Lydia Wilson Marshall, Center for Archaeological Investigations, Southern Illinois University Carbondale, occasional paper no. 41 (Carbondale: Southern Illinois University Press, 2014), 192-214.

Cana's rise to the international stage was made possible by families who had to travel hundreds of kilometers "to serve the interests of a revenue-hungry elite class." Many did so "through predatory slave raids by Dahomey." Cana's transformation into a major enslaving hub was a political process. It was not something native to the land. But because the process was shaped on the model of modern Western civil principles and not the kin-based joint family that had been widespread throughout the land, many Africans who were subjected to this type of new society mounted various forms of resistance.[23]

WEST AFRICAN RESISTANCE STRATEGIES

West Africans resisted the challenges to their freedom and their traditional way of life in several ways. The first was to create cities of refuge, places of sanctuary for those fleeing enslavement. These cities, places like the Wèmè kingdom, the Porto-Novo kingdom (which eventually became the capital city of the current Republic of Benin), Ekpe, and Badagry, transformed into new kingdoms under the control of those who settled in them, free of the oppressive rule of Dahomey. The turning of the refuge cities into independent kingdoms helped develop culturally integrated communities that shared the same linguistic group, the Aja-Ewe. A subgroup, the Gun people, enjoyed natural protection against continuous invasions from the kingdom of Dahomey thanks to surrounding lagoons. The Gun thereby succeeded in resisting Dahomean raiders, who were more effective on dry lands than on waterways: "The existence of Lake Nokoue, together with the marshes around the Rivers So and Wèmè . . . formed a barrier against the penetration by the more purely terrestrial [land-based] power of Dahomey, and so tended to preserve the political and cultural autonomy of the Gun."[24]

Over time, the protective nature of the marshes proved to be insufficient because the lagoon dried up. But the people, resolved to remain free from oppression, became creative. They relocated to new areas that also provided water protection, like the Ganvie and So regions, developing canoe-based warfare strategies for warding off raiders. They also consciously devised

---

[23]J. Cameron Monroe, "'When the King breaks a town he builds another': Politics, Slavery, and Constructed Urban Landscapes in Tropical West Africa," in *Landscapes of Preindustrial Urbanism*, ed. Georges Farhat (Washington, DC: Dumbarton Oaks Research Library and Collection, 2020), 281-82; Bernard-Copé, *Les Royaumes de Wèmè (1525–1779)* (Porto-Novo, Benin: Symboles de l'Amitié, 2012), 22-56.

[24]Manning, *Slavery*, 40.

mixed, diverse community living, thus emphasizing togetherness in the face of the ever-present threat of slave raids.[25]

Resistance to enslavement took place even within Dahomey itself. Before the European enslavers arrived, a solidarity had characterized residents as a kin-based people. But the growing new civic identity made the people citizens of a distant monarchy in which all individuals were considered *les choses du monarque*, or "the things of the monarch." Everything under the monarchy, from the slave raids to the shipment of people to the New World, hinged upon commodifying people. One way people were turned into "things" was the use of a census-tax-conscription pattern: the state would take a census and impose individual-based taxes, a practice previously unknown in kin-based communities. The taxes would enrich the royal family and feed the state's war machine, which was also fed by conscription as a way of asserting the state's dominance over the people. Such practice was continued throughout the colonial period that followed enslavement (1894–1960).[26]

Ordinary Dahomeans, however, resisted the new "thing-ification" of people, subverting the whole enterprise when census takers would visit. Treating state agents as outsiders, citizens resisted by keeping to themselves, giving incorrect information, and sharing the little resources they had among themselves, rather than paying taxes—essentially by doing just as they had done before the new state machine descended upon them. The state responded by cajoling some individuals, including village chiefs, luring them into service as lackey agents. This created internal conflicts among Dahomeans as individuals and joint families resisted other Dahomeans serving as state agents by refusing to pay those taxes. This was the case with Gnonhossou, my grandfather, who, based on my father's recollection, died from grave injuries to his feet for refusing to honor such taxations. The internal conflict also included the abuse of religion. The state used Vodoun priests, rites, and symbols for enslavement goals, such as when priests would coerce individuals to pay taxes on pain of illness or death by having stirred the displeasure of evil spirits or deadly snakes.[27]

---

[25]Elisée Soumonni, "Lacustrine Villages in South Benin as Refuges from the Slave Trade," in *Fighting the Slave Trade: West African Strategies*, ed. Sylviane A. Diouf (Athens: Ohio University Press, 2003), 3-14, 8-9.

[26]Diamond, "Dahomey," 36, 62, 67.

[27]Diamond, "Dahomey," 38, 48. The Vodoun way of life was deeply transformed during the slave trade to suit oppressive practices. It is to be understood as an elaborate system of priesthood including a seminary (*Hounkpamin*), something far more sophisticated than its magical portrayals

Guezo took control of indigenous justice courts and used them to exact sig-nificant portions of disputed money and property to run the state, keeping some of it for the royal family. The effect was to cause yet another aspect of Dahomean life—the consensus-based justice system—to descend into corruption, leading to legal arrangements that served as indirect means of levying taxes. He also created unnecessary laws under the pretext of protecting the citizens, with the real purpose of creating a new collective psychology of the people as "the things of the King." His new law against homicide was an example. Murders had been extremely rare in the preexisting kin-based communities of Dahomey, but Guezo created a law asserting that only the king had the right to take human life, thereby indirectly forbidding violent rebellion against state agents, something that became increasingly likely in the new oppressive climate.[28]

Kin solidarity was the people's most potent weapon of resistance. Aware of how powerful the people's loyalty to each other was, the state aimed to weaken it in any way it could. Kin-based attachment to land was one such example of their resistance. In the indigenous worldview, land was unsel-lable and not to be commercialized. So strong was this attachment that Glélé, the king who succeeded Guezo, turned down French colonizers' offer to buy Dahomean land even though he was in favor of colonization. The land united the people and they usually stood together to defend it.[29]

Any member of a joint family could inherit a piece of land as a caretaker, a practice that has survived until this day despite contemporary legal mea-sures that threaten it. My own father, tapping into this long-held value, ap-pealed to all eleven of his children to pay newly mandated government fees so that our family could hold on to the land that he had inherited from his father. Although our ancestral land is now divided up among the eleven of us, the pieces will continue to be held together within our extended family and passed down to the next generation.

Kin solidarity was significantly weakened in Dahomey over time and set the precedent for internal rivalries upon which post-slavery Western imperi-alism flourished. Nevertheless, in some areas, solidarity survived the years of

---

in the media. See Adjignon Débora Gladys Hounkpe, "Educational Practices in Voodoo Convents in Benin," in *Educational Theories and Practices from the Majority World*, ed. Pierre R. Dasen and Abdeljalil Akkari (London: Sage, 2008), 306-27; Diamond, "Dahomey," 49-52.

[28]Diamond, "Dahomey," 73-76.

[29]Diamond, "Dahomey," 72.

the slave raids and continued well into the early years of the formal European occupation of Africa. Writing in 1917, General George Joseph Toutee, a French colonial officer in Dahomey, witnessed that solidarity firsthand. French colonial troops experienced great difficulty in their movements from one place to another in occupied Dahomey. Surprised, General Toutee attributed the native resistance to *L'esprit de solidarité*, "the spirit of solidarity." He added that even the official Dahomean army did not fight against imperialism with the fervor of the popular resistance that he encountered among the people.[30]

During Guezo's reign, Thomas Birch Freeman, an Afro-British Methodist missionary whose mother was English and whose father was African, visited Badagry, Ouidah, and Popo, among other places in West Africa. Contrary to Francisco Félix de Souza, a mulatto (mixed-race person) who actively worked to increase the enslaving business in Dahomey, Freeman was a different kind of mulatto who actively countered enslavement. He did so through his introduction of a Wesleyan approach to Christianity. Freeman's method included an attempt to persuade Guezo to turn to agricultural business and away from enslaving and other dehumanizing practices, implicitly challenging the brutality that the pro-European monarch had carried forth. Perhaps as a sign of his change of heart, mixed with his reading of the political and economic international relations that were changing around him, Guezo eventually agreed to stop enslavement. He agreed that Wesleyan "missionaries should settle at Whydah." Even today in Benin (and all West Africa), resistance is still present wherever freedom-seeking Africans and African-descended persons stand against new forms of oppression.[31]

CONCLUSION

The enslavement that took place on the west coast of Africa was a dramatic story of injustice against Black bodies and souls, for whom living free and productively was as natural as breathing is to all human beings. European encroachments had the effect of destroying much of that African legacy, but the quest for freedom through resistance was also a natural response.

---

[30]Robin Law, "The Politics of Commercial Transition: Factional Conflict in Dahomey in the Context of the Ending of the Atlantic Slave Trade," *Journal of African History* 38, no. 2 (1997): 213-33; Diamond, "Dahomey," 42.

[31]Guezo, "From Guezo, King of Dahomey, to Her Majesty Queen Victoria," July 4, 1850, cited in Coates, *King Guezo*, 81.

The story of the capture of the *Ulysses* demonstrates that well-orchestrated resistance tactics within Africa against European enslavement did not always work; millions of Africans ended up being captured, enslaved, and coercively shipped to the Americas and elsewhere. Resistance, however, finds its value not only in how successfully it has achieved its goal but in the degree to which it expresses people's humanity, particularly when that humanity has been under assault. To resist is to be fully human. Many Africans survived the attempts to enslave them by creatively setting up refuge cities, building alternative kingdoms, and acting with a kin-based spirit of solidarity, thriving against all odds.

Even those who landed in new, unwanted places, such as James Bradley and other African Americans, enjoyed the solidarity of African-descended kinfolk, something that became evident for the 216 men, 107 women, 93 boys, and 117 girls aboard the *Ulysses*. Ten months after the *Ulysses* émigrés landed in Jamaica, "a considerable number of these people" experienced oppression from a White Jamaican landowner who exploited their labor through horrid working conditions in what was known as the "apprenticeship" system. According to a newspaper account of the incident, the émigrés were "charging him with cruelty." When they demanded a new workplace, a group of Black Jamaicans protested on their behalf. As newly emancipated people, one can imagine that the African-descended Jamaicans drew from their native sense of liberty and their powerful, kin-based solidarity to guide them. They may even have been immersed in the nonoppressive Christianity offered by the holiness perspective discussed in this book—a fuel for their resolve to live free, as people created in God's image.[32]

In the next chapter, David Daniels will explore how the main historical figures we are profiling in this book constructed their concepts of freedom, equality, and justice differently even from how their abolitionist counterparts did, drawing from their own perspectives, which were shaped by their lived experiences. In "thinking with" rather than just "thinking about" Nancy Prince and James Bradley, Daniels will ask how we as Christians can identify the opportunities and obstacles involved in the struggle to erect a more racially just society today.

---

[32]Ingraham, diagram with caption, in "Capture of the *Ulysses*," *British and Foreign Anti-slavery Reporter*, October 7, 1840, 262.

CHAPTER THREE

"LIBERTY, LIBERTY!"

WITNESSES TO A MORE RACIALLY EQUITABLE FUTURE

David D. Daniels III

It is well known that the color of one's skin does not prohibit [one]
from any place or station that he or she may be capable of occupying.

NANCY GARDNER PRINCE (REGARDING RUSSIA), 1850

Thanks to the Lord, prejudice against color
does not exist in Lane Seminary.

JAMES BRADLEY, 1834

Yet their present state is blissful, compared to slavery.

NANCY GARDNER PRINCE
(REGARDING EMANCIPATED JAMAICANS), 1853

WHAT A WORLD we would live in if racism no longer restricted people from flourishing as human beings. As part of the Dialogue on Race and Faith Project, which oversaw the production of this book, I read with amazement the testimony of Nancy Gardner Prince, an African American woman, and her personal experience of imperial Russia in the early nineteenth century as a "prejudice-free" society. Could such a world or society have existed in Western culture as far back as two hundred years ago? If it did, could it exist again in the United States in our lifetime?

Until I studied Prince and James Bradley my knowledge of revivalist abolitionists centered mainly around their critiques of slavery and their campaigns to end it. Even though I teach the history of Christianity in the United States, I understood abolitionists only narrowly. Weren't abolitionists focused almost solely on abolishing slavery? As I came to discover, it was not necessarily so. A second plank of the early-1830s abolitionist platform, for example, pointed to racial justice, the complete ending of discrimination. These abolitionists and others like them pursued racial justice in the Northern free states, a step beyond emancipation, while they also worked to end slavery in the Southern and border states where slavery was still in force.

This chapter will introduce an early revivalist abolitionism, one that aimed for more than merely the end of slavery, through the narratives of two abolitionists who intersected with David Stedman Ingraham: Nancy Gardner Prince, a revivalist laywoman, émigré to Russia, entrepreneur, philanthropist, abolitionist, and missionary; and James Bradley, a freed person, abolitionist, and revivalist clergyperson. Both explored the historical achievability of racial coexistence and caught glimpses of it as they worked for a racially just society. They each testified to having lived in interracial communities that gestured toward justice in their day, whether it was in imperial Russia, post-emancipation Jamaica, or the free states of the American North. Their experiences of "interracial" coexistence, as they saw them, offered glimpses of a more racially just future for the United States, one that went beyond the limits of the racist society in which they lived. The witness of the three abolitionists imagined a future in which slavery could be dismantled, opening spaces for freedom, equality, and a Christianity concerned with racial justice. Their testimony gives us the same foretaste today, while also illuminating the challenges that persist in our own time.

TWO FUTURES

Revivalist abolitionists like Bradley, Prince, and Ingraham recognized the twin problems of slavery and anti-Black racism. On the surface, it might seem that the Northern states of the 1830s and 1840s would have been thoroughly just environments. It's true that the North included places where African Americans could practice a range of freedoms. African American males could vote in Massachusetts, New Hampshire, Vermont, and Maine, and towns and settlements such as Brooklyn, Illinois, or Seneca Village in New York City were known as places of particular liberty for African Americans. In Ohio between 1800 and 1850, according to historian William Loren Katz, there may have been as many as thirty Black towns, what became known as "oases of freedom in the vast desert of slavery," a phrase employed by the mid-nineteenth-century author John Elliott Cairnes. Others sprung up in Illinois and Indiana after about 1830. James Bradley described an oasis of freedom within communities such as Cincinnati's Lane Seminary in the early 1830s, where "prejudice against color does not exist" and where he experienced racial equality.[1]

But some supposedly free states denied citizenship to African Americans. Ohio, Missouri, and Oregon had White-citizens-only state constitutions, and New Jersey, Pennsylvania, and California removed African American males from their voting rolls, effectively ending their citizenship in those states. The state of New York limited voting to an elite set of Black male property owners. Federal policy became overtly hostile, too, echoing in American law what had been playing out in cities and towns across the land for generations. A key passage of the 1857 Dred Scott decision by the US Supreme Court, which perpetuated slavery and denied Black federal citizenship, held that Blacks "had no rights which the White man was bound to respect." The day-to-day experiences of African Americans, even in supposedly free states like Ohio, included events like the 1829 Cincinnati White riot against Blacks, in which one thousand African Americans fled from the city to relocate to other towns, or the eviction of African Americans by White mobs, such as what happened in Plymouth, Ohio, in 1830, and in numerous similar events across the state.[2]

Christian abolitionists like Bradley, Prince, and Ingraham participated in antislavery societies that advocated for "the immediate emancipation of the whole colored race within the United States," and not just the abolition of slavery. These societies identified three key pillars of emancipation: "The emancipation of the slave from the oppression of the master, the emancipation of the free colored man from the oppression of public sentiment, and

---

[1]William Loren Katz, *Black Pioneers: An Untold Story* (New York: Atheneum, 1999), 26.
[2]Gary J. Kornblith and Carol Lasser, *Elusive Utopia: The Struggle for Racial Equality in Oberlin, Ohio* (Baton Rouge, LA: LSU Press, 2018), 21; Dred Scott v. Sandford (1857), transcript of US Supreme Court decision, National Archives online, www.archives.gov/milestone-documents/dred-scott -v-sandford.

the elevation of both to an intellectual, moral, and political equality with the whites." The end of slavery was tied to "freeing" the free African American population from civil inequalities due to "color, condition of birth, poverty," and other realities. The abolition of slavery on its own would have been insufficient for such abolitionists; they looked to the end of anti-Black racism altogether. These activists envisioned a society where African Americans, formerly enslaved and finally free, would be uplifted in status, able to enjoy equality within all spheres of life, whether intellectual, social, moral, civil, or political. That was the true goal.[3]

PATHWAYS TO POST-SLAVERY

From the vantage of Christian abolitionists like Prince and Ingraham, there were real-life examples of societies where life without racism could be realized: imperial Russia and post-emancipation Jamaica, each of which could model aspects of what a postslavery future for the United States could look like.

Nancy Prince wrote that she thrived as a Black woman in Russia in ways that she had been unable to in the United States. She attributed this to the suffocating effect of American racism. In Russia, she was a successful businesswoman, able to use her entrepreneurial acumen, interpersonal skills, and social networks in productive ways. As a society that (in Prince's telling) was without racism, Prince saw imperial Russia as a model for the United States in how to organize a society free from racial prejudice. Russia was a society in which Black people were not criminalized for being Black and where her full humanity as a Black person was affirmed as she lived and moved in daily life. She learned Russian, gained facility with French, and discovered a market for French and English styles of clothing for infants and children, which she began producing for sale. The empress, Alexandra, became one of her customers, as did others within the nobility who followed the empress's taste in fashion. The emperor, Nicholas I, and the empress gave her audiences. Prince also participated in philanthropic endeavors, donating and raising funds for Russian orphans and other projects, leading the charge to establish an orphanage in St. Petersburg.

---

[3]"Constitution of the Oberlin Anti-slavery Society" (1835), EOG (Electronic Oberlin Group) online, www2.oberlin.edu/external/EOG/Documents/OberlinAntiSlaveryCon.htm.

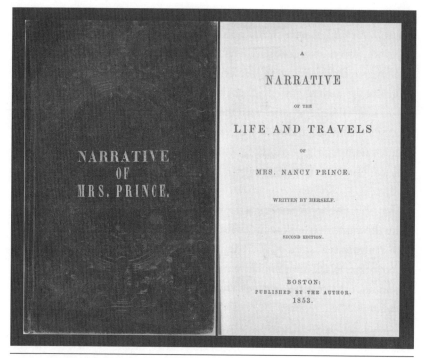

Figure 3.1. Cover and title page of Nancy Prince's *Narrative*, second edition, 1853

Russian Whites could relate amicably and fairly to Blacks, thought Prince; therefore so could White Americans if they wanted to. A society not organized by race was historically achievable. "It is well known," she wrote, that in Russia "the color of one's skin does not prohibit [one] from any place or station that he or she may be capable of occupying," even in such an overwhelmingly White country. To embark on a pathway toward a post-slavery society, Prince believed, the United States had to confess that it was not because of Black people—the idea that they were somehow infantile, pathological, or uneducable—that slavery and racism continued to exist. Instead it was a question of the will, specifically of Whites, to embrace racial equality rather than continuing to believe in the supposed inferiority of people of African descent. For the United States to become a supposedly racism-free nation, Prince held, skin color had to stop being a determiner of one's station in life. It also had to stop being the thing that admitted or prohibited a person from occupying specific social locations or that determined life outcomes. In the United States, interracial coexistence had to become the norm to yield a society that was absent a racial hierarchy.[4]

Prince also depicted post-emancipation Jamaica as a story of progress, a place where the formerly enslaved had been given a chance to govern their own lives. Watching emancipated Jamaicans live out their freedom, Prince was convinced that they possessed the skills to succeed: they were enterprising, intelligent, and responsible; they exercised self-determination, serving as magistrates and other government officials; and some had become property owners. It was all a far cry from popular portrayals in the United States of free Jamaicans as "lazy" and emancipation as having "been of no benefit" to freed persons, according to Prince.[5]

But how could such a culture of freedom and progress be built on American soil? Prince was convinced that education had been one of the keys for racial uplift in Jamaica, and it could be in the United States as well. Nearly nine thousand students were educated in schools funded by a foundation called Mico, and more students received schooling from mission societies and the national government. The Afro-Jamaicans she met welcomed the books she distributed, and she spoke of having encountered an effort in Jamaica to increase the literacy of children and adults. Christianity would also be a pivotal component toward establishing a post-slavery society in America. Prince described the Christianity that she saw lived out among Afro-Jamaicans: "There are many places of worship of various denominations," she wrote, "namely, Church of England, and of Scotland, Wesleyan, the Baptist, and Roman Catholics." Christian denominations in Jamaica "differ from what I have seen in New England, and from those I have seen elsewhere" such as in other parts of the United States and Russia. Among the Baptists, she identified a denomination led by Afro-Jamaicans whose houses of worship held four to six thousand people and featured a unique combination of practices, including class meetings, which were associated with the Methodists rather than the Baptists. Emancipated Jamaicans didn't abandon Christianity; they embraced it more fully. Prince thought that it must have been a crucial steppingstone toward establishing a post-slavery nation.[6]

---

[4] Nancy Prince, *A Narrative of the Life and Travels of Mrs. Nancy Prince* (Boston: published by the author, 1850), 16.

[5] Prince, *Narrative*, 50.

[6] Prince, *Narrative*, 72-73; Nancy Prince, *The West Indies: Being a Description of the Islands, Progress of Christianity, Education, and Liberty Among the Colored Population Generally* (Boston: Dow and Jackson, 1841), 8.

If Americans could gain "a true representation" of the progress of emancipated Jamaicans, Prince believed, they could more readily embrace the idea that emancipation would benefit all Americans. The transition from slavery to freedom in the United States could take place through embracing the virtue of racial equality, securing opportunity without regard to race, making education readily available to the whole population, and strengthening the Christian church among all races.[7]

Not that Jamaica provided a perfect image of how to make those things happen. While progress did exist among the emancipated Jamaican population, Prince wrote, it might have been even more pronounced if the efforts of the people hadn't been subject to hampering by hostile cultural forces within Jamaica. Emancipated Jamaicans had "many obstacles to contend with," wrote Prince, "and very little to encourage them; every advantage is taken of their ignorance; the same spirit of cruelty is opposed to them that held them for centuries in bondage." These Jamaicans, according to Prince, were victims of Western missionaries and British former enslavers. Anti-Black racism was still at play even after the end of the system of slavery. The United States would have to reject those attitudes if it was to have a fighting chance of building a just society.[8]

Prince held that the British two-stage emancipation protocol, by which adults were freed first in 1834 and youth four years later, had created new problems while it sought to set enslaved people free. The initial plan, later abandoned in favor of a single cutoff date on which youth slavery would end, had been for young people to achieve emancipation upon reaching a designated age. Prince saw the grief that adults experienced while that policy was in force, being compelled to watch their children remain enslaved while they, the parents, entered freedom for the first time. *Abolish slavery for all, immediately*—that was best, in Prince's view. She also wrote that the American government needed to prepare for White backlash after slavery was abolished. Once the enslaved youth of Jamaica were emancipated by the British Parliament, the former slaveholders violently attacked and plundered the communities of the formerly enslaved. "What little the poor colored people had gathered during their four years of freedom," Prince wrote, "was

---

[7]Prince, *West Indies*, 11.
[8]Prince, *Narrative*, 53; Prince, *West Indies*, 10.

destroyed by violence; their fences were broken down, and their horses and hogs taken from them."[9]

Another hindrance against full justice that Prince identified in Jamaica was that freed persons were being underpaid for their labor due to a system that set wages uniformly across the island, blocking opportunities for formerly enslaved persons to negotiate what they would earn for the work they did in freedom. Certain Afro-Jamaican entrepreneurs felt forced to "sell at a loss." The consumer side of the economy had its issues too, as merchants routinely extorted Afro-Jamaican customers with higher prices than they charged Whites. "An extraordinary price is asked of them for every thing they may wish to purchase," wrote Prince. The exploitation extended into church life too, where, according to Prince, at least one Baptist denomination required payment for religious services such as baptism and Communion.[10]

Jamaica was far from completely just, in Prince's telling, even though its racial environment was nowhere near as extreme as the viciousness and biting inhumanity of slavery as it existed in the United States. There was a long way to go in Jamaica toward true, thoroughgoing justice. "Yet their present state," she concluded of freed Afro-Jamaicans, "is blissful, compared with slavery," and the American society had an example to follow in Jamaica, at least as the first steps. By learning from post emancipation Jamaica, the United States could make the transition from slavery to freedom, said Prince. But it would have to abolish slavery all at once, anticipate and overcome White resistance, ensure a living wage, and establish fair prices of goods. And it would all have to come in tandem with good education, a robust Christian component in the fabric of the culture, and a renewed movement toward racial equality among the people. Only then could the United States take meaningful steps toward inaugurating a post-slavery way of life on its shores.[11]

VISIONS OF FREEDOM

The racially inclusive future that Prince and Bradley envisioned was shaped by concepts of freedom, equality, and Christianity that were more expansive than what the US government and the majority of Americans adopted

[9]Prince, *Narrative*, 58.
[10]Prince, *Narrative*, 53-54; Prince, *West Indies*, 8.
[11]Prince, *Narrative*, 53; Prince, *West Indies*, 10.

during the 1830s and 1840s. The fullest expressions of freedom were reserved for White adult males, with White adult women just behind them in perceived rank. The Dred Scott decision simply codified the way that Americans were already living. As the Supreme Court concluded in its ruling, free Blacks possessed no legal rights that the courts had to honor. Freedom and equality were reserved for White Americans, those who had the only citizenship that was recognized by the federal government, effectively making those priceless ideals of freedom available to Whites only.

That wasn't good enough for Prince and Bradley, who had encountered those "oases of freedom" in Russia, Jamaica, and Ohio. Drawing from the well of their Christian faith, they joined the political, religious, and legal struggle for justice, redefining freedom and equality with referents and content that went further and deeper than the dominant society did, holding up African Americans as *equals* in all aspects of life. An antislavery ethic was a hallmark that distinguished their Christianity from the proslavery religion of their opponents. The ethic of proslavery Christians was grounded in a logic that excluded enslaved persons from the realm and rights of full humanity by deeming them property, not fully human. That logic was applied to Christian morality itself, which was understood (in such thinking) not to extend to enslaved Africans. The result was that Christians could violate such persons with complete impunity not only in society but within the church itself, since the enslaved (it was said) were not true humans in the first place. The act of depriving people of African descent of freedom, equality, and citizenship was a natural implication of that dehumanizing ideology.

The Christianity of Bradley and Prince challenged that exclusionary logic. Their Christianity rejected proslavery tenets that sanctioned that a human could be "owned" by another human as property. For these revivalist abolitionists, that humans were created in the image of God precluded genuine Christianity from legitimating slavery on any level. Bradley held that freedom was a mark of the image of God. Prior to experiencing freedom from enslavement himself, Bradley noted that when enslaved persons were outside of the company of White people, "all their talk is about liberty, liberty!" He contended that all enslaved persons "long for liberty." They "long to be free," he wrote, and "they desire liberty more than anything else, and have, perhaps all along been laying plans to get free." Bradley held that

God created humans with the knowledge of freedom, which meant that even enslaved persons who had never experienced liberty knew to desire it.[12]

That longing for liberty grew out of hope. As Bradley noted, enslaved persons possessed the "hope of liberty," a hope that informed their visions of freedom and emboldened their wills to escape slavery, that "hopeless bondage" and "oppressed" condition, even knowing the terrible risks. Freedom and hope were intertwined with one another, a powerful and sometimes irresistible contrast to the prospect of life in slavery.

Figure 3.2. Statue, erected in 1988, depicting James Bradley looking across the Ohio River toward Cincinnati (the site of Lane Seminary) and the free state of Ohio

James Bradley identified 1828 as the date of his conversion to Christ. At the center of his Christianity was the "cross of Christ" and the "resurrection of the just," anchoring a faith through which the "walls of prejudice are broken down" and "men [and women] of color meet at the feet of Jesus." Christians were understood as people who look "upon each other in love," unlike enslavers' culture of violence, including such oppressors who called themselves Christians. For Bradley, a Christian's belief in Christ had to be manifested by practices of Christian virtues such as love, which were not

---

[12]James Bradley, "Brief Account of an Emancipated Slave Written by Himself, at the Request of the Editor," in *The Oasis*, ed. Lydia Maria Child (Boston: Benjamin C. Bacon, 1834), 111.

some exclusive possession of the dominant race. They applied to all people. Bradley manumitted himself through his earnings in 1833, five years after his conversion, buying the freedom that he already knew for having been created in God's image.[13]

For Nancy Prince, freedom was also a mark of the image of God. In her reading of Scripture, God was a freedom-loving God who included people of all races in the divine vision of freedom, rather than just the single dominant race of Whites. Slavery was a violation of the norms that God established at creation, not least because it caused Whites to inflate their authority beyond what God had given them. God granted authority or "dominion" to all humans, but only over animals and "no farther." God did not grant any group of people authority over any other. To violate those limits would result in one group's oppression of another group, which would contradict the idea that all people are made "in the image of God." Prince was adamant that people of African descent were part of God's creation, God's inheritance, and she called Whites out for their enslavement of Blacks, asking them such questions as, "Who made them [White people] Lord over God's inheritance?"[14]

Prince held that in addition to violating God's principles and commands, slavery also distorted God's original creation of humanity, as seen in the lives of both slaveholders and enslaved persons: "It makes master and slaves knaves." She reminded White Americans who enslaved African Americans that, in the words of a woman she knew, "God spoke very loud to . . . (the white people,) to let us go." Prince concluded that "if they [Whites] believed there was a God," then "why not obey him" and end slavery?[15]

The Christianity of Bradley and Prince challenged the status quo of White supremacy and Black subordination, touching both the enslavement of African Americans and their presumed racial inequality with Whites. Prince in particular contended that the church and the surrounding culture *were* separable from White supremacy, that they could be dislodged from one another, and she called for a Christianity marked by egalitarianism and compassion. Bradley advocated a Christianity that espoused liberty for all. Each of them saw a racially inclusive Christianity as the necessary foundation of the racially inclusive society that was within reach.

[13]This paragraph and the one preceding: Bradley, "Brief Account," 108-12.
[14]Prince, *Narrative*, 43.
[15]This paragraph and the one preceding: Prince, *Narrative*, 42-43, 62, 66, 77, 78.

THE OASES OF TODAY

Bradley's and Prince's witness to the possibility of full equality and freedom in America calls us to envision a more racially just future. Do "oases of freedom" exist in our lives, places where a greater range of freedoms exist for all races than is generally true in the communities where we live? We must ask ourselves: Are our congregations among those places? Our denominations? The other spaces where we spend our time and energy as disciples of Jesus? If we stop and reflect long enough, we may recognize these places as social workshops of the future where we can experiment with robust racial coexistence, cultivate knowledge about how to live as postracist Christian communities, and generate new narratives of a future with racism completely gone. How do such places in our lives widen our understanding of Christian faith and of the future?

Bradley and Prince bore witness to locales where interracial communities were achievable. These were more than far-off, imaginary utopias or unrealistic, unachievable communities; they lived in such places. We might join Prince in confessing that a society or various societies exist that are not organized around race. Prince held that one's skin color, be it White or Black, should not determine a society's patterns of relationships. There is no inherent value in the color of one's skin; rather, value is bestowed by people, by the culture in which one lives. Imperial Russia found it possible to resist conferring special value on White skin and organizing its society around race. I wonder whether it was because Russia was not part of the transatlantic slave trade, the oppression of Black people, or the colonization of Africa. Prince does note that while race was not an organizing factor for Russia's society, class and serfdom were. But standing outside of the history of the middle passage might have created in Russia a certain set of historical conditions that inhibited or precluded anti-Black racism from emerging as a controlling force the way it had in America and the Caribbean.

Taken together, Prince's depictions of Russia and Jamaica suggest a multidimensional approach to achieving a racially just future. First, Prince might suggest, we must affirm that skin color is not the issue. The crux of the question is the *value* we place on skin color, the meaning and associations that *we* impose on our experience of the color of human skin. Being White is not the problem; it is *the construction of whiteness* that is the problem, heralding whiteness as the color of a superior race, of those who ought to run the world. Prince and Bradley rejected such notions. All peoples, all races, are equal, they believed, and all should co-lead together—an echo of Prince's concept of authority as grounded in a theology of creation. Second, there should be a focus on the means to achieve racial progress with a gradual movement toward racial justice. We must clear out other impediments to racial justice, such as racially biased employment, wage, and pricing practices, lingering colonialism, and other systemic issues, asking ourselves where unfair and unequal practices occur in our world, and what we might do to address them. These were key questions for Prince; they are also profoundly Christian questions, as they are framed by a theology of Jesus' liberative life, death, and resurrection for the transformation of the world. Third, as Prince and Bradley embraced an abolitionist ethics that called for an immediate end to slavery, Christians today are called to embrace an antiracism ethics, one that focuses on addressing racial consequences such as outcome disparities in wealth, health, and employment, as the approach to ending racism.

As we seek to construct an antiracist ethics and a concept of what racial justice can look like, what do we do when we discover that one congregation's definition of justice differs from that of another? We can start by listening attentively to one another, challenging each other with both grace and truth. We should lay on the table our respective definitions for the terms that we use when talking about racial justice, bearing in mind that different people and communities use the same terms to mean different things, sometimes vastly different things. Plenty of differences between communities, whether sociological, political, psychological, or theological, influence how those misalignments come to be. We should probe those origins to understand them and each other as we search for justice, asking all the while how our varying life experiences lead to differences in how we think about justice and envision what true freedom means. We should ensure that the life experiences that we include in the conversation reflect people of differing races, genders, classes, and Christian traditions, and be very careful as to whether any perspectives are to be privileged.

To advance racial justice, we might need to raise up more leaders—both from within the church and from outside of it—who have been shaped by a vaster range of social interactions than those available in communities that are restricted by race. That diversity of lived experience can become the moral epicenter for the communities in which such leaders serve, transforming them into flourishing places where Christians practice justice, solidarity, and racially diverse leadership, showing those ideals in how they worship, fellowship together, and order the church's common life. In these communities, racial justice would be rehearsed, practiced, and lived, rather than remaining an abstract principle, and resources would be distributed in such a way as to achieve equality and secure equity for all races and peoples without prejudice.

For Bradley and Prince, issues like slavery and racism were weighty and urgent enough to supersede debate, dialogue, and consensus making. Such issues demanded concrete action, and urgently. Love between the races, as Dr. King said, cannot be legislated. But racial justice can. We should strive to anticipate and build an alternative vision for the future of American society where racial justice is the norm, not an exception—a postracist future, built where prejudice and structural injustice once stood but have since been annihilated. It will take compelling vision and boldness. But if Bradley and Prince's witness is to be taken seriously, we've already seen glimpses of such a world before. Perhaps we can again, even in the United States, if we have the courage, humility, and devotion to Jesus that it will take to build it.

This chapter has offered a connection between Christianity and racial justice, especially as viewed through the experiences of Nancy Prince and James Bradley. But it is not just Christian belief that creates that bond. Christian *practice*, particularly the practice of worship in the church, can be a means of solidifying the link between faith in Jesus and the pursuit of racial justice in the world. As we turn to chapter four, the connection between racial equity and worship will become even more explicit, drawing again on the historical contexts of Bradley, Prince, and David Ingraham. A worshiping community is compelled by the love of God to act in service to the world, where new creation brings visions of a restored social order. That is the example that these three revivalist abolitionists and others like them have given us. It serves as a model for how we might worship God and seek God's justice today.

CHAPTER FOUR

"Reviving Our Spiritual Strength"

WORSHIP, JUSTICE, AND SALVATION

R. Matthew Sigler

This is a pleasant [Sabbath] day for many reasons. First, it is
the resurrection day of the blessed Savior, which is a warrant
that all true believers shall rise and live with him. "Because I
live ye shall live also." And, second, because it is the time when
the Christian world assemble to honor Christ, and revive their
spiritual strength and gain new converts to their Master. And,
third, because it is a day of rest to the Body and mind from
the labors and cares of life which mankind so much need.

DAVID INGRAHAM, 1841

Should dangers thick impede my course,
O let my soul sustain no loss;
Help me to run the Christian race,
And enter safe my hiding place.

NANCY PRINCE, 1853

"WORSHIP HAS NEVER ELIMINATED WORLD HUNGER," a fellow
doctoral student told me after I shared that I was pursuing a degree in the
history of Christian worship. I was taken aback. I could only stand silent in
reply, and not because of the curtness of his observation, but because I was
wrestling with the critique myself. Does worship matter, I wondered, for the

dozens of unhoused men and women two blocks away from my church building? Wouldn't our time on Sunday be put to better use and become more reflective of the kingdom of God if we were to do something other than worship, like hosting a banquet for those in our community who were hungry? I could hear Scripture passages—James 1:27, Micah 6:8, Amos 5:23—reverberating in my thoughts as I stood there wordlessly flipping the question over in my head.

Less than a decade after that exchange, the question of whether worship is relevant for the world's most daunting struggles seemed even more pressing in the wake of the 2020 unrest surrounding police shootings, mass protests, and the construction of border walls. During that time I heard a self-described "liturgist and activist" challenge our students at Seattle Pacific University, where I teach, with an observation: "We're in love with the work of God," she said, referring to justice, "but not the God of the work." Worship is fuel for the work of justice, she argued, and it sustains our efforts. Her message hit home with many of our students, who were willing recipients of the word that day, having chosen to attend a noncompulsory worship service. But is that the purpose of worship, to provide sustenance for our efforts at enacting social change? My Reformed friends would quickly pull out the Westminster Shorter Catechism and remind me that humanity's "chief end" is to "glorify God, and to enjoy him forever." Worship, they would say, is never a means to an end.

To question how worship and social action interface with each other is not new to Christianity. In the fourth century, Saint John Chrysostom argued that the church was in error because it lavishly "clothed" the altar for the Lord's Supper but left Christ naked in the street. Methodist theologian Georgia Harkness wrestled with the role of prayer in fighting the social ills of the twentieth century. "Unless we do the works that ought to be the fruit and accompaniment of prayer," she once wrote, "we cannot hope that in response to even the most fervent prayers God will implant order in the world." While the abolitionists at Oberlin Collegiate Institute in the nineteenth century did not address such questions directly, their witness and

---

[1]Westminster Shorter Catechism, answer 1, available in various locations online; see, e.g., "The Shorter Catechism," in *The Constitution of the Presbyterian Church (U.S.A.)*, pt. 1, *The Book of Confessions* (Louisville: Office of the General Assembly, 2004), 175, www.pcusa.org/site_media /media/uploads/oga/publications/boc.pdf.

practice held worship and social action together. In this chapter we will explore how our three revivalist abolitionists practiced worship both publicly and devotionally, what their writings reveal about how they understood the purpose of worship, and how these practices connected to their efforts to enact social change. Finally, we will consider how these insights might renew our congregations as we seek to be faithful in our worship and witness today.[2]

COMMON WORSHIP PRACTICES AMONG OUR THREE REVIVALIST ABOLITIONISTS

What was worship like for these three revivalist abolitionists? Most of the evidence comes from journal entries, which bear witness to a vibrant devotional life for each of them. Both Nancy Prince and David Ingraham frequently used hymnody to express their faith. Their writings teem with glimpses into corporate worship practices and anecdotes about daily prayer. We will consider these in greater detail in a moment.

Gathering for worship on Sunday was essential for these abolitionists. Ingraham's journal contains several entries about worship on "the Sabbath." On Sunday, March 14, 1841, he listed three reasons why Sunday worship is so essential for the life of the believer. Sunday "is the resurrection day of the Blessed Savior," he wrote, "which is a warrant that all true believers shall rise and live with him." For Ingraham, Sunday was not merely a commemoration of Christ's resurrection but a venue through which the believer was brought into union with Christ's saving work. Yes, Christians meet on the first day of the week because through the resurrection God in Christ has intervened decisively in human history. The day remembers God's past deeds. But Sunday also orients us to God's redemptive future.[3]

---

[2] "Do you wish to honour the body of Christ? Do not ignore him when he is naked. Do not pay him homage in the temple clad in silk, only then to neglect him outside where he is cold and ill-clad. He who said: 'This is my body' is the same who said: 'You saw me hungry and you gave me no food,' and 'Whatever you did to the least of my brothers you did also to me.' . . . What good is it if the Eucharistic table is overloaded with golden chalices when your brother is dying of hunger? Start by satisfying his hunger and then with what is left you may adorn the altar as well." Saint John Chrysostom, "Homily 50 on Matthew," trans. George Prevost and rev. by M. B. Riddle, in *Nicene and Post-Nicene Fathers, First Series*, ed. Philip Schaff, vol. 10 (Buffalo, NY: Christian Literature, 1888), rev. and ed. for New Advent by Kevin Knight, quoted in New Advent, accessed August 4, 2022, www.newadvent.org/fathers/200150.htm; Georgia Harkness, *Prayer and the Common Life* (New York: Abingdon, 1948), 203-4.

[3] David Ingraham, manuscript journal, Adrian College Archives, 101.

Ingraham continued, remarking that Sunday is a seminal time for Christians to "honor Christ," "revive their spiritual strength," and "gain new converts." On first read we might wonder why he listed those three aspects in a single point. Upon closer consideration, all three of them are oriented toward God's saving work in the life of the believer. In effect, Ingraham pointed out that Sunday is essential for the Christian because we corporately proclaim that Jesus is Lord ("honor Christ"), are sanctified into Christ's likeness ("revive their spiritual strength"), and proclaim the good news of redemption in Christ Jesus ("gain new converts"). Sunday worship is a primary venue in which God's saving work is made real in the community of faith. These three aspects, reasoned Ingraham, are founded on and flow from God's redemptive work in Christ Jesus through the resurrection.[4]

Last, Ingraham offered that Sunday worship is essential in the life of the believer "because it is a day of rest to the Body and mind from the labors and cares of life." While he did not fully develop a theology of Sabbath, Ingraham's writing reflected a view common among Christians of his day that Sunday was to be the day both of resurrection and of rest.[5]

While we cannot say for certain what the order of service looked like for our three figures, we do have evidence from several sources that give us insight into what probably happened on Sundays. Historians have often focused heavily on worship that occurred at camp meetings in particular; Charles Finney promoted these occasional services as vital means of bringing sinners to repentance. But we would be wrong to assume that every Sunday looked like a camp meeting. There were certainly some similarities between worship practices at a camp meeting led by Charles Finney and the elements of worship at the churches he pastored: hymn singing, preaching, altar calls, and so on. When one examines an order of service that was likely used at First Congregational Church in Oberlin during Finney's tenure, however, it looks like many other Protestant services of the nineteenth century:

- Prelude
- Invocation
- Anthem (by the choir)
- Scripture reading

---

[4]Ingraham, journal, 101.
[5]Ingraham, journal, 101.

- Pastoral prayer
- Hymn
- Offering
- Sermon
- Altar call (on occasion)
- Prayer
- Hymn
- Benediction

The Doxology was included each Sunday, too, but its location varied, falling after the invocation or the pastoral prayer or prior to the benediction.[6]

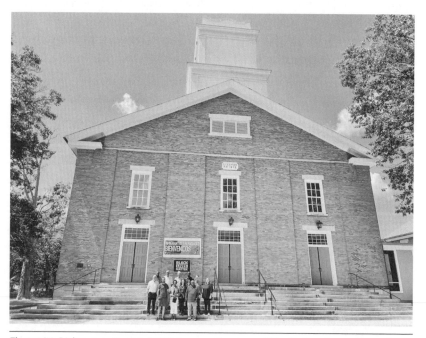

Figure 4.1. Dialogue on Race and Faith team on the steps of Oberlin First Congregational Church, built in 1842 as the largest structure west of the Alleghenies to accommodate the crowds drawn by its first pastor, Charles G. Finney

[6]We have no surviving orders of worship from either of Charles Finney's pastorates, but we do have many anecdotes about times of worship. In what follows I am drawing from orders of worship dating from the 1890s under Finney's successor at First Congregational Church in Oberlin, James Brand. Notably, these look very similar to sermon notes from the 1850s that were written by Finney's son-in-law, a man named James Monroe. Given the similarities it is likely that what is presented here is very similar to how the order of service was shaped during Finney's time at First Church.

Of course, there would have been differences between the order from First Church Oberlin and the services that Ingraham led in Jamaica. Ingraham most likely did not have an organ or a small orchestra for the prelude or anthem, as would have been the case at First Church. We do, however, see plenty of similarities between the two contexts from accounts in Ingraham's journal, such as the public reading of Scripture, preaching, hymn singing, and the Lord's Supper. The latter would have been a regular, though not weekly, practice at First Church, and we know that Finney often celebrated the Lord's Supper while pastoring in New York. Ingraham also made multiple references in his journal to taking Communion in worship.

How did the abolitionists of the revivalist tradition understand the Lord's Supper? Ingraham's journal offers several glimpses into his theology of Communion. First, it is a memorial of Christ's atoning work. "I have had the privilege," he wrote, "of sitting at the table of my Master to commemorate his dying love." He continued: "O may it be a permanent blessing to me. I need the assistance of all grace and every help that Christ has left for his Church to keep me in his Son and from being buried in the world." For Ingraham, Communion was not simply a practice that helped to recall Christ's sacrifice, but an act of worship by which God provided "blessing" and a means of "grace" to the partaker. Finally, Ingraham believed that the sacrament of the Lord's Supper points toward Christ's second coming. In one of the earliest entries in his journal, Ingraham noted that his congregation in Jamaica "once more celebrated the Lord's death till he come." In this paraphrase of 1 Corinthians 11:26, Ingraham showed that the sacrament was not merely observed as a somber affair commemorating Christ's death, but "celebrated," as the church awaited Christ's return.[7]

Beyond these Sunday gatherings, we find references to many other acts of worship and forms of pastoral ministry. Ingraham wrote throughout his journal about visiting the sick, welcoming new members, and marrying couples. A monthly "concert of prayer" was referenced on multiple occasions. These prayer meetings likely included a Scripture reading, a hymn, and an extended time of intercession with prayers offered spontaneously by anyone who felt led to do so.[8]

---

[7] Ingraham, journal, 3, 95.
[8] Charles Finney records one such "concert of prayer" in his autobiography. See *Charles G. Finney: An Autobiography* (Old Tappan, NJ: Revell, 1908), 42-43.

While these public venues of worship were clearly important to Nancy Prince, David Ingraham, and James Bradley, the three of them also gave witness to vibrant personal devotional lives. Each provided evidence of spiritual disciplines that undergirded their faith. First, each practiced a stalwart commitment to reading Scripture devotionally. "Oh, how I longed to be able to read the Bible!" wrote Bradley in his "Brief Account" of his life. Prince and Ingraham quoted Scripture regularly. Prince did not mention the practice of reading Scripture as often as Ingraham spoke of it, but that is probably because her autobiography was not a journal. She clearly was well-versed in Scripture and cited passages frequently, along with the paraphrased psalmody of Isaac Watts, a Congregationalist minister who was a prolific hymnist. Watts's hymns became extremely popular among revivalists, and both Prince and Ingraham frequently cited them.[9]

Ingraham's journal, like Prince's writing, is filled with scriptural allusions as well as entries that note his practice of regular Scripture reading. "On Sab[bath] morn [September 4, 1839] I read the passage 'Jesus hath done all things well,'" he wrote. "My mind seemed to dwell upon the glorious savior." For all three abolitionists, reading the Bible seems to have been much more than a rote exercise in piety. It was a discipline born out of a deep hunger to know and follow God.[10]

Second, vibrant prayer infused the devotional lives of Prince, Ingraham, and Bradley. What did they pray for? Nancy Prince offered prayer in lyrical form in her autobiography. She included a poem, probably her own, at the end of her book, asking God for protection and strength that she might faithfully "run the Christian race." She called the poem "The Hiding Place," drawing from several Scripture passages such as the description of God in Psalm 32:7.[11]

David Ingraham's journal includes glimpses into his prayer life as well. His writing contains prayers of supplication for his own needs, including petitions for physical and spiritual strength, guidance in decision-making, and a greater sense of God's presence. Notably, Ingraham often prayed that God would allow him to remain faithful in following Christ and witnessing to God's work in the world. He also offered intercessory prayers for others, including for his parishioners. He prayed for his father's salvation, for fellow

---

[9]James Bradley, "Brief Account of an Emancipated Slave Written by Himself, at the Request of the Editor," in *The Oasis*, ed. Lydia Maria Child (Boston: Benjamin C. Bacon, 1834), 110.
[10]Ingraham, journal, 7-8.
[11]See appendix E for the full text of the poem.

ministers who refused to give up alcohol (the inclusion of such prayers shows the influence of the temperance movement on Ingraham), and that God would bring about justice for the oppressed. "O who can measure the guilt or sound the iniquity of this nefarious traffic and its twin sister slavery," he wrote. "O that I may pray <u>often</u> and with more <u>faith</u> for the oppressed."[12]

Last, hymns featured prominently in the writings of both David Ingraham and Nancy Prince. At least thirteen different songs were mentioned by Ingraham, and five were quoted in Prince's memoir, one of which was likely her own composition. Their use of hymnody demonstrates what is true for most of us, that songs remain with us in ways that prose or speech do not. The songs that we use in worship form our thoughts about God. In multiple places in their writings, Prince and Ingraham turned to lyrics when they seemed to lack other words.

Consider how Ingraham referred to one of Isaac Watts's hymns:

Feb 20th [1840] In looking back upon my past life it seems to have been one of toil, care responsibility and hurry—and I feel that I need a little time for calm and sober reflection and to wash the feet of that blessed Savior whose goodness has been so great to me and whose love has been so boundless. Surely and truly I can say "Thus far the <u>Lord</u> hath led me on."[13]

The full text of Watts's hymn "Thus Far the Lord Hath Led Me On" reads like this:

Thus far the Lord hath led me on,
Thus far His pow'r prolongs my days;
And ev'ry evening shall make known
Some fresh memorial of His grace.

Much of my time has run to waste,
And I, perhaps, am near my home;
But He forgives my follies past
And gives me strength for days to come.

I lay my body down to sleep;
Peace is the pillow for my head;

---

[12]Ingraham, journal, 24, emphasis original.
[13]Ingraham, journal, 31, emphasis original.

His ever-watchful eye will keep
Its constant guard around my bed.

Faith in Thy name forbids my fear;
O may Thy presence ne'er depart!
And in the morning may I bear
Thy loving-kindness on my heart!

Ingraham referred to this hymn during a multiday illness, most likely the effects of tuberculosis. We can imagine how this hymn echoed in his mind as he labored in ill health. In offering a single line in his journal, "Thus far the Lord hath led me on," Ingraham pointed to these lyrics, which brought him hope in God's faithful care. Similarly, Nancy Prince turned to hymnody in her writings to express feelings and thoughts amid significant trials. In one such moment, feeling betrayed and neglected by some members of the Christian community in Boston, she quoted a paraphrase of Psalm 94, also by Isaac Watts.[14]

The Christian abolitionists that feature in this book practiced regular rhythms of public and private worship. Gathering with the community of faith on Sundays, they sang hymns, heard the Word of God publicly read and expounded on, engaged in fervent prayer, and partook of the Lord's Supper on occasion. Outside these corporate times of worship, they practiced a regular habit of devotional Scripture reading, prayer, and hymn singing. These elements of worship are certainly not exclusive to these three abolitionists of the revivalist tradition. But the fact that they practiced them gives us a deeper appreciation for what was unique about their approach to Christian worship and how it interplayed with answering God's call to work for justice.

THE MEANING AND PURPOSE OF WORSHIP

The understanding of worship that framed the practices of Oberlin revivalists like Ingraham and Bradley was forged in the fires of the Second Great Awakening (ca. 1790–1840), a transatlantic movement that was characterized by spiritual renewal and evangelistic fervor. Many people attending public worship meetings or revivals in those days experienced an "awakening" and

---

[14]See Nancy Prince, *A Narrative of the Life and Travels of Mrs. Nancy Prince, Written by Herself*, 2nd ed. (Boston: published by the author, 1853), 84; see also Isaac Watts, "Psalm 94 part 1," Poetry Nook, accessed March 6, 2023, www.poetrynook.com/poem/psalm-94-part-1.

professed life-changing encounters with God. By the time Ingraham began ministry in Jamaica the movement had reached its zenith, but its effects were still reverberating in the work of the abolitionists we have been profiling. Worship in the Second Great Awakening stood on a firm belief that God was in the midst of the worship assembly. Journal entries of participants in these revivals are full of descriptions of God's dynamic activity among those gathered for worship. Put quite simply, worship was understood to be an encounter with the living God.

The arena for that encounter, the place where God's saving work would take place in a person's life, was understood to be the heart. In times of worship, those whom the Holy Spirit convicted of sin would often fall to the floor or cry aloud for mercy. Then when the sinner received assurance of salvation, she would often sing or shout for joy. Meanwhile, other worshipers might travail in fervent prayer to be sanctified in Christ. Participants in the worship service would be immersed in vibrant preaching aimed at awakening the sinner to his need for God's saving grace. Singing not only accentuated this aim but also provided the grammar for those experiencing the full sweep of God's saving work in their midst.

We should clarify that in speaking of the role of the affections in worship we are not talking about emotionalism or what was called "enthusiasm" at the time. The latter would be understood as contrived or manipulated emotion. Rather, the revivalism of the Second Great Awakening emphasized the belief that a person's spiritual senses could be awakened and respond to the triune God's work in the person's very being.

God's saving activity could be experienced in both public and private worship. On July 27, 1840, David Ingraham wrote that he

> spent the Sabbath very pleasantly and this morn I left at 6 o clock with a prayerful heart for home. During my passage up the lake I was much affected by reading the feelings and dealings of God with his ancient people, when they had time and again gone away from God and were sorely oppressed in consequence—they cried to God and often at first refusing to hear them, when He saw them put away their idols and sins—His feelings are beautifully and meltingly expressed in the following language "His soul was grieved for the misery of Israel." O what compassion!! O what love!! I can't express what I feel as I look at this trait of His character. I can only weep wonder and admire.

O what God is the Christian God¡¡ God forbid that I should ever offend such a being. O <u>Bind</u> me to the <u>cross</u> by <u>love</u>.[15]

Notice that Ingraham emphasized first God's desire ("feelings") that God's people should reject idolatry and be set free from oppression. He then reflected on his own affective response to the text he had read. Ingraham employed the word *meltingly*, which many revivalists used when referring to their affective experience of God. Prince and Bradley also frequently used similar language when speaking of their faith. The accounts of all three abolitionists are peppered with phrases like *feel*, *longed for*, and *heart*.

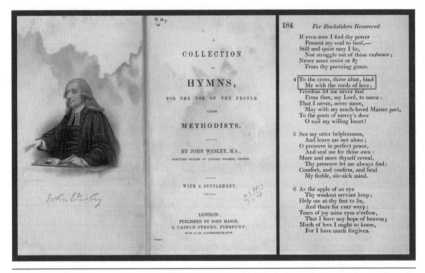

Figure 4.2. Excerpt from a hymn by Charles Wesley, which David Ingraham may have alluded to in his diary

Finally, revivalist worship, both public and private, was centered around God's salvation. When the community of faith gathered, it sought to participate in nothing less than the totality of God's saving grace. Worshipers prayed for the unconverted, that they might experience conviction for their sin followed by repentance and justification by faith. Those who had already

---

[15]Ingraham, journal, 58, emphasis original; quotation is from Judges 10:16 KJV. It's possible that Ingraham is echoing a Charles Wesley hymn: "To thy cross, thy altar, bind / Me with the cords of love." John and Charles Wesley, "After a Recovery," in *Hymns and Sacred Poems* (Bristol, UK: Farley, 1742), (repr., ed. Randy L. Maddox; Durham, NC: Center for Studies in the Wesleyan Tradition, Duke Divinity School, 2021), 72, https://divinity.duke.edu/sites/divinity.duke.edu/files/documents/cswt/10_Hymns_and_Sacred_Poems_%281742%29_mod.pdf.

been justified in Christ sought sanctification in God's perfecting love. Through preaching, singing, praying, and the Lord's Supper, worshipers encountered God in their midst, a God who had the singular aim of bringing about the salvation of the world.

At this point we need to pause to address a common mischaracterization of revivalists' worship in the first half of the nineteenth century. In his "new measures" to promote revivals, Charles Finney argued for a specific approach to Christian worship that had as its goal the salvation of the individual. We have already touched on some of the elements that Finney championed in his camp meetings: extended preaching, hymn singing, dedicated time and space for the penitent to respond to God's convicting grace, and so on. Scholars have often suggested that Finney's approach to worship instrumentalized such practices as means to the specific end of saving souls from hell. They argue that such an approach reduces Christian worship to a gimmicky performance aimed at manipulating the emotions. It also, the critique goes, holds an otherworldly escape to be the goal of the Christian life. But thinking of Finney and revivalism in such terms fails to consider the emphasis that the abolitionists of the revivalist tradition placed on sanctification. God's end goal, they would have said, is not simply to save us from the penalty of our sins, but to transform us into the image of Jesus Christ.

It is also essential to consider the revivalists' understanding of God's future (what we call eschatology). The abolitionists of the revivalist tradition held to a postmillennial view of Christ's return. That is, they believed that Christ would return after the millennium referenced in Revelation 20. In that passage the devil is restrained for a thousand years, a good thing for those living. Postmillennialists of the nineteenth century looked for a soon-coming time in which humanity would enjoy peace, joy, and righteousness as well as a renewed devotion to Christ. For the abolitionists of the revivalist tradition, personal sanctification, along with its consequent effect on society, was the method by which the millennium would be ushered in. Crucially, the location for the thousand-year period was understood to be the earth, not heaven.

To characterize the revivalism of the early 1800s as focused narrowly on escape from the world through conversion is to overlook some key features of the theological underpinnings of the movement. For abolitionists of the revivalist tradition, the goal of God's salvation was the renewal of the image of Christ in the human person (sanctification). Rightly understood, sanctification is always outward-facing and animated by holy love for God and neighbor. And for the revivalists, the scene of God's redemptive work was this earth, the site of the soon-coming millennium. When we characterize worship among the abolitionists of the revivalist tradition as being immersed in the story of God's salvation, we must remember the end goal and locus of God's redemption: holy, outward-facing love flowing through sanctified Christians on the earth. From this perspective, worship is anything but an escape from the world. It is profoundly for the good of the world.

LESSONS WE CAN LEARN

"Turn your eyes upon Jesus, look full in His wonderful face," the refrain of the hymn tells us. "And the things of earth will grow strangely *dim*," it continues. But shouldn't the things of this earth grow strangely *clear* as we gaze upon Jesus Christ? This was the question a former teacher of mine asked our worship design team as we considered singing that hymn in a chapel service at Asbury Theological Seminary. He understood the rhetorical thrust of the song: in Christ's presence we find care amid the pains of this world. But for many Christians, it is more than a lyrical turn of phrase. It's the foundation of a distorted image of God's plan: worship is viewed as an escape from this world, a way to avoid it. "Look full in His wonderful face" and forget that George Floyd spent the last minutes of his life gasping for air and crying out for his mother. "Look full in His wonderful face" and avoid acknowledging that many of us still benefit from a system that privileges White bodies. "Look full in His wonderful face" and be lulled into complacency that dilutes the Christian witness against injustice.[16]

On the other hand, many American churches have pushed back against escapism by orienting their worship services around the latest news headlines and calls to activism. In some cases, there is little difference between these services and community service organizations. If we turn our eyes to Jesus at all, it's only to find motivation to carry on the work of activism.

In naming these two approaches to worship we return to the competing aims from the story at the beginning of this chapter. Is the practice of

---

[16]Helen Howarth Lemmel, "Turn Your Eyes upon Jesus" (1922), hymnary.org, Calvin University, accessed August 4, 2022, https://hymnary.org/text/o_soul_are_you_weary_and_troubled, emphasis added.

Christian worship an end unto itself? Or is it a means to a different end? These might seem to be the only options. But if our study of the abolitionists of the revivalist tradition teaches us anything about worship, it's that there is another way of thinking about those two aims, even if they appear at first to contradict.

First, we have seen that the abolitionists of the revivalist tradition held to the essentiality of corporate worship. For as much as they organized for social action, worship on Sunday was something quite different. Worshiping with the community of faith was neither an optional activity nor a mere obligation that a person needed to fulfill each week. The abolitionists gathered for worship with an expectation of encountering the living God, taking seriously the promise of Jesus that "where two or three are gathered in my name, I am there among them" (Matthew 18:20). God was to be encountered not only in the mind but in the affections and the spiritual senses. The abolitionists of the revivalist tradition reveled in God's presence made manifest in the lives of those who experienced salvation.

As Christians, most of us hope to encounter God in worship together. But our language often fails us when we try to articulate *how* we encounter God in worship. When we describe times of worship, we tend to default to words like *lively* and *inspiring* or *boring* and *lifeless*. The abolitionists of the revivalist tradition remind us that we are to bring the full gamut of our humanity before God in worship—our joys, fears, questions, everything. But they also remind us of the importance of encountering God with the *spiritual* part of who we are. If you strike a tuning fork and hold it next to another one that has been tuned to the same frequency, the second one will begin to vibrate with sound like the first. The revivalist abolitionists understood the Spirit's role to include awakening a person's spiritual senses, like one tuning fork awakening the resonance of another. The language of Romans 8:16, the idea of the Holy Spirit's witnessing to our spirit, featured prominently in this perspective.

That still leaves us with the question of how and when we encounter God in the act of worship. Does it happen at a particular moment in a service? Or does it come through a particular practice, like singing? The example of the revivalist abolitionists seems to suggest that God is present in several ways when Christians gather. Hymn singing certainly featured prominently in the practices of Ingraham and Prince; even more foundational for them were Scripture reading, preaching, prayer, and the Lord's Supper. All these various acts represented habits of a vibrant devotional life. To the revivalist abolitionists, private devotion and the gathering of the faithful were not two separate disciplines but a singular, seamless practice of a life of worship, one lived in the faith that God was active in their midst.

Second, worship for these Christian abolitionists was about experiencing and participating in the full sweep of God's saving work. As the community gathered for worship, it expected to experience God's awakening, justifying, and sanctifying grace. In holding to an expansive view of God's work, the abolitionists of the revivalist tradition believed that the goal of God's grace is not only to forgive us of our sins but also to sanctify our sinful nature. Simply put, the triune God is making us look like Jesus. When we take that idea to heart, it leads us to expect God to do something both inward *and* outward with us at the same time, in line with the greatest commandment (see Matthew 22:37-40). We must resist the critique that worship among the abolitionists of the revivalist tradition was primarily about being saved *from* the world. To them, salvation was squarely *for* the world.

What might it look like to recover this expansive understanding of God's salvation in Christ Jesus as a centerpiece of Christian worship? Our context, of course, is quite different from the world that Ingraham, Prince, and Bradley encountered every day. For one thing, most believers in the West would agree that we now live among the ruins of Christendom, and the unawakened are much less likely to show up in church on a Sunday now than they would have been in the middle of the nineteenth century. In increasingly post-Christian and unchurched contexts, first encounters with faith in Jesus will not take place in a pew on a Sunday but outside the church altogether. Some Christians, sensing a decrease in the church's relevance to a culture that seems to have no use for it, have argued that the worship gathering is even less important than they already thought it was. But our study should remind us of the essential nature of God's story of salvation, which must include the Holy Spirit's power to bring transforming grace into our lives as we encounter what God wants to do in us and in our world. The changing relationship between the church and culture is an occasion to consider how the full story of God's salvation can be proclaimed and experienced in our worship services. Do we leave worship gatherings captivated by God's story of salvation? Does the scope of that story include the audaciously optimistic claim that God the Father, through the redeeming work of God the Son and the regenerating work of God the Spirit, is transforming us into a signpost of God's new creation?

The abolitionists of the revivalist tradition offer a perspective that worship is neither an escape from the injustices of the world nor merely a means to sustain activism. If Christian worship is the primary place where we encounter the living God by God's Spirit and participate in the story of God's full salvation in Christ Jesus, and if we broaden our vision of salvation to include God's desire to transform us in holy love for a future that is profoundly "for the life of the world" (John 6:51), perhaps there is nothing more essential to justice than worship. This is a lesson the church might heed today as its people seek to be faithful ambassadors of the new creation in the midst of a broken world.

The next chapter will take up the responsibility of connecting more precisely revivalist theology to the justice efforts of revivalist abolitionism. We have seen in this chapter that what we believe about God and how we worship God have effects on how we treat our neighbors. The theology of the revivalist abolitionists was an action-oriented holiness theology, one that affirmed that God is deeply at work in the hearts of dedicated Christians, transforming them into Christ's image. It is from a changed condition of the heart that love for others flows, especially toward the oppressed and outcast. Just as God's grace overflows toward us despite our brokenness and sin, this theology has a profoundly optimistic paradigm. It not only includes a Spirit-empowered ability to love all individuals but has a goal of changing the structures that keep persons, any persons, from full freedom. A theology so integrated between belief and action and among diverse peoples found expression in the writings of Ingraham, Bradley, and Prince. As chapter five will show, that same theology continues to call us to integrated lives of discipleship today.

"This Holy Cause"

REVIVALIST THEOLOGY AND JUSTICE ADVOCACY

Douglas M. Strong

*God preserve you and strengthen you in this holy cause, until
the walls of prejudice are broken down, the chains burst in pieces,
and [people] of every color meet at the feet of Jesus, speaking
kind words, and looking upon each other in love—willing to
live together on earth, as they hope to live in Heaven!*

JAMES BRADLEY, 1834

*Such a kingdom rises in grandeur as we contemplate it. And what
an enlarged view does this give us of the wisdom of God. . . . Such
a kingdom will indeed be glorious. Every man we meet will be a
brother; every woman a sister; and every child a child of God.*

JONAS W. HOLMAN, 1838

*O that we may all be encouraged to walk nearer to God
and do more for the salvation of the oppressed. . . .
O for more and more of the spirit of consecration till
my whole being is lost in God and his cause.*

DAVID INGRAHAM, 1839

AFTER THE MURDER OF GEORGE FLOYD in 2020, millions of protesters demonstrated around the United States for racial justice. For Blake
Dahlin, one of my theology students at Seattle Pacific University and the

photo editor of the campus newspaper, photojournalism became a means of expression through which he hoped to offer a Christian witness. Documenting the civil unrest in Seattle, Dahlin observed that the great majority of protesters marched peacefully and that the movement's leaders actively worked to forestall violence. Most photographers, however, rushed to capture the few random scenes of conflict or destruction. "That wasn't the angle I wanted," he said later. "I thought that it matters where I stand as a journalist, as it completely shapes the story that's told. We need people who can stand in the gap and build bridges between sides so that people don't move further apart."

Where Dahlin stood, both physically and theologically, mattered. It mattered that he placed himself among people whose lived experiences were unlike his own. Location makes a difference when we engage in intentional, sustained relationships, especially with those who've endured discrimination. It also mattered that Dahlin embodied ideas that he had heard in his theology courses. His classroom learning helped to graft what was, for him, a new emphasis on the Holy Spirit's sanctifying love onto his long-established emphasis on justification in Christ. The Spirit's love became a grounding for social activism just as Jesus' work of conversion was a grounding for Dahlin's spiritual growth.

What we believe about God affects our actions toward God and other people. For twenty-first-century Christians such as Blake Dahlin, and for nineteenth-century Christians such as James Bradley, David Ingraham, and Nancy Prince, specific theological convictions have provided the resources necessary for the work of racial justice. As this book's introduction points out, Bradley, Ingraham, and Prince lived in an era of revivalism. But even though they manifested a revivalist spirituality, some of the convictions they articulated about the comprehensiveness of God's love, holiness, justice, and companionship weren't promoted by other revivalists. Most nineteenth-century White Christians didn't resist the racist prejudices of their era. A few revivalists who were also abolitionists, however, such as the highlighted figures in this book and some of their colleagues, expanded the meaning and implications of standard revivalist beliefs. Their enlarged theological understanding predisposed them to engage in social justice initiatives.

This wasn't just about having a strong theological foundation for one's spiritual life, though such a foundation is crucial and is sometimes missing in contemporary justice work. This is something more dynamic, more profound: these abolitionists expanded revivalist spirituality into something bigger than it had ever been, like a balloon increasing in volume. They took the theological underpinnings they had already confessed as revivalists and made them larger, more effective, more prophetic, through the way they lived out Christ's mission in the world. This chapter explores how they went about doing that, or rather, how God did those things through them.

What were their expanded beliefs? These bold nineteenth-century abolitionists claimed that God's love includes all people; that God empowers Christians to live a holy life; that God sides with the oppressed; and that we're called to have proximate, vulnerable relationships with others. When such abolitionists applied these theological convictions to the wider social order, they recognized that the institution of human slavery and the practice of racial discrimination were affronts to God's holiness, so they became champions for racial equity. They advocated for dramatic changes in unjust social structures, even against formidable opposition.

Each of the featured people in this book received training in the study of theology and thus learned how to articulate their convictions with depth and precision. James Bradley and David Ingraham obtained their theological educations at Lane Theological Seminary and Oberlin College. Nancy Prince lived for seven years at the Boston residence of Free Will Baptist pastor Jonas W. Holman, where she informally acquired theological knowledge by being immersed in a religiously conversant home environment. Yet despite the three abolitionists' commitment to education and their exposure to extensive intellectual formation, none of them aspired to be full-time academics or to write scholarly tomes. Instead, as practical theologians, they insisted that beliefs should be applied immediately and pragmatically within the larger community. They assumed that what they held to be true should have a direct effect on how they lived out their lives in the world. Recognizing that beliefs have consequences on the everyday behavior of men and women, they boldly asserted the relevance of Christian theology in all spheres of life.

FOUR CORE REVIVALIST BELIEFS

As enthusiastic participants in the religious awakenings of their era, Bradley, Ingraham, and Prince held tenets in common with other contemporary revivalists, beliefs shared by the majority of pre–Civil War Protestants. In their writings, each of the abolitionists featured in this book expressed typical revivalist ideas. The conventional revivalist concepts that they affirmed can be summarized by four theological characteristics: the belief that God initiates a relationship with individuals through a transforming experience with Jesus Christ (experiential conversion); the sentiment that Christians should practice a piety shaped by Scripture (biblically based devotion); the insistence that every person needs to turn away from their sin (repentant redemption); and the commitment that Christians need to express their faith publicly by sharing the gospel message with others and by conducting their everyday lives ethically (holy activism).[1]

The first characteristic that nineteenth-century revivalists, including Bradley, Ingraham, and Prince, expressed consistently was the insistence that God reaches out to people *personally*, enabling them to be converted. This new-birth conversion would be evident in believers' lives through their ongoing relationship with God (experiential conversion). Put simply, God is a divine Being who relates intimately to human beings. Revivalists stressed the inner work of the Holy Spirit, the breaking in of God's life to the present. Such a transformation produces inner serenity, exuberant joy, and zealous enthusiasm.

All three of our featured abolitionists demonstrated this type of life-changing encounter with God. James Bradley, for example, narrated how some "Christians talked with me concerning my soul," and how their conversation led him to commit his life to Christ. Nancy Prince wrote about the vicissitudes of being an African American woman and how "care after care oppressed" her. "All hope but in God was lost." Searching for relief from the difficulties of her distressed life, Prince resolved "to seek an interest in my Savior and put my trust in Him; and never shall I forget the place or time

---

[1]The four core theological beliefs of revivalism that I describe are derived from the "four main characteristics" named by historian David Bebbington in his influential study of the British evangelical revival. See his *Evangelicalism in Modern Britain: A History from the 1730s to the 1980s* (London: Unwin Hyman, 1989), 2-17, though I have nuanced Bebbington's characteristics to fit the American revivalist context.

when God spake to my troubled conscience. Justified by faith I found peace with God."[2]

Similarly, David Ingraham experienced multiple encounters with a close, indwelling Savior whom he called the "personal God of compassion and love." Ingraham conveyed his thoughts and prayers in a private diary. He recorded his fervor, for instance, when "the Lord wonderfully filled my soul" and his delight that "the blessed Savior has seemed very precious to my soul." He affirmed that "I know he [God] is a hearer of prayer." Ingraham described repeatedly how he longed for further spiritual experiences: "O," he wrote once, "for more of the presence of God." He wanted to "grow in grace and daily experience more and more of the fullness of the Blessed Savior." Such intimacy with God was not for himself alone; it was a privilege available to everyone: "O for peace and love to reign over all and then we shall see the salvation of God." He was convinced that all ministers should "preach the gospel from experience"—an ongoing, lived relationship with God.[3]

For nineteenth-century revivalists, their affective experiences with God led to a second trait, a revivalist characteristic that referred to the depth and breadth of their faith practices. Revivalists lived out a vital piety that manifested in a range of habitual disciplines such as prayer, hymn singing, communal worship, and small accountability groups, all centered around a spirituality that was grounded in Christian Scripture (biblically based devotion). Bradley, for example, "longed to be able to read the Bible" as soon as he was converted. Prince and Ingraham repeatedly alluded to biblical verses throughout their narratives, illustrating their dependence on the witness of Scripture. Ingraham found solace "meditating on the Word" and in "many happy hours praying." For these social reformers, the practice of the spiritual disciplines was not individualistic: Ingraham, for instance, enjoyed the Lord's Supper in corporate worship, at one point gushing, "How sweet is the communion of saints." He also relished the time he spent in a small group "meeting for our mutual improvement" because the fellowship was so "precious."[4]

---

[2]James Bradley, "Brief Account of an Emancipated Slave Written by Himself, at the Request of the Editor," in *The Oasis*, ed. Lydia Maria Child (Boston: Benjamin C. Bacon, 1834), 110; Nancy Prince, *A Narrative of the Life and Travels of Mrs. Nancy Prince, Written by Herself*, 2nd ed. (Boston: published by the author, 1853), 17.
[3]David Ingraham, manuscript journal, Adrian College Archives, 3, 7, 11, 20, 45, 54, 57, 58, 64, 65, 95.
[4]Bradley, "Brief Account," 110; Prince, *Narrative*, 83-88; Ingraham, journal, 5, 37, 46, 67, 72, 73, 95.

Revivalists stressed, third, the importance of asking forgiveness for their sin, believing that Jesus' death on the cross offered them mercy and pardon (repentant redemption). Such repentance was not a one-time event, they believed, but a continual disposition of reliance on God's mercy. "O bind me to the cross by love," wrote Ingraham in his diary. "I repent. I long to be fully delivered from . . . every sinful indulgence." Prince likewise found "forgiveness of sin through Jesus Christ my Lord." Bradley recognized "the sinfulness of my nature," which "led me to the cross of Christ." He confessed that he "must repent and live to do good."[5]

The connection that Bradley made between repentance and ethical living ("live to do good") highlights the fourth typical revivalist characteristic evidenced by these abolitionists: an activist faith (holy activism). Revivalists demonstrated their "doing good" through evangelism and by living a moral life, as shown by one's personal behavior and compassion toward others. The gospel, they determined, needed to be expressed practically—what Nancy Prince referred to as "usefulness."[6]

All three of our abolitionists, for instance, spoke about their commitment to evangelize others. Bradley hoped that his Lane Seminary education would provide him with an opportunity to "prepare to preach the gospel." Prince went to Jamaica to "raise up and encourage the emancipated inhabitants, and teach the young children to read and work, to fear God, and put their trust in the Savior." In the pages of his journal, Ingraham rejoiced that Jamaicans "publicly consecrated themselves to God and his cause" as "disciples of Jesus" when they joined his congregation.[7]

Revivalist activism included compassionate deeds on behalf of those who were disadvantaged. Prince cited biblical examples of holy actions: "The poorest can do something for the cause of Christ; even a cup of cold water." Quoting Matthew 25, Prince wrote admiringly about people who gave food to those who were hungry. Likewise, Ingraham prayed "for more active faith in his [God's] love and mercy to his children," linking devotion to God with care for God's people.[8]

---

[5]Ingraham, journal, 44, 46, 59; Prince, *Narrative*, 17, 89; Bradley, "Brief Account," 110.
[6]Prince, *Narrative*, 43.
[7]Bradley, "Brief Account," 110; Prince, *Narrative*, 45; Ingraham, journal, 5.
[8]Prince, *Narrative*, 87; Ingraham, journal, 27.

EXPANDING REVIVALIST BELIEFS

None of those four theological emphases, as shown through the writings of Bradley, Ingraham, and Prince, differed one bit from similar characteristics demonstrated by other revivalists of their era. But to accompany these standard revivalist tenets, Christian abolitionists extended the core commitments in ways that spurred revival-minded Christians to press for social justice concerns. They magnified several revivalist beliefs that allowed them to exhibit a distinctive witness for their time.

What theological wisdom mobilized a few revivalists, especially people associated with Oberlin and other abolitionist communities, to advocate for racial justice? In the memoirs of Bradley, Ingraham, and Prince, several biblically derived enlargements of the four core theological convictions can be identified: that God's image abides in all human beings (all-embracing love); that the Holy Spirit fills men and women so that they are enabled to consecrate themselves to God and are empowered to assist in bringing about a sanctified society (sanctifying holiness); that God supports the oppressed and judges those who oppress others (prophetic justice); and that Christians can embody God's overflowing love by expressing love for their neighbors, especially the marginalized, through proximate, open-hearted fellowship and concrete acts of righteousness (humble companionship).

First and foremost, the abolitionists forcefully asserted the implications of the truth that *all* people are created in God's image (all-embracing love). This concept amplified and made tangible the general revivalist concept that God initiates life-changing experiences with people through conversion to Jesus Christ. Ingraham declared that the comprehensiveness of God's compassion and love was the most evident "trait of His character."[9]

When taken seriously and applied to actual social situations, the belief in God's all-embracing love resulted in interracial teamwork. Nancy Prince, for instance, typically found Whites, including some of her fellow missionaries, to be patronizing opportunists who took advantage of her. She once described how "the weight of prejudice has again oppressed me, and were it not for the promises of God, one's heart would fail, for *He* made man in his own image." Despite such discrimination, she experienced self-worth in knowing that she was God's good creation. But surprisingly (and uncharacteristically),

---

[9]Ingraham, journal, 58.

Nancy Prince also received confirmation of her divine image-bearing from one of the White missionaries, David Ingraham. Due to Ingraham's Oberlin-sparked conviction regarding the intrinsic worth of all people, he affirmed Prince's "usefulness" and her calling to be a teacher. Ingraham's extended family welcomed Prince "with much encouragement," and another White abolitionist colleague and financial supporter of Oberlin, Lewis Tappan, became her "kind friend."[10]

Christians, both Black and White, who took the risk of enacting God's all-embracing love in real times and places established spaces of sanctuary for African Americans, a rare occurrence in antebellum America. James Bradley exclaimed that "prejudice against color does not exist at Lane Seminary," at least among his fellow students, who treated him "just as kindly, and as much like a brother," as though he were like them in appearance and educational background.[11]

Oberlin was one of the first towns to put the concept of crosscultural fellowship to the test. Oberlin and other small communities used the image of God's comprehensive, unconditional love as a motivational driver for their idealism. Frequently, though not always, these towns were the sites of abolitionist colleges, places like Adrian, Michigan; Berea, Kentucky; McGraw and Whitesboro, New York; Tabor, Iowa; and Galesburg, Jacksonville, and Wheaton, Illinois. As outposts of Christian community development, they manifested the hopeful, historical possibility that safe, nondiscriminatory spaces could be created.[12]

These localities were able to exhibit the inclusion of all people because they were explicit about who and what they wanted to become as a community. They practiced specific activities through which they could learn to love their neighbors, in whom they believed they would encounter Christ. Intentional interactions between races—eating meals together, residing in the same houses, praying and studying Scripture together—became deeply transformative. Their goal was to be sanctified, individually and communally, in order to become more like Jesus.

Not all White students at Oberlin agreed with the school's experiment in interracial fellowship. Delazon Smith, a disgruntled and disaffected Oberlin

---

[10]Prince, *Narrative*, 42, 55-56, 82, emphasis original.
[11]Bradley, "Brief Account," 110.
[12]Oberlin Anti-slavery Society, "Constitution of the Oberlin Anti-slavery Society" (June 1835), II.1.

Figure 5.1. Pre–Civil War racially integrated, abolitionist Christian schools

dropout, wrote a degrading exposé of the community in 1837, right after he left the college. Among other complaints, Smith said he became "disgusted" with the inclusive "reception and treatment" of African Americans. Smith's critique charged that "the conduct of some leading abolitionists" in Oberlin could "be contrasted with the avowed principles" of other prominent American abolitionists. Apparently, the radicalism of Oberlinites went beyond the relatively modest reform ideas then current among most White abolitionists. (Many Whites in the broader abolitionist movement wanted to end slavery but still asserted White privilege and superiority over people of color.) "Oberlin abolitionists," he wrote, "not being satisfied with the standard of abolitionists generally," advocated for racial equity and not simply the abolition of enslavement. Caustic in tone, Smith wrote incredulously that "amalgamation [the social mixing of races] is carried out at Oberlin." It seems that students were engaging in racial intermingling in their everyday relationships. Smith's blatant racism is evident in a description of one aspect of campus life: "At table [in the dining hall], they [African Americans] were interspersed among the [White] brethren and sisters that all might enjoy the privileges as nearly equal as possible, of glorifying and deifying the negro species." Smith intended his phrasing ("glorifying" and "deifying") to be sarcastic and insulting, but his description inadvertently confirms that a significant number of White Oberlinites were putting into practice their theological conviction of God's all-embracing love. For these revivalist abolitionists, all people, including their African American neighbors, were made in God's image (and therefore could be "glorified") and had sanctified potential by the power of the Holy Spirit to become more Christlike (and therefore could approximate being "deified").[13]

Smith's last comment alludes to the second distinctive theological trait of revivalist abolitionists: their belief that Christians can receive a fullness of divine love (sanctifying holiness). Once God's perfect love is received by "consecrating" (explicitly devoting and dedicating) one's life fully to Christ, then it can be poured out to other people. David Ingraham and James Bradley arrived in Oberlin in the mid-1830s during a season of revival throughout the United States. The holiness emphasis was growing. In Oberlin and many other places, people from all walks of life and a wide range of denominations consecrated their whole selves to God. Charles G. Finney, the famous evangelist and newly installed Oberlin professor, obtained a fresh empowerment of the Holy Spirit at this time. Asa Mahan, the first college president and a theological mentor to Ingraham, also had a spiritual breakthrough regarding the experience of entire sanctification. Mahan asserted that "in our efforts after holiness, we may attain to a state of entire consecration to Christ." For Mahan, holy consecration resulted from God's action and not from human effort alone: "Our hope of attaining this state rests not at all upon a view of our own natural powers as moral agents, but upon the provisions of divine grace for our redemption from all iniquity." This stress on consecrating oneself to sanctified holiness intensified the commitment to biblically based devotion (the second core revivalist belief) that characterized all nineteenth-century revivalists.[14]

Writing in his journal, Ingraham exemplified the holiness emphasis, basing it on God's gift of sanctifying grace. "I pray that I may be holy," he wrote. "God

---

[13]Delazon Smith, *A History of Oberlin: or New Lights of the West. Embracing the Conduct and Character of the Officers and Students of the Institution, together with the Colonists, from the Founding of the Institution* (Cleveland: S. Underhill and Son, 1837), 57–59, 64. Smith later moved to Oregon and was elected to the United States Senate as a proslavery Democrat.

[14]Asa Mahan, *Scripture Doctrine of Christian Perfection: With Other Kindred Subjects, Illustrated and Confirmed in a Series of Discourses Designed to Throw Light on the Way of Holiness* (Boston: D. S. King, 1839), 172-73. The holiness emphasis, both as a doctrine to be believed and a blessing to be experienced, proliferated throughout many denominations in the middle third of the nineteenth century, including Methodists, New School Presbyterians, Congregationalists, Free Will Baptists, Quakers, and Franckean Lutherans. See Douglas M. Strong, *Perfectionist Politics: Abolitionism and the Religious Tensions of American Democracy* (Syracuse, NY: Syracuse University Press, 1999), 31-37, 53-62, 91-115.

Figure 5.2. Asa Mahan, 1850s

send down his Spirit," "O for entire submission and perfect love and confidence in God," "O for more and more of the Holy Spirit to enlighten, lead, strengthen, and sanctify us all that we may be holy and without blemish before Christ in love." After reading Charles Finney's lectures on sanctification published in the *Oberlin Evangelist* newspaper, Ingraham stated that "nothing but unbelief hinders me from the enjoyment of this great and glorious privilege." He desired for others to experience this gift from God as well: "O for a spirit of consecration to rest upon them." Regarding "these doctrines" of holiness and sanctification, he wrote excitedly: "Blessed be that some are longing for a perfect knowledge and love of Christ and his Gospel."[15]

In his diary entries, Ingraham repeatedly combined two commitments, the sanctified consecration of one's soul and "God's cause" of social justice, viewing the concepts as inseparable. He was encouraged because his Jamaican congregants "consecrate themselves to God and his cause." He implored, "O for more and more of the spirit of consecration till my whole being is lost in God and his cause." And again: "O for more entire consecration that my entire influence might be for God. O that I might breathe nothing but love." Bradley, too, connected the work of "those who take part with the oppressed" to "this holy cause" of bringing racial justice to "the poor broken-hearted slave and free men of color."[16]

Nancy Prince's theological background also incorporated a stress on sanctification. Her primary denominational association, the Free Will Baptists, sent several of its pastors to Oberlin for training, who then proclaimed a holiness message. And just prior to Prince's sojourn to Jamaica, Jonas W. Holman,

---

[15]Ingraham, journal, 3, 10, 14, 36, 46, 77, 93.
[16]Ingraham, journal, 3, 45, 77; Bradley, "Brief Account," 111.

the Free Will Baptist pastor at whose residence she lived, preached a sermon about "the necessity of holiness." Holman directly blended sanctification with abolitionism when he chastised the sinfulness of any "unsanctified" person who "traffics in human flesh and makes merchandise of the souls of men."[17]

Holman's linkage of holiness to social reform represented the revivalist abolitionists' assertion that sanctification could be applied to the entire society as well as to individuals. In a typical example from 1839, Jonathan Blanchard (later to assume presidencies at two abolitionist colleges) gave a rousing commencement address at Oberlin about God's desire to erect a "perfect state of society." Clearly, the Oberlinites took seriously the promise of God's hopeful future.[18]

Figure 5.3. Photograph of Oberlin College around 1860, with First Congregational Church and Tappan Hall

What was the future they foresaw? Holman spoke about "an enlarged view" of God's glorious intent for the "reign of Christ," when "every man we meet

[17]J. W. Holman, *The Glory of the Church. A Sermon, Delivered at the Dedication of the Free-Will Baptist Meeting-House, on Bunker's Hill, April 17, 1838* (Boston: J. N. Bang, 1838), 6, 9, 11. Fittingly, Holman published a religious journal called the *Revivalist*.

[18]Jonathan Blanchard, *A Perfect State of Society* (Oberlin, OH: James Steele, 1839).

will be a brother; every woman a sister; and every child a child of God." Antici-
pating the fulfillment of God's promises, he believed that "amidst the groans
and cries of the oppressed," the time of "jubilee is at hand" and "the long night
of oppression is receding." James Bradley foresaw a day when "the walls of
prejudice are broken down, the chains burst in pieces, and men of every color
meet at the feet of Jesus, speaking kind words, and looking upon each other in
love willing to live together on earth, as they hope to live in Heaven!"[19]

The vision of a sanctified society included an assertion of God's righteousness, which points to the third theological characteristic of abolitionists
such as Bradley, Ingraham, and Prince: God takes the side of the oppressed
and calls out the iniquity of oppressors (prophetic justice). This conviction
is an extension of the third common revivalist belief, in repentant redemption. Abolitionists noted that the concept of justice as described in the
Scriptures was grounded in practices that maintained and restored fairness
and well-being (shalom) for the community, including the ministries of supporting the oppressed and confronting oppressors. Biblical justice required
concrete actions, such as opposing social structures that produced inequity.
David Ingraham understood this requirement. He acted on his justice principles and used his privileged position to establish a night school to provide
literacy for formerly enslaved people. He also pressed for fair wages for freed
Jamaicans and wrote articles that blasted slavery and the racism of White
Americans. In one of the articles, he stated his purpose plainly: he hoped
that "the facts I have stated, may make a deep and lasting impression upon
all who may read them, and that . . . many hands be opened for the relief of
the oppressed. . . . And when they *think*, may they *feel*; and when they *feel*,
may they *act*; and when they *act*, may God's blessing attend their efforts."[20]

James Bradley similarly stated forthrightly that "God will help those who
take part with the oppressed." Nancy Prince declared that "God speaks very
loud, and while his judgments are on the earth, may the inhabitants learn
righteousness!" When accosted by a group of White racists, Prince boldly
raised her voice and shouted: "There is a God, and a just one, that will bring
you all to account." Writing in his diary, David Ingraham was appalled that

---

[19]Holman, *The Glory of the Church*, 11-13; Bradley, "Brief Account," 111-12.
[20]D. S. Ingraham, "West Indies," *Oberlin Evangelist*, March 27, 1839; D. S. Ingraham, "Capture of
the *Ulysses*—Suffering of the Slaves," in *The Colored American*, April 4, 1840; Ingraham, journal,
47, 50, 88, emphasis original.

"our world seems to be one great slave plantation—a part [one portion] living at the expense of the oppressed." Given the suffering caused by such injustice, he asked himself several rhetorical questions: "O when will men learn that God is on the side of the poor, friendless, and oppressed?" "Where are the exertions for their liberation?" and "O who can measure the guilt or sound the iniquity of this nefarious [slave] traffic?" Ingraham's answer: "Slavery must fall and may the time come soon. The Lord executeth judgment for all that are oppressed. . . . O that the oppressor may see and repent ere it be too late."[21]

Based on their understanding of God's righteous requirements, revivalist abolitionists weren't afraid to demand that their country come to terms with its racism. They cherished the United States, and their patriotic admiration led them to expect that their nation would live up to God's standard of justice and repent of its wrongdoing. Nancy Prince did not shy away from calling out "the disadvantages and stigma that is heaped upon us [African Americans] in this our professed Christian land." She wrote that "God has in all ages of the world punished every nation and people for their sins. The sins of my beloved country are not hid from his notice." David Ingraham believed that the law of God took precedence over the laws of the United States. In his journal, he wrote his opinion bluntly: "America—You've many things to love and many things to hate, and while I would rejoice in all that's good and praise God as the Author, I would mourn that there are so many great sins about that God must ere long pour out his fury unless they [the majority of White Americans] repent and reform."[22]

The fourth theological characteristic of Oberlin abolitionists and their colleagues connects to the fourth commonplace core belief of revivalists, holy activism. The abolitionists, however, widened the scope of holy activism, moving beyond acts of compassion to acts of justice, propelling them forward toward racial equity. They believed that God's example of vulnerability and friendship through the life, death, and resurrection of Jesus Christ (see Philippians 2:1-11 and John 15:15) and the indwelling of the Holy Spirit (see Acts 2:1-18, 42-47) gave Christians the power to act with similar vulnerability. Bradley, Ingraham, and Prince became convinced that God's sanctifying love would be manifest when people who were previously estranged from one another opened themselves up to cherished relationships of mutual trust (humble companionship).

---

[21]Bradley, "Brief Account," 111; Prince, *Narrative*, 67, 78; Ingraham, journal, 24, 50, 79.
[22]Prince, *Narrative*, 43, 84; Ingraham, journal, 83-85.

Because of the history of discrimination, relationships that are both proximate and trusting can be difficult to establish and require sustained effort.
White people have a particular obligation to act without pride, arrogance,
superiority, or paternalism in their interactions with people of color, taking
on a posture of respect and humility like what David Ingraham exhibited.
Ingraham traveled to Jamaica as a missionary ready to replicate the interracial community he had known at Lane and Oberlin. When Delazon Smith
(the Oberlin dropout) mockingly described how Oberlinites structured their
table fellowship—remember that seats were arranged so that "all might
enjoy the privileges as nearly equal as possible"—he indicated not only that
African Americans and Whites sat next to one another, but also that they
prioritized relationships based on equality. When Ingraham and his wife
were students, they had experienced such equitable companionship with
African Americans and they were eager to develop similar, positive relationships with Black Jamaicans. But relationships of this sort couldn't be formed
at a distance or by living in a separate compound, as some White missionaries would. The Ingrahams understood that they needed to live among their
congregants and get to know them well, which is evidently what occurred,
because David Ingraham commented that in addition to preaching and
teaching he also "advises, counsels, and prays" with his church members.[23]

Sadly, we know from David Ingraham's journal that over a couple of years
he became increasingly sick, probably from tuberculosis. Eventually he could
no longer speak. His journal indicates that during the time that he was ill, he
was also "wounded" and disappointed by complaints brought by two of his
White missionary colleagues, who accused him of misconduct. We don't know
exactly what concerned the other missionaries, but it may have been their
perception that Ingraham welcomed Jamaicans into church membership too
leniently. But despite Ingraham's discouragement from fellow Whites, he
chronicled ongoing fellowship with his Jamaican congregants and the assistance they gave him in his days of illness. Indeed, his evolving need for physical
and emotional aid increased his dependence on them and the feelings of love
they shared for one another. He recorded in his diary that his congregants
laughed with him, wept and prayed with him, and kissed and embraced him.
They provided his family with gifts of food, herbal medicine, and money on

---

[23]Smith, *A History of Oberlin*, 64; Ingraham, journal, 87.

multiple occasions. They "all know me and love me," he confided in his diary. "My dear church were much overjoyed to see me."[24]

Apart from his sickness, Ingraham also made frequent note of his spiritual inadequacy due to sin. His longing for God's mercy allowed him to maintain a repentant temperament: "I need the assistance of all grace." His humble disposition before God, being "poor in spirit" (Matthew 5:3), combined with his frailty caused by chronic ill health, may have inclined him to be especially open to receiving support from Black Jamaicans and to identifying (though incompletely, of course) with their vulnerabilities. Perhaps only those who themselves have been vulnerable, those who understand their own brokenness (be it spiritual, physical, or emotional), are able to recognize when oppression has affected others.[25]

Ingraham clearly cherished fellowship with people of African descent. Connecting his own faith with that of his Black congregants and viewing his discipleship on the same level as theirs, Ingraham prayed "that Christ may be formed in them and me." It gratified him to know that his church folk "manifest the strongest love and attachment toward me and seem to be earnest in prayer" for him. Ingraham gained comfort knowing that "my dear church feel a deep interest for me and are incessant in prayer." He felt close to his congregants, and according to their testimony, he was "much loved" by them.[26]

Never once did Ingraham indicate in his diary that he looked down upon the race of his church folk. In his journal, his Jamaican Christian congregants were not labeled with racial descriptors, such as *Black*. Rather, his church members were consistently referred to as "dear church," "my dear people," or "God's dear people." While scores of individuals are mentioned in Ingraham's hundred-page journal, the adjective "dear" appears only in reference to a few cherished relationships: to Jesus Christ ("dear Savior"); to his family members ("dear Betsey," "dear parents"); to his associates from Oberlin ("God's dear people"); to his missionary colleagues ("dear brethren"); and most especially to his Jamaican congregants ("dear church"). Ingraham used one phrase, "the dear

---

[24]Ralph Tyler to Henry Cowles, March 20, 1842, alumni records, Oberlin College Archives; Ingraham, journal, 35, 87, 94, 96-100.

[25]Ingraham, journal, 44, 46, 95.

[26]Ingraham, journal, 19, 21, 41, 86, 87; Sarah Ingraham Penfield, letter, January 3, 1859, in Thornton Bigelow Penfield and Sarah Ingraham Penfield, *Letters from Jamaica 1858–1866*, ed. Charles G. Gosselink (Silver Bay, NY: Boat House, 2005), 26, Penfield Family Web Site, www.penfield.fm /jamaica/jamaica.pdf.

bond of love," to refer solely to his wife, his children, and the African-descended members of his church. In his mind, they were all of one heart. Frequently he wrote in the same breath about "my dear family + church" or "my dear family and dear people," a connectedness built on proximity and vulnerability.[27]

Using similar terminology, James Bradley encouraged people "of every color" to look "upon each other in love." The impact of Spirit-empowered, experiential relationships mobilized revivalist abolitionists to work for the "holy cause" of emancipation and racial equity. Likewise, the Spirit can sanctify us with an ongoing, affective love of God and neighbor that compels us to pursue justice for all of God's people.[28]

CONCLUSION

Neither the three highlighted figures in this book nor their revivalist abolitionist peers were well-known in their day, and their witness to racial equity has remained virtually unnoticed until now. Fortunately, the newly discovered journal (for Ingraham) and rediscovered autobiographical narratives (for Bradley and Prince) provide us with a window into the perspectives of these ordinary Christians who responded to the challenges of their culture in extraordinary ways. As twenty-first-century heirs of our nineteenth-century forebears, it behooves us to recognize that the beliefs of otherwise unheralded people can make a difference in our own lives and in our society.

What are these beliefs? Over and above the standard marks of a revivalist Christian—conversion, biblically based devotion, redemption, and activism— Bradley, Ingraham, and Prince also emphasized all-embracing love in concert with holiness, justice, and companionship. We should teach and preach these convictions—an "enlarged view" of Christian faith, in Holman's words—convictions that mobilized the Oberlinites and their colleagues to advocate for racial justice. Most Christians in their era, including other revivalists, didn't profess the expanded beliefs. Most of antebellum White Christianity was committed to personal spirituality and evangelism but not to social reform. Then and now, it takes courage to hold unswervingly to a theological balance

---

[27]Only once in his journal did Ingraham use the term *Black* to refer to African Americans, and then only to describe the racism he observed; after witnessing the beating of "colored or black" crew members by a group of racist White sailors aboard a ship, he lamented that African Americans "suffer because they are black." Ingraham, journal, 78-79; see also 45, 46, 77, 89.
[28]Bradley, "Brief Account," 111-12; Ingraham, journal, 45, 46, 77.

that refuses to separate deep devotion to Jesus Christ from unflinching advocacy for social justice. Such a combination is unpopular in polarized times, even though it reflects the witness of the Bible.

The revivalist abolitionists conveyed a practical theology that seamlessly wove together faith in God with social activism on behalf of the poor and oppressed, not an either-or but a both-and. Ingraham's journal entries often mention prayers, hymns, Scripture passages, evangelistic appeals, and praises to God, followed immediately by pleas for the White church, in which he included himself, to wake up to the reality of its complicity in oppression. "O for the freedom of the world. For this let me labor—for this let me pray," he wrote. "O that we may all be encouraged to walk nearer to God and do more for the salvation of the oppressed." May Ingraham's theological convictions, simultaneous commitments to a transformed life with God and to racial justice, be our hallmark as well.[29]

To move from racial equity to gender equity is a natural step. The first wave of the twentieth-century women's movement used many of the same arguments that had been used in abolitionism. Rhetoric that appears in calls for justice for African Americans is easily transferable to calls for justice for women. It is no coincidence that Oberlin's vision for desegregation in its student body was accompanied by a decision to admit female students. These students included David Ingraham's future wife, Betsey, and twenty years later their daughter, Sarah Ingraham Penfield. From its genesis in the holiness revivalism that Oberlin represented, a recognition of the call of women to preach and to minister like their male counterparts made its way into the theology and structures of the same holiness denominations that had become abolitionist on principle. Chapter six will give us a glimpse into the experiences of Black women in Jamaica, including Nancy Prince. It will also discuss the perspective of Sarah Penfield, a White woman who returned to Jamaica as a missionary some twenty years after her parents' deaths. She and her husband Bigelow served during the years between emancipation in Jamaica and emancipation in the United States. They also represented the holiness revivalism that expressed itself resolutely in a spirituality that sought justice for all, regardless of race or gender.

---

[29]Ingraham, journal, 3, 4.

CHAPTER SIX

"Purified Through Fire"

THE PIETY AND POWER OF FEMALE AFFLICTION

Diane Leclerc

---

*O Father, fearful indeed is this world's pilgrimage, when the soul has
learned that all its sounds are echoes, all its sights are shadows. But
lo! a cloud opens, a face serene and hopeful looks forth and saith, "Be
thou as a little child, and thus shalt thou become a seraph, and bow
thyself in silent humility and pray, not that afflictions might not visit,
but be willing to be purified through fire, and accept it meekly."*

Sorrow connects the soul with the invisible.

Nancy Prince, 1853

*I feel more and more like laying myself out for the
people here, like living and dying for Jamaica.*

Sarah Ingraham Penfield, 1858

It was 1977 when the TV miniseries *Roots* first aired. As our
family gathered around the television for eight consecutive nights, my
fourteen-year-old self first awakened to the history of enslaved people. Was
the story of Kunta Kinte true? The emotional impact of the narrative would
stay with me for a very long time, even after I realized that it was historical
fiction. I've come to realize that fiction based on history is a necessary genre

given that so much of what really happened in the days of American slavery was lost. What would we do if we could retrieve actual accounts of the thousands upon thousands of injustices and atrocities that were committed during centuries of bondage on these shores?

When I first encountered David Ingraham's sketch of the *Ulysses*, I was in shock. Five hundred and fifty-six enslaved persons endured fifty days of appalling, suffocating conditions before the ship was captured and unloaded in Kingston, a year after full emancipation came to Jamaica in 1838. These passengers, these prisoners, were human beings, and they endured true horror. What happened to them? Much of the content of their stories we can only surmise. But we do know that the 556 people were real. This book is, in some sense, an attempt to remember them with dignity.

The purpose of this chapter is to look at the lives of women in and around the narratives we have focused on in this book, examining the particular ways they experienced suffering. What do we know about what enslaved women endured in Jamaica, either before or after emancipation? What were the experiences of both Black and White women in Ingraham's journal? What does the autobiography of Nancy Prince, a freeborn Black woman, add to the discussion? And what might an extensive collection of letters written by David and Betsey Ingraham's daughter, Sarah Ingraham Penfield, tell us about women's lives twenty years later? We will take up these questions, while also calling to light the suffering that many women endured through birthing and mothering during slavery and the abolitionist period, and we will ask what we can learn from these stories today as we seek repentance and justice.

THE EXPLOITATION OF BLACK MOTHERS IN JAMAICA, CA. 1800–1840

Rhoda Reddock, a scholar of the Black Caribbean of the early nineteenth century, reminds us that the study of history is important not just for its own sake "but in order to acquire an understanding of the workings of society that we can apply to our present experience. In the women's movement throughout the world, women have had to re-examine and re-interpret history and often re-write it in order to make women visible." Reddock tells us that on Jamaican plantations, enslaved girls began forced labor at age four. Most women worked in the fields until the age of fifty-five, planting and harvesting sugar cane. A typical workday was twenty hours in length for both men and women, with women working during all nine months of pregnancy. It was common for enslaved persons of middle age or younger to die under such harsh and rigorous work conditions. The discipline that kept them working included daily whippings, whether they had "erred" or not. The whip was always there to remind them that they were not their own.[1]

In early-1800s Jamaica, history records a pregnant enslaved woman named Hetty who received punishment for failing to secure her master's cow, which later got loose. She received a brutal beating, including the whip, during which her "master flew into a terrible passion, and notwithstanding her pregnancy, ordered the poor creature to be stripped quite naked and to be tied to a tree in the yard." There he beat her relentlessly. The unborn baby did not survive the beating. A few days later Hetty died too.[2]

At the peak of the slave trade in the late eighteenth century, plantation owners generally believed that buying more enslaved persons was cheaper than raising them and could easily replace those who died from overwork or at the hands of their oppressors. Female labor was in huge demand, and slaveowners worked their women extremely hard. If a female laborer became pregnant, it was considered a problematic distraction from maintaining profits. Jamaican slave trader John Barnes stated that "the Child is some years before it can be put to labor." Historian Sasha Turner writes that "Jamaican slave holders were largely unwilling to sacrifice losing women's labor in the fields during pregnancy and childbirth or wait long-term for rearing children into capable workers," a wait of at least four years. When women gave birth, no profit could be "expected for many years to come."[3]

But once trading enslaved people became illegal in British territories in 1807 (and in 1808 in the United States), the supply chain suddenly disappeared, meaning that breeding more enslaved persons became paramount. Black women's bodies were seen not only as a source of economic profit in sugar *production* as they acted as field laborers, but as laborer makers and the source of *reproduction*, adding to the labor force through the labor of

---

[1]Rhoda E. Reddock, "Women and Slavery in the Caribbean: A Feminist Perspective," in *Freedom Road*, ed. James Millette (Kingston, Jamaica: Arawak, 1988), 152.

[2]Sasha Turner, "Home-Grown Slaves: Women, Reproduction, and the Abolition of the Slave Trade, Jamaica 1788–1807," *Journal of Women's History* 23, no. 3 (2011): 39.

[3]Turner, "Home-Grown Slaves," 40. Barnes is quoted in Turner.

The driver's whip unfolds its torturing coil.
"She only Sulks___ go lash her to her toil."

Figure 6.1. An enslaved mother in the British West Indies is forced to return to manual field labor after nursing her baby, 1826

childbirth. "Enslaved women's reproductive capabilities," writes Turner, "were pivotal for slavery and the plantation economy's survival once legal supplies [of people] from Africa were discontinued." After the end of the slave trade, a fertile woman's value increased; when she was sold, a woman's capacity to birth children had a proportional impact on her monetary value.[4]

It took a while for plantation discipline to catch up after slave trading became illegal. At first, slaveowners punished women just as severely as before, whether the women were pregnant or not. But as evidence of the effects of beatings and floggings on pregnant women and their unborn children mounted, such as in Hetty's case, enslavers began to connive and contrive new "protections" of their property. One such scheme was to whip a pregnant woman while she was lying down. The enslavers would dig a hole where the woman's belly would fit, thus enabling them to flog only her back. Later, slaveholders became more knowledgeable about the effects of work and nutrition

---

[4]Turner, "Home-Grown Slaves," 40.

on women who were pregnant or of childbearing age. Their concern for profit regulated the treatment they gave to Black women, if slightly. Even so, in owners' eyes, "black women could balance the most demanding manual labor alongside bearing children," a reflection of a racist stereotype, that Black women's bodies are exceptionally hardy, that continues to this day. Black women themselves, according to Reddock and other scholars, understood their exploitation and the intent of their "breeders," the slaveholders who used them to increase their wealth and power. "All data then available," she writes, "indicated that enslaved women disliked having children. . . . As a result of this, [self-inflicted] abortion and, to a lesser extent, infanticide were widely practiced." Many observers today believe that these were acts of resistance.[5]

THE MOTHERING PRACTICES OF NANCY PRINCE

Nancy Prince never had children of her own, but she was a mother none-theless. Her autobiography, published in 1850 with a second edition in 1853, speaks to her persevering faith, a sense of Christian calling, and a strong sense of identity as a freeborn Black woman. Growing up, she heard stories of her grandfather, who "was stolen from Africa" but escaped a slave ship, swam to shore to the beaches of New England, and fought at Bunker Hill for the freedom of the colonies. While many of Nancy's relatives were sailors, an occupation that promised "comfort and respectability," her growing-up years were very difficult, marked by severe poverty and significant loss. She never knew her father, who died when she was an infant. Her mother's third husband, also stolen from Africa, died during the War of 1812, leaving Nancy's mother with eight children that she could not care for, either finan-cially or emotionally. Prince's narrative is filled with descriptions of her mother's bouts of immobilizing depression. "My mother," she wrote,

> was again left a widow, with an infant six weeks old, and seven other children. When she heard of her husband's death, she exclaimed, "I thought it; what shall I do with these children?" She was young, inexperienced, with no hope in God, and without the knowledge of her Saviour. Her grief, poverty, and responsibilities, were too much for her; she never again was the mother that she was before.[6]

---

[5]Turner, "Home-Grown Slaves," 49; Reddock, "Women and Slavery," 156.
[6]Nancy Prince, *A Narrative of the Life and Travels of Mrs. Nancy Prince, Written by Herself*, 2nd ed. (Boston: published by the author, 1853), 7-8, https://archive.org/details/narrativeoflifet 1853prin/page/8/mode/2up.

The children then moved from household to household, separated from each other as they went to live with relatives and strangers. One little boy died of consumption. As one of the oldest siblings, Nancy wrote, she left her mother's house to work at the age of eight and began a years-long quest to take care of her siblings herself when she was only a teenager.

At age fifteen, she heard that her older sister Silvia had moved to Boston and become a prostitute. Nancy left her home in Salem, Massachusetts, and journeyed on foot to Boston in a New England February. With the help of a stranger, Nancy was able to rescue Silvia from the "mother of harlots" and returned to Salem, aided by another stranger, a "colored man" who paid their fare. At about the same time, Nancy and her brother George "were very desirous to make our mother comfortable." George "went to sea" for a time, but returned home. Nancy supported him, as well as another brother, whom she "boarded out for one dollar a week. . . . He expected to be supported by my brother George and myself."[7]

It was all part of her motherly sense of responsibility for the other children. "I could not see my mother suffer," she wrote.

> In the Spring, I returned to Boston, and took my brother Samuel with me; soon after, my sister Lucy left her place and went to her mother, but was not permitted to stay; my mother wrote to me, requesting me to take care of her. I then determined, in my mind, to bring her to Boston, and if possible, procure a place for her; I then had Samuel and John on my hands; Lucy was not nine, and very small of her age, I could not easily get her a place, but fortunately obtained board for her and Samuel for one dollar a week. My brother John, whom I had boarded, at last got a place where he had wages. . . . [He] left his place, and was several months on my hands again.

Then, after two more pages describing the never-ending work of looking after her siblings in this way, she wrote that she realized it was time to make a change. "In 1822, with a determination to do something for myself, I left my place . . . and made up my mind to leave my country." That was when Nancy Prince married her husband, a man many years her senior, and left with him to live in Russia for about ten years.[8]

Her concern for children continued in Russia, where she set up an orphanage, but an illness forced her to return to the United States alone in 1833

---

[7]Prince, *Narrative*, 16-19.
[8]Prince, *Narrative*, 16, 18-19, 20.

to recover. Prince and her husband intended that he would follow her home in two years' time after accumulating "a little property," but he died before he could make the trip. Now widowed herself, it was not long before Nancy Prince acted again on behalf of children, believing that God was guiding her. "I am indebted to God for his great goodness in guiding my youthful steps," she wrote.

> My mind was directed to my fellow brethren whose circumstances were similar to my own. I found many a poor little orphan destitute and afflicted, and on account of color shut out from all the asylums for poor children. At this my heart was moved, and I proposed to my friends the necessity of a home for such, where they might be sheltered from the contaminating evils that beset their path.

She opened such a home in Boston with an inaugural group of eight children but was only able to keep its doors open for three months before "want of funds" forced its closure.[9]

Prince then began to wonder about overseas missions. "My mind, after the emancipation in the West Indies," she wrote, "was bent on going to Jamaica. While I was thinking about it, the Rev. Mr. Ingraham, who had spent seven years there, arrived in the city." David Ingraham met Prince in Boston and convinced her to come to Jamaica to help him, and she set out on November 16, 1840.[10]

The rest of her journal often reads as a travel guide, recalling the many adventures that Prince experienced during her time in Jamaica. But it is prefaced by the sense of hope that she felt in going there. "I will mention my object in visiting Jamaica," she wrote. "I hoped that I might aid, in some small degree, to raise up and encourage the emancipated inhabitants, and teach the young children to read and work, to fear God, and put their trust in the Saviour." Later, "I continued with the same opinion, that something must be done for the elevation of the children, and it is for this that I labor." She finally settled into work at a missionary school, the Mico Institution in Kingston.[11]

On one occasion, Prince met with the American consul, who told her that the emancipated people did not want Black Americans to come to Jamaica

---

[9]Prince, *Narrative*, 40-41.
[10]A minor historical correction here: David Ingraham had spent not seven years in Jamaica when he met Nancy Prince in Boston, but three.
[11]Prince, *Narrative*, 43, 45, 47.

in order to "better their condition; he said they came to him every day praying him to send them home." It is clear that Nancy, even as a Black woman, did not include herself among these Americans. She believed that the color of her skin would make her efforts more effective for evangelism and education. Like a proud mother, she was able, we might infer, to see the freed persons for who they were. Repudiating the racist, proslavery contention that Africans were ignorant, she wrote that "they are not the stupid set of beings they have been called; here we surely see industry; they are enterprising and quick in their perceptions, determined to possess themselves, and to possess property besides, and quite able to take care of themselves." She went on: "I told them we had heard in America that you are lazy, and that emancipation has been of no benefit to you; I wish to inform myself of the truth respecting you, and give a true account on my return." Like a protective mother, she was bold in recounting their continued mistreatment even after emancipation. "The same spirit of cruelty is opposed to them," she wrote, "that held them for centuries in bondage."[12]

Alongside this theme of the true character of Jamaican Blacks, Prince's narrative also conveys a deep, motherly concern for children who were not in school. She decided to return to America to raise funds for an institution she wished to found, to be known as the Free Labor School. She visited Boston, New York, and Philadelphia to collect money and sailed for Jamaica once more on April 15, 1842, intending to start the school. But it was not to be, as conditions in Jamaica prevented the school from opening its doors before it could ever get off the ground.

Prince did not fade into the woodwork after her return to Boston in 1842. Not only did she write and publish her autobiography, but she also actively engaged in abolitionist work, showing a fierce maternal protectiveness toward individuals who had escaped from Southern bondage. On one memorable occasion, Prince (at the age of forty-eight) fearlessly tackled a notorious slavecatcher as he closed in on a victim. "Only for an instant did the fiery eyes of Mrs. Prince rest upon the form of the villain," eyewitnesses recalled, before she "grappled with him," enlisting the help of another woman to drag him into the street. Prince commanded the gathering crowd of women and children to pursue the slavecatcher and pelt him with stones,

---

[12]Prince, *Narrative*, 48, 50, 53.

an order "they proceeded to obey with alacrity." The slavecatcher fled in terror and did not return to that neighborhood for several years. Although the announcement of Nancy Prince's death in 1859 at the age of sixty occupied only two lines of a newspaper issue otherwise focused on the high-profile execution of abolitionist leader John Brown, her courage, dedication, faith, and self-sacrificing spirituality were no less profound.[13]

SARAH INGRAHAM PENFIELD AND DYING FOR JAMAICA

The dozens of letters that Sarah Ingraham Penfield and her husband Thornton Bigelow Penfield (known to his family as "Bigelow") penned between 1858 and 1886 recount their experiences as ministers in Jamaica. It was a long, difficult road for them to get to serve there. After the tragic, early deaths of David and Betsey Ingraham, Sarah, who had been born in Jamaica, grew up in the care of a relative in upstate New York. In young adulthood she made her way to Oberlin College as a student like her parents before her. Bigelow, her future husband and also a student at Oberlin, graduated in 1856, the same year that Sarah graduated from Oberlin's Ladies' School. They each moved to New York after finishing at Oberlin, Bigelow to spend two years at Union Theological Seminary, Sarah to work at the Home for the Friendless, where Bigelow's sister Josephine also served. When Sarah and Bigelow married in 1858, they immediately received a call from the American Missionary Association to Jamaica, an invitation to return to the land of Sarah's birth.[14]

Bigelow had long sensed a vocation to missions, having testified to a call to be a missionary in India when he was twelve. His mother and her first husband, Bigelow's father, had moved to Oberlin seeking a spiritual community, and Bigelow grew up immersed in the ethos of Oberlin holiness and social justice, such as when his mother presided over the first meeting of the

---

[13]Thomas B. Hilton, "Reminiscences: Woodfork and Nancy Prince," *Woman's Era* 1, no. 5 (1894): 4-5, https://archive.org/details/womans-era-1.5/mode/2up?; "Died," *Liberator*, December 2, 1859, 191, http://fair-use.org/the-liberator/1859/12/02/the-liberator-29-48.pdf.

[14]Thornton Bigelow Penfield and Sarah Ingraham Penfield, *Letters from Jamaica: 1858–1866*, ed. Charles G. Gosselink (Silver Bay, NY: Boat House, 2005), Penfield Family Web Site, www .penfield.fm/jamaica/jamaica.pdf. In addition to publishing the letters, the Penfield family also preserved all of Thornton Bigelow's and his second wife Charlotte's letters from India, which when transcribed run to hundreds of pages altogether. Charlotte E. Mertz, ed., *Only for Jesus: The Penfield Correspondence 1866–1872*, rev. ed. (Silver Bay, NY: Boat House, 2011), Penfield Family Web Site, www.penfield.fm/Only-for-Jesus.pdf. Prints of these books are held at the Oberlin College Archives.

Figure 6.2. Photograph of Oberlin Ladies' Course Seniors, 1857. Sarah Ingraham (later Sarah Ingraham Penfield) is on the far right of the top row.

Ohio State Temperance Convention. After her husband died in an accident, she remarried Henry Cowles, a theology professor at Oberlin and later the editor of the *Oberlin Evangelist*. He was a staunch abolitionist, even before joining the Oberlin faculty.

"Sarah's letters," writes the editor of the Penfield family's collection, "show her sensitivity to the issue of women's rights, especially when she experienced the patronizing attitude of her older male colleagues in Jamaica, who may not have been aware of the changes that were taking place in Oberlin." Female graduates, for example, were first allowed to read their own essays at commencement in 1858.[15]

Many of Sarah's letters describe her living situation in Jamaica, where she and Bigelow were extremely poor. In her daily life, she felt torn. On one hand, she was very concerned to fit a romantic ideal of the domesticity that

---

[15]Charles G. Gosselink, introduction, in Penfield and Penfield, *Letters from Jamaica*, 18.

was common in the United States during the Victorian era. She gave detailed reports of her housework and her care for the several Black children she had taken in at any given time almost since the moment they first landed. At the same time, Sarah strove for an empowered role, something she had learned during her Oberlin days. She spent much of her time making pastoral calls, even alone, until her health prevented her from doing so. Her ministerial presence made an impression on those who lived near her. "Since we came we have opened a female prayer meeting. . . . Some of the sisters are very much attached to me and I to them," she wrote. In 1860, when Bigelow was often away during worship time in his work to maintain contact with three mission sites, Sarah remarked that she read sermons to the congregation. "I have done this a good many times lately," she wrote, "and have been blessed myself by it and a blessing to others in it, I hope."[16]

Sarah did make friends with other missionaries at first, but none of the friendships lasted very long. Reading her letters, one senses isolation. Much of this must have been due to the lifestyle and justice-driven decisions that she and Bigelow had made as they entered the mission field, choices that were at odds with the practices of other missionary families at the time. Both Bigelow and Sarah commented in their letters that the other missionaries had abandoned "Oberlin principles" as they "in no way acknowledg[e] them [Blacks] as equals." Sarah complained that her coworkers, whose "conduct is so utterly adverse to our Oberlin training," were morally lax, not only practicing bigotry but also drinking too much. Prejudice became a point of great tension among the missionaries. It came to a head when colleagues came for meals in the Penfield home and discovered, to their aghast offense, that the Penfields included their Black children at the same dinner table with them, even when other missionaries were visiting. The issue eventually blew up, to the surprise and grave disappointment of Sarah and Bigelow. The young couple was not the first to challenge a missionary culture that had strayed from its ideals; a single woman before them, Sarah remarked to her mother-in-law, was sent home for being too ardent about practicing racial equality.[17]

---

[16]Sarah Ingraham Penfield to Mary Louisa Cowles, February 5, 1859, in Penfield and Penfield, *Letters from Jamaica*, 31; Sarah Ingraham Penfield to Mary Louisa Cowles, October 14, 1860, in Penfield and Penfield, *Letters from Jamaica*, 99.
[17]Sarah Ingraham Penfield to Mary Louisa Cowles, March 4, 1859, in Penfield and Penfield, *Letters from Jamaica*, 37.

The letters give an image of other missionaries as difficult, meanspirited, ineffective, and racist, the latter in contrast to the Penfields' principled attempts to demonstrate equality. Early in their stay, Bigelow criticized the other clergy directly, creating tension between the Penfields and the other families that lasted the duration of their seven-year stay in Jamaica. At moments the missionary establishment even seemed to punish Bigelow by failing to provide ample financial resources and by passing him over for opportunities to further his career.

Meanwhile, from the very first year in Jamaica onward, Sarah's health suffered as her father's had. Aside from a cough horrible enough to produce blood, she endured a long chain of fevers and seemed to be sick more often than she was well during her years on the island. She blamed poverty, the weather, and the workload. The family's financial situation, she wrote, was challenged by their care of Jamaican children, and she suggested to her mother-in-law that people in Oberlin might like to sponsor one or more of the children for twenty-five dollars. She was not alone in her sickness. As Sarah prepared to return to the United States for treatment in 1863, her second daughter, Ellen Josephine (nicknamed Nellie), who was only a year old, developed a fever and cough and died within hours. Nellie's sudden death prompted Sarah to adjust her plans and take her older daughter Mary with her to America.

Despite the difficulty of life and ministry in Jamaica, the Penfields were optimistic at first, believing that the emancipated Jamaicans would heartily receive the gospel and work to better themselves. Toward the end of their time in Jamaica, they perceived Black Jamaicans as increasingly riotous and became outraged at the continued harsh treatment and discrimination that the White population continued to give them. At the beginning of their time there, the Penfields saw conversions and revivals; at the end, they felt as though they had only lost ground in the churches, and despaired.

After leaving Jamaica in September 1863, Sarah went to a sanatorium (a facility for those attempting to recover from tuberculosis) in Saratoga Springs, New York, for a planned six-month stay, while Mary went to live with her grandparents in Oberlin. Sadly, Sarah's treatment was ineffective. When she returned to Oberlin in 1864 she was dying, and Bigelow rushed home from Jamaica to be with his wife in her final days. The illness took her life on April 21, 1864, very much like it had taken her parents' lives.

The letters that Sarah and Bigelow wrote included accounts of their spiritual lives. The daily suffering they endured, mentally and physically, made the doctrine of entire consecration (a core belief of revivalist abolitionists, as described in chapter five) real to them. Their discipleship came at a cost. "I feel more and more," wrote Sarah in February 1859, "like laying myself out for the people here, like living and dying for Jamaica. I do hope the Lord will spare our lives to accomplish something for these people." Five years later, she very much had died for Jamaica. The terrible brevity of her life is perhaps redeemed through the lives of those children that she raised in her own home, or through her preserved letters, which show the incredible fortitude of faith that she possessed despite physical, mental, emotional, and social affliction. The connection that Sarah, like David and Betsey before her, felt between her vibrant faith and the social activism that she carried out is abundantly clear to anyone who encounters her heart in the pages of her letters.[18]

THE PIETY OF AFFLICTION

Each of the narratives that we have studied in this chapter contains some element of affliction, a particular kind of suffering that, according to Simone Weil, has three essential dimensions: the physical, the psychological, and the social. It is common for nonphysical trauma to cause physical pain, just as physical pain can cause psychological and emotional turmoil, especially if the pain is chronic. The social dimension comes from an experience of alienation and degradation. Suffering can bring a kind of loneliness, not only because others often withdraw from those who suffer, but also because every experience of suffering is unique. Abuse, as one form of affliction, elicits suffering in all three dimensions.

To cause affliction deliberately in another person's life cannot be justified. It's true that Christian reflection on suffering can point to elements of redemption in the meaning-filled wounds of Jesus. Yet even as we see redemption along those lines in the writings of Nancy Prince and Sarah Penfield, the experience of enslaved women offers a different perspective.[19]

---

[18]Sarah Ingraham Penfield to Mary Louisa Cowles, February 7, 1859, in Penfield and Penfield, *Letters from Jamaica*, 36.

[19]This paragraph and the one preceding are indebted to Simone Weil, *Waiting for God*, trans. Emma Craufurd (New York: G. P. Putnam's Sons, 1951), originally published as *Attente de Dieu*

Sarah Ingraham Penfield's life and death. Of the two children that Sarah Penfield birthed, one died only a year after she was born, a parallel to the experience of Sarah's mother, who had also lost a child in Jamaica. Sarah's experience of motherhood came at great cost. She wrote in sad detail of the extreme difficulty she faced in her excruciating attempts at breastfeeding and of the financial difficulty of raising the Jamaican children she adored and cared for. Her health, which was almost always precarious, often kept her from fully engaging in the missionary work to which she was called and from the quality of ministry she must have envisioned. Yet her letters betray a depth of spirituality within her that was strengthened, not diminished, by her plight.

In a way, her afflictions enveloped her life. They had begun when she herself was orphaned as a child upon David and Betsey Ingraham's deaths of tuberculosis at young ages and ended with her own death from the same disease. What might be called a "dying spirituality," nurtured during her short life by her sick parents, her relatives, and the ethos of Oberlin, led her to commit to a life of costly self-sacrifice, called entire consecration, and to frame her affliction as being endured for Christ's sake. That theological narrative gave her courage to bear the pain she carried across the span of her life. "My own soul," she wrote in 1862,

> has been greatly blest of late. When we first came here I was in a very unhappy
> state of mind—dissatisfied with myself and everybody else, and restive under
> the dealings of my Heavenly Father with me. But a crisis came, and by God's
> help I was able to say "not my will but thine be done," and my soul has rested
> calmly and quietly on God ever since. I think I can say my peace has been as
> a river, though sometimes for the moment ruffled on the surface, down deep
> in my heart it has flowed steadily on.

Like her father David, Sarah was a true example of the wedding of personal piety, pursued in spite of affliction, and social activism.[20]

Nancy Prince's acts of "sharing in the suffering of Jesus." At the end of her narrative, Nancy Prince took several pages to reflect on how the pain

---

(Paris: La Colombe, 1950), 117; see also Bessel van der Kolk, *The Body Keeps the Score: Brain, Mind, and Body in the Healing of Trauma* (New York: Penguin, 2015).

[20]Sarah Ingraham Penfield to Mary Louisa Cowles, January 29, 1862, in Penfield and Penfield, *Letters from Jamaica*, 132.

and difficulties of her life were evidence of having shared in the sufferings of Jesus. She associated herself with the characters of several Scripture passages that spoke to the discipline of suffering. "In the hands of the Lord," she wrote, "there is a cup; the Saviour drank it to the dregs." So did she. With Paul's discourse in Philippians and Peter in his first epistle, she wrote that "what things were gain to me, I counted loss for Christ, in whom I suffered all things; and do count them nothing, that I may win Christ and be found in him . . . thinking it not strange concerning the fiery trials, as though some strange thing happened; for saith the apostle, it is better if the will of God so be that ye suffer for well doing, than for evil." She saw herself in Romans 8, Isaiah 53, and Matthew 25, identifying with Paul and with Christ in her circumstances. She sensed God saying to her out of Matthew, "Come ye blessed of my Father, inherit the Kingdom prepared for you. . . . Inasmuch as ye have done it unto one of the least of my disciples, ye have done it unto me." Ultimately, she saw herself as God's child, as she showed in her magnificent final paragraphs:

> I am a wonder to many, but the Lord is my strong refuge, and in him will I trust. I shall fear no evil, for thou, O Lord, art ever near to shield and protect thy dependent children. . . . Sorrow connects the soul with the invisible.
>
> O Father, fearful indeed is this world's pilgrimage, when the soul has learned that all its sounds are echoes, all its sights are shadows. But lo! a cloud opens, a face serene and hopeful looks forth and saith, "Be thou as a little child, and thus shalt thou become a seraph, and bow thyself in silent humility and pray, not that afflictions might not visit, but be willing to be purified through fire, and accept it meekly."

There is no doubt that Nancy Prince lived her life drinking from the "dregs" like her Savior, Jesus. In her view, her "self-sacrificing spirituality," characterized by a deep, "sanctified" commitment to the well-being of others, especially children, redeemed her affliction. Hers is another poignant example, with Sarah Penfield's, of what a life can look like when it marries personal piety with social activism.[21]

"Suffer not a Black woman." The institution of slavery combined systemic, state-sanctioned, structural abuse with the daily indignities that were endured by Blacks in all parts of the New World. It resulted in

---

[21]Cf. Philippians 3:7-9; 1 Peter 4:12, 3:17; Matthew 25:34, 40 (KJV); Prince, *Narrative*, 83-84, 86-88.

devastating, penetrating consequences both while slavery was active and down through history to today. Enslaved persons, traded from Africa and brought as prisoners to the New World, suffered an immensity of affliction unparalleled in modern history and difficult to fathom. Some 160 years after emancipation in the United States, there is still generational scarring among Black people, and there are countless instances of race-based abuse and murder even now.

Yet despite the millions of people whose lives and selves have been formed and shaped by slavery and its legacy, their point of view and experience has largely been ignored in most theological study and reflection. By contrast, womanist theology in particular centers the experiences and perspectives of Black women, arguing that they are a valid and valuable starting place for doing theology. Focusing on their experiences, writes theologian Delores Williams, can help to "bring back women's social, religious, and cultural experience into the discourse of theology, ethics, biblical and religious studies" today. To center the stories and personhood of marginalized human beings in our theology means not only joining Christ in his preference for the poor and oppressed but also claiming that our own personhood can be realized, in the words of theologian M. Shawn Copeland, "only in solidarity with the exploited, despised, poor 'other.'"[22]

Among its many sins and atrocities, North American slavery saw the exploitation of Black female bodies and their organs of reproduction, their very motherhood, at the behest of their "owners" in acts of unspeakable dehumanization. The prejudice that women experienced in such cases was magnified on account of being both Black and female. Bigotry and misogyny combined to make these women's terrors all the more terrible. Such abuse, if we have eyes to see, necessarily reveals a stunning "spirituality of inno-cence" in its victims. These women did not deserve to suffer or die. With great theological delicacy, we should affirm that in the bodies of these Black enslaved women we see the body of Jesus on the cross. He was whipped and stripped naked, weighed down by the sins of others, and laid in death before his time. So were these enslaved women. Copeland writes that opening our

---

[22]Delores S. Williams, "Womanist Theology: Black Women's Voices," in *Black Theology: A Documentary History*, ed. James H. Cone and Gayraud S. Wilmore, vol. 2, *1980–1992* (Maryknoll, NY: Orbis, 1993), 266; M. Shawn Copeland, *Enfleshing Freedom: Body, Race, and Being* (Minneapolis: Fortress, 2010), 89.

eyes to Christ's own suffering in the bodies and faces of these women "exposes the way in which we *all* have betrayed the very meaning of humanity—our own, the humanity of exploited, despised, poor women of color, and the humanity of our God." This confession is the beginning of true solidarity.[23]

Acknowledging that Christ shared the suffering and anguish of enslaved women is not synonymous with claiming that their suffering is redemptive. To say that their pain can be redeemed would only serve to co-opt, even to romanticize, the suffering of generations of enslaved persons and their descendants. Instead, as we affirm Jesus' solidarity with those who suffer in innocence and see his face in theirs, we find that our own "praxis of solidarity is made possible by the loving self-donation of the crucified Christ, whose cross is its origin, standard, and judge." This praxis of solidarity calls for us to not only see and intentionally remember the exploited victims of history, but also, in the words of Copeland, to shoulder the responsibility "to stand between poor women of color and the powers of oppression in society, to do all that we can to end their marginalization, exploitation, abuse, and murder. In memory of the cross of Jesus, we accept this obligation, even if it means we must endure rejection or loss."[24]

Yes, in the faces of Black women, men, and children, we can see the face of Christ—"despised . . . rejected . . . a [person] of suffering, and familiar with pain," one who was thought "punished by God, stricken . . . and afflicted," and "pierced," "crushed," punished, and wounded (Isaiah 53:3-5 NIV). If there is ever to be racial reconciliation within the church or in spite of it, we must come to see each other clearly in the hope that God, in God's wisdom, will deal wisely with the overwhelming torrent of such grievous sin. "I think some people would understand the quintessence of sanctifying grace if they could be black [for] about twenty-four hours," said Amanda Berry Smith, a Black Methodist abolitionist preacher, in the late 1800s. If we have any abolitionist sensibility today, may our attempts at piety, our very sanctification, not be holiness for our sake, something to wrap around ourselves like a coat, but a life of solidarity and active love toward those who suffer injustices at human hands.[25]

---

[23]Copeland, *Enfleshing Freedom*, 90.

[24]Copeland, *Enfleshing Freedom*, 99, 101.

[25]Amanda Smith, *An Autobiography: The Story of the Lord's Dealings with Mrs. Amanda Smith the Colored Evangelist* (Chicago: Meyer and Brother, 1893), 116-17.

The quest to free enslaved people was, of course, the primary goal of abolitionism. But even in the nineteenth century, it was clear that the institution of slavery generated economic, social, and cultural conditions that continued to oppress individuals after their legal bondage was behind them. Therefore, a determination to improve the kinds of lives that freed persons had available to them and to ameliorate the negative byproducts of slavery was also at the forefront of abolitionists' mission and purpose. Chapter seven will explore how Christian abolitionists used the tools of charitable aid and philanthropy, their money and their time, to institute progress toward racial equity by addressing gaps in education, job training, and land acquisition for those who had been emancipated.

"Organized Efforts to Educate and Elevate"

CHARITABLE AID AMONG CHRISTIAN ABOLITIONISTS

Esther Chung-Kim

I needed all the hospitality that was extended to me.

Nancy Prince, 1853

The time has arrived when organized efforts should be used to educate and elevate the free-colored population. Motives that should induce abolitionists to undertake this work of philanthropy are numerous and . . . weighty.

Lewis Tappan, 1836

A SIMPLE GOOGLE SEARCH for *abolitionist leaders* yields names like Harriet Tubman, Frederick Douglass, Sojourner Truth, and William Lloyd Garrison—men and women remembered for eloquently swaying public opinion against slavery or risking their lives to help others escape bondage. They modeled racial justice in a very visible way, through organizing protests, mobilizing support, publicly speaking and writing for the abolitionist cause, and directly challenging or flouting laws that protected slavery. Their work was essential and courageous, but they did not stand alone. The cause was supplemented and made possible by a much greater number of individuals and faith communities who labored behind the scenes, supporting abolitionists and helping freed men and women with the resources they needed to build new lives and flourish.

From the 1830s through the Civil War, Christian abolitionists, from public figures to community supporters, worked as the nation's conscience for the ethics of antislavery. The abolitionist movement was primarily religious in its leadership and its methods of reaching people, stressing the spiritual as much as the civil damage that was being done to enslaved persons and the nation. The antislavery cause originated and was strongest in the middle class, particularly in the religious sector of New England and its westward extension into places such as upper New York State, Ohio, and Michigan. Both Whites and freed Blacks worked as missionaries, attempting to improve the lives of emancipated persons through education and job training. They also worked as administrators, fundraisers, and organizers of antislavery societies dedicated to the abolition of slavery and the improvement of living conditions for Blacks. Lewis Tappan, for example, a Christian abolitionist and businessman, urged that practical piety, including charitable aid, hospitality, and fundraising, be preached from every pulpit. It was an idea that undergirded much of the antislavery effort. This chapter will examine these behind-the-scenes contributions as a key aspect of the abolitionist movement.

ABOLITIONISTS AS MISSIONARIES: DAVID INGRAHAM AND NANCY PRINCE

When the British government passed the West Indies Emancipation Act in 1833, American abolitionists paid careful attention to the emancipated people of Jamaica, seeing the British example as a model for freeing enslaved people in the United States. Many American abolitionists, experiencing a new sense of enthusiasm when the law was passed, served as missionaries in Jamaica to help the emancipated transition to their new lives. David and Betsey Ingraham were among the vanguard of abolitionist missionaries to Jamaica, and David's journal shows how he worked to improve the situation of Blacks through establishing a church and a school. He also sought to convince those back home to adopt an antislavery ethic, publishing a denunciation of the inhumane trade. He described the forced splintering of families as "fathers robbed of their wives and children—children torn from the embrace of their mothers, and every relation and feeling dear to the human heart, severed and mangled." After working three years there (1837–1840), he returned to the United States to recruit other missionaries. It was on this trip that he met widowed Nancy Gardner Prince—whose mind was already set on serving in post-emancipation Jamaica—and persuaded her to help bring moral education to the mission near Kingston.[1]

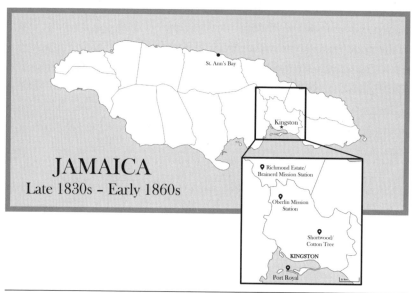

Figure 7.1. Sites in Jamaica connected with Oberlin-influenced missionaries, late 1830s to early 1860s

When Prince first arrived in Jamaica in December 1840, she taught for a season at a school at St. Ann's Bay on the north shore before traveling to Kingston and working at the Mico Institution, which had been established in 1836 and was now devoted to instructing emancipated Blacks in the British colonies. Prince soon discovered the harsh conditions of Jamaica and the high mortality rate from sickness among Americans who emigrated there. But as the previous chapter narrates, she also saw the entrepreneurship of Black men and women and proudly described them as industrious, enterprising, and perceptive, thus countering a stereotype of Whites in the United States who questioned Blacks' capacity or desire for independence. Resolved to continue her mission, Prince decided to establish a Free Labor

---

[1] D. S. Ingraham, "Capture of the *Ulysses*," *The Colored American*, April 4, 1840.

School in Jamaica for poor girls. She formed a society (charitable organization) to contribute to the cause and returned to the United States to raise support and funds.

While in the United States, Prince met the Anti-slavery Society at the home of Lucretia Mott and learned that Ingraham had just died from tuberculosis and that his family was staying with Theodore Weld, a Lane Rebel who would later train Oberlin students to become antislavery activists. Prince received an invitation to stay at the home of the late Ingraham's cousin, where she received much encouragement from missionaries who took great interest in her cause. She received donated funds for her Free Labor School in Boston, New York, and Philadelphia. But when the funds turned out to be insufficient, she took fifty dollars from her own purse, thinking that the society would refund her the money. When she returned to Jamaica on May 6, 1842, the colony was in a state of political and social instability. Disillusioned by the greed of White landowners and the deceit of some Blacks who sought to plunder her, she made plans to leave.[2]

Prince returned to New York in October 1842, her resources depleted. Several people tried to help her raise the twenty-five-dollar cost to unload her baggage from the vessel, without much success. When someone introduced her to Lewis Tappan, he himself raised the money and went with Prince to the ship to retrieve her luggage. She returned to Boston the next summer, "poor in health and poor in purse, having sacrificed both, hoping to benefit my fellow creatures." Whether it was through hospitality, charity, fundraising, or simply service to those around her, Prince understood that practical godliness meant doing whatever she could for someone else in need—and she was, in turn, supported and upheld by Christians in Jamaica and the United States who shared her mission.[3]

FUNDING ANTISLAVERY MOVEMENTS—LEWIS TAPPAN

In their work as publishers, administrators, and financiers of antislavery efforts, the Tappan brothers supported various institutions that promoted abolitionism. Lewis Tappan and his brother shared a vision together for the

---

[2]Fifty dollars in 1842 is equivalent to $1,806 in 2022.

[3]Nancy Prince, *A Narrative of the Life and Travels of Mrs. Nancy Prince, Written by Herself*, 2nd ed. (Boston: published by the author, 1853), Internet Archive, https://archive.org/details/narrativeof lifet1853prin/page/8/mode/2up, 82–83.

antislavery cause but accomplished different goals. Arthur Tappan took several steps to organize antislavery groups. He paid for the printing of over 7,600 copies of the *Emancipator*, a Christian antislavery newspaper, and to have it distributed to Northern clergy. He also dispatched William Lloyd Garrison to England to obtain the blessing of British antislavery leaders. Arthur's involvement meant that many of his distinguished friends would eventually also get involved. Many, such as Gerrit Smith, also shared Arthur's revivalist bent.

Lewis Tappan served as a bridge between the more radical Garrisonians and the socially "respectable" element of society. As a founder of the New York Anti-slavery Society and the American Anti-slavery Society, Lewis Tappan contributed monetarily and morally to further the abolitionist cause. He helped to establish Oberlin Collegiate Institute (later known as Oberlin College), wrote and published antislavery materials, assisted in securing freedom for refugees from the *Amistad* slave ship (as we will learn later in this chapter), organized the American Missionary Association (AMA) to educate the emancipated, and raised funds for various efforts to improve the condition of freed Blacks. In doing all of this, he mobilized many churches and religious societies to lend their aid to the abolitionist movement and to support the economic independence of persons who were newly emancipated. The massive enthusiasm of both Lewis and Arthur Tappan for re-sourcing the antislavery movement traced its origins back to Theodore Weld.

Oberlin College. In 1831, Weld convinced the Tappan brothers to join the abolitionist movement and contribute to the building of Lane Theological Seminary. Weld considered Lewis a needed administrator for the movement, someone who could make the cause of antislavery flourish not just as a movement but also organizationally.

As we saw in chapter one, after the contentious debate on slavery, Weld and a majority of the Lane Seminary students, including James Bradley, David Ingraham, and trustee Asa Mahan, left the school. A few of these Lane Rebels scattered to other institutions, but a bulk of them formed a seminary-in-exile at a sympathizer's spacious house. Arthur Tappan supplied five thousand dollars to find and pay for their housing on the outskirts of Cincinnati, meanwhile seeking a site for a new seminary for this group of students who wished to finish their studies. Asa Mahan, the supportive trustee,

Figure 7.2. Engraving of Lewis Tappan, 1854

and John Morgan, the only supportive professor, served as advisers for the group, which carried out a variety of charitable, religious, and social activities in service of Cincinnati's impoverished Black population during the summer and fall of 1834. Weld and his abolitionist friends established a learning center for evening reading classes, a lending library for the benefit of Cincinnati's Black residents, Sunday schools, and a Bible class. Back in

New York, the Tappan brothers, pleased with Weld's reports of these education programs for Blacks, published accounts of the antislavery revival in the *Emancipator* and the *Evangelist*, two local newspapers that promoted the abolitionist cause. The brothers also supported the effort in Cincinnati by sending out bundles of tracts and primers along with clothing and money. Lewis Tappan paid to transfer several schoolteachers from the Northeast to Cincinnati to assist and sought to replicate Weld's Cincinnati activities in majority-Black slums in Manhattan.

In January 1835, Asa Mahan, along with Oberlin founder John Shipherd, met with the Tappan brothers to convince them to settle the Lane Rebels at Oberlin. In the new arrangement, Arthur Tappan selected Mahan to become Oberlin's president, while Charles Grandison Finney would lead the theology department. By autumn, the first of the Lane Rebels arrived at Oberlin College. Arthur Tappan watched keenly from New York. He took more interest in Oberlin than in any other project in his antislavery career because he believed the instruction there would bring the moral reform needed to end slavery in America. In 1835 alone, Arthur donated over seven thousand dollars, and together with two other businessmen in a joint arrangement, he lent the school ten thousand additional dollars to construct a four-story brick building to house classrooms and a dormitory. Meanwhile, Lewis and other businessmen agreed to pay eight professors six hundred dollars a year to cover their salaries, and Arthur and several friends bought a huge circus tent for seven hundred dollars to provide a place for Finney to preach. Until First Congregational Church was built near Tappan Hall in Oberlin, the tent served as a prefabricated college chapel that the seminarians would raise and dismantle once a week for Finney's services. Weld traveled to Oberlin to give a series of lectures and trained the students as antislavery agents, enabling them to spread out and influence many nearby communities for the antislavery cause.[4]

Publications for persuasion. All of those developments at Oberlin were taking place at the same time that Lewis Tappan was helping to oversee an enormous, multipronged publishing strategy in New York. When the second annual meeting of the American Anti-slavery Society convened in May 1835,

---

[4]One thousand dollars in 1835 is equivalent to over thirty-five thousand dollars in 2024. Thus, the Tappan brothers were giving substantial donations to make it possible for Oberlin College to incorporate the Lane Rebels.

Tappan and other leaders set a goal of investing thirty thousand dollars to finance one of the most ambitious national pamphlet campaigns in revivalist history. As chairman of the Society's publications committee, Tappan worked on fundraising and created a strategy for disseminating antislavery literature far and wide. The committee proposed issuing four journals each month, one every week: first, *Human Rights*, a four-page sheet; second, the *Anti-slavery Record*, embellished with woodcuts; third, the *Emancipator*, demoted from a weekly but lively in its appearance and layout; and fourth, the *Slave's Friend*, a children's magazine. The papers would be sent to key leaders all over the country. In response, the delegates enthusiastically pledged an initial $14,500 for the effort.

Tappan spent many hours in the feverishly busy atmosphere of the Anti-Slavery Rooms (offices) in New York City, assisting with the publication of the first *Human Rights* journal, the most spirited of the series, and preparing the children's magazine himself. To achieve nationwide coverage, he also aided his publishing agent in fundraising campaigns and paying bills, helping to defray monthly costs that could reach nearly a thousand dollars for printing between twenty-five thousand and fifty thousand copies of each weekly publication. By July 1835, huge bundles of paper piled up in the New York City post office awaiting delivery to hundreds of communities. By the Society's third annual meeting in May 1836, Tappan's publication board had issued over a million antislavery pieces.

Amistad *defense*. In the summer of 1839, a Spanish ship assisting in the transport of fifty-three enslaved persons from Havana to Puerto Principe, Cuba, was overtaken by its captives. Tricked or kidnapped and sold into slavery, these Africans, from the Mendi (Mende) tribe of West Africa, mutinied, killed the captain and cook, and attempted to steer the ship back to Africa, but sabotage by the remaining Spanish crew landed them on the East Coast of the United States. When the *Amistad* landed at Long Island, the mutineers were transported to New Haven, Connecticut, to be tried for piracy and murder.

The incident attracted national attention to Lewis Tappan's work. On hearing of the arrests, Tappan formed a legal defense team, including AMA cofounders Joshua Leavitt and Simeon Jocelyn, and arranged for Yale divinity students to provide spiritual instruction for those awaiting trial. His work to publish articles about the Africans' plight and raise funds for their legal defense, which produced evidence to compel their release, may have been primarily responsible for the court's ruling in favor of "the Amistads," as they came to be known, and ordering them set free.

The prosecution appealed, eventually bringing the case as far as the Supreme Court. Because of growing national publicity for the *Amistad* case and Tappan in particular, slavery proponents began to inundate his mailbox with threatening letters. As the date of the hearing before the Supreme Court got closer, Tappan became convinced that the defense needed an additional lawyer on its team and approached former President John Quincy Adams. Adams's eloquent appeal for justice persuaded a majority of justices to rule in the defendants' favor, and they were declared free by the nation's highest court on March 9, 1841. When Tappan thanked Adams for his contribution to the victory, Adams deferred back to Tappan's own work. "The captives are free," Adams wrote. "Thanks, in the name of humanity and justice, to you!"[5]

Tappan traveled to New Haven to arrange accommodations for the liberated Amistads. He and James W. C. Pennington, a Black Congregational minister in Connecticut, had formed a special society to sponsor the repatriation of the Mendi captives and envisioned providing a way for them to return to Africa as missionaries rather than as freed slaves. In August 1841, a few months before their departure, Pennington founded the Union Missionary Society (the forerunner of the AMA) to support the effort to help the Mendi Africans and establish other antislavery missions at home and abroad. Tappan hoped to raise the full amount by autumn of that year to provide for the Amistads' journey. He also knew that he had to address the difficulty of finding the exact location in Africa from which they had originated and of preventing their re-enslavement once they arrived home.

Although Lord Aberdeen, the British foreign secretary, promised to assist the group once they arrived in African waters at Sierra Leone, US President John Tyler refused to transport them on an American warship, adding an unexpected expense to the process. With only a few weeks of good sailing weather left to find a private vessel, Tappan toured churches in New Hampshire and Massachusetts, collecting $1,300 during a depression year for the

---

[5]John Quincy Adams to Lewis Tappan, March 9, 1841, Tappan correspondences, Amistad Research Center, Tulane University.

Amistads and those who would accompany them. The thirty-five surviving Mendi Africans finally reached the coast of Sierra Leone in January 1842. Although most of them dispersed to find their families and vanished from the historical record, the Mendi Mission, founded by American abolitionist missionaries and the remaining Mendi veterans, became the flagship outpost for the AMA for the next four decades.

The Richmond Estate. In 1846, Lewis Tappan, George Whipple, and Simeon Jocelyn organized the American Missionary Association to connect antislavery churches, carry on mission work in Africa and the Caribbean, and establish education centers, such as Berea College in Kentucky. The organization advocated from the start for an unconditional and universal abolition of slavery, but its broader impact went beyond antislavery through a later emphasis on the education of emancipated men and women. Tappan sought through the AMA's work to support abolitionist pastors who were suffering financially because of their unpopular principles. For example, John G. Fee, a Presbyterian pastor, told Tappan that he might have doubled his salary by accepting a position in a slaveholding church but chose instead to build up his little abolitionist congregation in Kentucky and spread antislavery sentiment, despite the persecution he knew would come.[6]

By 1860 the association had contributed more than a million dollars to over one hundred antislavery missions in the United States and abroad, including the one at Oberlin Station in Jamaica where Sarah Ingraham Penfield served. Although not every effort proved successful, the association laid the groundwork for wartime and Reconstruction-era efforts to provide religious and secular education for Black people. Few abolitionists had Tappan's long-range perspective, which included a vision not only for eliminating the injustices of his day but also for improving life for freed persons after emancipation.

The AMA and other revivalist societies established a significant higher education presence in the South, eclipsing the half-dozen or so schools that secular societies had formed. Between 1865 and 1869, the association reopened Berea College (founded in 1855, reopened in 1866) and founded six chartered colleges: Fisk University, Atlanta University, Hampton Institute,

---

[6]John G. Fee to Lewis Tappan, July 22, 1846, Tappan correspondences, Amistad Research Center, Tulane University.

Talladega College, Tougaloo College, and Straight University. It also helped to establish Howard University in Washington, DC.

Lewis Tappan spent considerable energy on fundraising for land acquisition and job training because he recognized the immediate need for emancipated persons to make their living. Looking to the earlier emancipation in British territories for possible ideas, Tappan asked Amos Phelps, a fellow abolitionist who had visited Jamaica, for his recommendations. After returning from Jamaica in 1847, Phelps had suggested that missionaries deal with emancipated persons as men and women, not as subordinates, training them to be self-sufficient. He meant that the missionaries should encourage the development of family farm life, with Blacks owning land, improving it, and taking pride in their efforts to attain economic self-sufficiency and independence. Missionaries, he insisted, should receive training in how to work the land so that they could identify with the work of the people they were serving, hence missionaries ought to have their lodging stations on the same farming lands as freed persons. Everyone would be developing their farming skills at the same time.

Although Phelps was keenly aware of the obstacles in such a plan, Lewis Tappan was intrigued by the notion of the farming community as an avenue for Blacks to establish themselves as landowners. He sought to test those ideas in what would become known as the Richmond Estate experiment.

In 1854, a plantation located near the AMA missionaries' Brainerd Station in Jamaica came up for sale at the bargain price of $2,500. Known as the Richmond Estate, the plantation covered 1,090 acres and included a sugar mill, a mansion, and other buildings, and had been worth fifty thousand dollars in better economic times. Based on reports from AMA missionaries, Lewis Tappan surmised that it would be an ideal spot to try out Phelps's ideas. The missionaries would sell the land to emancipated Blacks in small lots, laying the groundwork for demonstrating to White Jamaicans that emancipated persons could truly become independent, industrious, and resolute farmers when given the chance.

Tappan's job was to raise the funds to buy the plantation, a task that proved difficult, partly because his British friends were sensitive to the failures of their colonial policy and took little interest in the project. But he made a down payment of five hundred dollars from the AMA's treasury, then set about selling shares in the enterprise to antislavery friends to obtain the remaining sum. It took several years, but the effort was successful in the end. Gradually, the New York headquarters of the AMA was able to increase support for the Richmond venture, and soon an industrial school appeared in the large mansion as segments of the estate began to pass into the hands of emancipated Blacks in lots of five or ten acres at low interest. Tappan told the readers of the AMA's *American Missionary* magazine, one of the most important journals for supporting education for the emancipated, that the British had compensated the wrong individuals in Jamaica, White landowners, under the terms of the Emancipation Act of 1833. According to Tappan, justice required that part of the compensation should have been expended to supply freed persons with education, agricultural implements, and small lots on reasonable terms. He saw the work of the AMA as a matter of justice for fellow human beings, a pursuit born out of the love that received such heavy emphasis in revivalist views of holiness. The AMA continued to support work among emancipated people in Jamaica, such as through the missionary work of Sarah Ingraham Penfield.

Freedmen's Aid Society. During the Civil War, William Goodell, editor of the *Principia*, a weekly abolitionist newspaper in New York, wrote that "as soon as slavery shall be abolished, there will be an opportunity for Christian philanthropists to commence the arduous work of educating and guiding the emancipated colored people." Most of the larger aid societies for freed African Americans published monthly or quarterly journals recording their activities and exhorting the faithful to contribute money. Abolitionists argued from multiple platforms, whether from the pulpit, in the press, or at meetings, that a hostile environment had created the servile, comic creature that was the White racist American caricature of enslaved Blacks. They asserted that if the social climate were to be transformed through the abolition of slavery and the ending of racial discrimination, Blacks would become constructive, capable, and creative members of society (just as Nancy Prince had affirmed about Jamaica, as we read in chapters three and six).[7]

By June 1861, the abolitionist-dominated AMA was planning to send teachers and books to educate the seven hundred Blacks living behind Union lines in Virginia. The AMA also helped the Union to provide for the

---

[7]William Goodell, "Work Ahead!," *Principia*, October 23, 1862.

physical needs of freed African Americans. The Boston Auxiliary sent more than one hundred barrels of clothing to the contrabands during the winter of 1861–1862. In January 1862, Treasury Secretary Salmon P. Chase sent abolitionist attorney Edward Pierce to investigate the condition and needs of the freed African Americans at Port Royal Island, South Carolina, one of the first territories captured by Union troops in the South. Pierce wrote to Boston pastor and abolitionist Jacob Manning to request aid, at which Manning called a meeting in his home to form a society to send supplies, teachers, and labor superintendents. By February, Manning had organized the Boston Educational Commission to aid those who became emancipated during the war. In New York City, Reverend Mansfield French, an abolitionist and a friend of Chase, organized the National Freedman's Relief Association. Meanwhile, in Philadelphia, abolitionist J. Miller McKim argued for colleagues to convert their societies into freedmen's aid associations so that they could move on from the "pulling-down," iconoclastic focus of the abolition movement (crushing the institution of slavery) to a new "building-up," constructive stage.[8]

Tappan's letters reveal that he inspired many donors to give money to help the emancipated. Abolitionist writer Lydia Maria Child (editor of the book in which James Bradley's autobiographical account was published) thanked Tappan for "The Song of the Contraband" (an antislavery song) that he had sent to her, mentioning that she had inherited one hundred dollars and used it entirely to help the "contrabands." In March 1862, the antislavery societies resolved to prepare freed persons to become self-supporting citizens because they believed that "no government could ever turn its back on [its citizens]."[9]

These and many other such efforts across decades were examples of how abolitionism played an important part in bringing education and land to the emancipated. Reverend Fee, who cofounded Berea College, also organized

---

[8]*Contraband of war* was a term used by the United States military during the Civil War to describe the status of previously enslaved individuals who sought protection behind Union lines. "Living Contraband—Former Slaves in the Nation's Capital During the Civil War," National Park Service online, last updated August 15, 2017, www.nps.gov/articles/living-contraband-former-slaves-in -the-nation-s-capital-during-the-civil-war.htm; "J. M. McKim and the Pennsylvania Anti-slavery Society," *National Anti-slavery Standard*, May 3, 1862.

[9]Lydia Maria Child to Lewis Tappan, March 23, 1862, Lewis Tappan papers, Library of Congress, via Slavery and Anti-slavery: A Transnational Archive; Edward L. Pierce, "The Freedmen at Port Royal," in *Enfranchisement and Citizenship: Addresses and Papers*, ed. A. W. Stevens (Boston: Roberts Bros., 1896), 88-89.

several schools, hospitals, and churches for freed African Americans in his native Kentucky. In 1865, Fee purchased 130 acres and resold the land in small tracts to freed African Americans, who established a village on the property. By 1891, forty-two families were living there. Fee also urged the AMA to go into the business of selling land to freed persons. As early as 1868, the AMA started purchasing plantations in the South for resale to working Blacks, and on each tract of land the AMA established a church and a school. Several small agricultural villages in the South grew up around these AMA centers.

In the early postwar years, freedmen's aid activities expanded greatly among societies that were connected to churches, whether the congregations were White or Black. The Baptist Educational Commission for Freedmen was one example, as was the Methodist Freedmen's Aid Society, which partnered with the Freedmen's Bureau (the government agency tasked to assist struggling freedmen with necessities and services) to educate Southern Blacks. From 1861 to 1893, the various Northern missionary societies and freedmen's aid groups and the Freedmen's Bureau spent more than thirty-one million dollars on Southern education, mostly for African Americans. Through all these efforts, abolitionist individuals and communities made it clear that their work would not end with legal emancipation. Their goal was racial equity and the flourishing of free human beings, and they were willing to shift their focus and efforts in order to see it through.

CONCLUSION

The US Senate adopted the Thirteenth Amendment to end slavery in the United States on April 8, 1864, but the measure failed to obtain the necessary two-thirds vote since the Republicans only had a bare majority in the House of Representatives. Most Democrats voted against the amendment, hoping to preserve slavery, but President Abraham Lincoln's reelection victory in 1864 convinced many Democrats that public opinion favored emancipation, and the House passed the amendment on January 31, 1865. Though the tide of public opinion (at least in Northern states) had turned toward emancipation, the job of transitioning four million emancipated people to independent life required the partnership of churches, auxiliary groups, missionary societies, and the government. Blacks were now faced with the complexities that came with gaining sudden freedom (slavery had not equipped most of them with education, property, or financial resources, and White landowners continued to hold the lion's share of power and resources in their communities); but the AMA and various freedmen's aid societies had already developed structures of education and support to help with the change to a new way of life. Countless advocates served as missionaries, teachers, donors, and fundraisers for the constructive work of rebuilding.

Contrary to the rhetoric of superiority and inferiority that was common in the United States at the time, David Ingraham, Nancy Prince, the Tappans, and other abolitionists believed that all people were created equal and that a systematic plan for education would ultimately erode prejudice and increase respect for people of color. More than a century before integration and equal rights were enacted into federal law, these abolitionists prophesied that a world without racism was possible and looked to build schools and provide resources and training for the emancipated to support themselves as they made their way into new lives of liberty.

Lewis Tappan used his privilege to work for racial justice, motivated by the same Christian value of charity that inspired the revivalist abolitionists highlighted in this book. His example offers a model for how Christian individuals and communities of various levels of privilege today can have important philanthropic roles in the quest for racial equity. A 2016 study showed that religious organizations in America had tripled the amount of money spent on social programs in the preceding fifteen years, regardless of whether the churches and groups that were included in the study were growing or shrinking in population. Of the various programs provided by religious organizations, fifty-six thousand of them focused on race relations. That focus suggests that the contemporary church is in a unique position to address injustice, especially in light of precedents set by Ingraham, Prince, Tappan, and others like them. The church in America bears social witness when it channels its resources to work for justice—helping the unemployed, providing food for the poor, offering programs for recovery, addressing mental illness, or any of countless other possibilities.

Nineteenth-century abolitionists were creative and innovative in their efforts toward racial justice and equity, and their example challenges our Christian communities today to listen to new ideas, take chances, accept out-of-the-box ideas, and partner with diverse groups in our mission to promote the flourishing of all human beings. Some programs I have been involved with support after-school tutoring, summer camps, and scholarships for underprivileged students, aiming to increase their opportunities for college and career development. The Christian commitment to care for one's neighbor encourages churches to work at breaking down barriers, promoting greater understanding across lines of difference, and combating hindrances to racial equity. But these are hardly twenty-first-century ideas.

We find ourselves facing the question of what we will do to advance God's inclusive reign. For the Tappan brothers, the answer included giving priceless connections in influence and millions in money toward fighting injustice. For Nancy Prince, it was to give fifty dollars as she could. For the widow, it was to give her last two small coins. In the same way that a boy's loaves and fish nourished thousands of hungry people when he gave what he had to Jesus, all of our contributions, no matter how large or small they seem when given, can play essential roles in God's work of establishing justice on earth. The cause of racial equity and reconciliation takes much more than money and power. All the resources of a sanctified life must be given to God as a form of practical godliness, and no less urgently today than in the nineteenth century, if we too will heed the call.

In the next chapter we will turn to notions of a fully integrated society. The particular case of Oberlin, Ohio, both the town and the college, is central to the themes of this book and directly influenced David and Betsey Ingraham, their daughter Sarah Ingraham Penfield, and James Bradley; the college was also a focus of the Tappans' aid and was known for its influence on many people whom Nancy Prince encountered. Chapter eight will review the history of Oberlin and its original quest for racial equity as well as the challenges that arose in sustaining that pursuit. What we learn from those obstacles and others like them can apply to any of us who seek to build up interracial Christian communities today.

"MADE WELCOME AS EQUALS"

THE OBERLIN EXPERIMENT IN INTERRACIAL CHRISTIAN COMMUNITY

Albert G. Miller

---

*The treatment accorded colored people in Oberlin socially at this time
[the 1830s–1840s] was most remarkable; in keeping, however, with
the professions religiously, politically and educationally made by the
founders of the community. Every Sunday colored persons could be
seen seated in conspicuous eligible places in the only church in the
town, worshiping after the manner of those in whose midst they
lived, and no one molested or disturbed them. Such persons were
made welcome as equals in the best families, as they were in every
part of the institution, and thus were given the best social, as they
were the highest educational advantages. Such was the recognition
and the consideration accorded the colored American, whether
student or resident, in Oberlin, in the earlier days of its history.*

JOHN MERCER LANGSTON, 1894

A RUDE AWAKENING

In 2000, my wife, Brenda, and I purchased a plot of land that had previously
been owned by Oberlin College, intending to build a home on Hollywood
Street on the west side of Oberlin. Historically, this area had been de facto
segregated and populated mostly by White residents, and we remembered

having arrived in town in 1991 to find very few African American families on the west side. When we were ready to buy and were negotiating a sale price, the seller's finance officer ordered a customary title search. As we read the report, we were shocked to find a racial covenant built into the property deed from the early 1900s. "As a further additional and valuable consideration for the above sale and conveyance," it read,

> it is stipulated, covenanted and agreed on the part of the Grantee, for himself, his heirs and assigns that . . . nor shall said premises be sold, rented, or conveyed to anyone belonging to the negro or colored race and that the foregoing covenants, stipulations and agreements shall run with the land and that if the Grantee, his heirs or assigns shall violate the foregoing covenants and agreements that said property shall at once revert to the Grantors herein.[1]

We were in our tenth year of living in Oberlin at the time we saw those words in print. We had learned from local Black folklore about the fight to desegregate the Hollywood Addition in the late 1950s, an effort led by Eva Mae Crosby, an Oberlin College graduate (1933) and the first African American woman to graduate from The Ohio State University's law school (1936). But this was Brenda's and my first documentary proof that the Black lore was correct, that racism had been baked into the culture and customs of the village of Oberlin and Oberlin College, the great symbol of liberal education and social life.[2]

Oberlin, the bastion of nineteenth-century abolitionism and revivalism and the first (still-operating) college in the United States to admit African Americans "irrespective of color," was not the racial utopia that it touted itself to be. How did Oberlin become so racially divided by the early twentieth century, when it had started as a signpost for revivalism, the abolition of slavery, and the protection of equal rights for all people?

THE ROOTS OF AN INTEGRATED COMMUNITY

Two great American movements, revivalism and abolitionism, converged with the founding of the Oberlin community. While not identical in their

---

[1] Warranty Deed 533151, Lorain County Deed Books, Lorain County Recorder's Office, Elyria, Ohio, 114:418.

[2] "Eva Mae *Parker* Crosby," Find a Grave profile, www.findagrave.com/memorial/50006489/eva-mae-crosby. Eva Mae Crosby was married to the Reverend Normal Cyric Crosby, pastor of Mount Zion Baptist Church of Oberlin. She was also a local real estate broker, attorney, and elementary school teacher.

origins or composition, they evolved alongside each other in the landscape
of the growing American nation.

In 1833, in large part through Charles Grandison Finney's revival influence, the missionary fervor of the Second Great Awakening became the
spark for the founding of Oberlin (both the village and the college). The
awakening movement would sweep into the northeastern part of the United
States and move across the Allegheny Mountains into the Ohio Valley and
beyond. One fruit of this revival was Oberlin's founding father, John Jay
Shipherd, who was converted to faith at age seventeen after being thrown
from a horse in Washington County, New York, in 1819.[3]

Shipherd believed that Jesus had called him to "preach my Gospel." In
1830 he moved with his family to Elyria, Ohio, to pastor a Presbyterian
church and further the revival. In his lament as to what he saw as "the de-
generacy of the church and the deplorable condition of our perishing world,"
he, his wife Esther, and a protégé, Philo Stewart, gathered likeminded revivalists to develop a religious "colony" (community) and educational institution in nearby Oberlin. Their covenant indicated that the Oberlin Colony
would devote itself to "spread the Gospel" and "maintain deep-toned and
elevated personal piety, to 'provoke each other to love and good works,' to
live together in all things as brethren, and to glorify God in our bodies and
spirits, which are His."[4]

Another ingredient in Oberlin's evangelical passion was the rising influence of abolitionism and its attendant commitment to racial equality.
Many revivalists were convicted to gradually or immediately abolish slavery,
and some were also committed to the broader notion of racial equality.
Shipherd, who had been raised in a slaveholding family, would come to
abhor slavery and racism. In his letter to Oberlin Collegiate Institute trustees
regarding their debate over admitting African Americans, he admitted his
sinful attitude toward people of another race and spoke of his repentance. "I
was brot [sic] up with blacks & slaves," he declared, "& would choke with
thirst before I would drink from the same cup with them; but God has
shown me that it was an *unholy pride* & *sinful prejudice* which I dare not

---

[3]Robert Samuel Fletcher, *A History of Oberlin College from Its Foundation Through the Civil War*,
vol. 1 (Oberlin, OH: Oberlin College, 1943), 58.
[4]Fletcher, *History*, 61; "The Oberlin Covenant," in J. H. Fairchild, *Oberlin: Its Origin, Progress, and
Results* (Oberlin, OH: Shankland and Harmon, 1860), 5.

cherish longer through fear of his displeasure." The connection of slavery and racist prejudice with sin and the need for repentance was at the heart of the religious drive of the abolitionist movement.[5]

African Americans who had been impacted by the institution of slavery were the first to lead the movement for abolition. Whether enslaved or free, whether in the North or the South, African Americans continually struggled for self-determination. It was Northern free Black leaders who helped convince William Lloyd Garrison, the titular leader of the abolitionist movement, to oppose the efforts of the American Colonization Society to remove and resettle free American Blacks to Liberia and to push instead for racial equality on American shores. The early Blacks who arrived in Oberlin were driven by this spirit of self-determination. They built lives for their families and contributed significantly to the ethos of a racial utopia that Oberlin was intended to exemplify.[6]

Chapter one of this book tells the story of how the Lane Seminary Rebels challenged and energized Oberlin, bringing the powerful revivalism and abolition movements together. Yet the decision to recruit thirty-two Lane students to Oberlin, including David Ingraham and especially the African American James Bradley, would test the moral fiber and commitment of the college. It would not be easy to convince the Oberlin community to subscribe to all the demands of the Lane Rebels and their faculty and trustee supporters. Specifically, their request that the college commit to admitting "students irrespective of color" caused consternation among some Oberlin students, faculty, and trustees. The student body was split regarding the admission of African Americans. Of fifty-eight students polled, thirty-two were against admitting Black students and twenty-six were in favor. David Ingraham's future wife, Elizabeth "Betsey" Hartson, was one of the Oberlin

---

[5]John Jay Shipherd to the Trustees of the [Oberlin Collegiate] Institute, January 19, 1835, in Fletcher, *History*, 59, emphasis original. The original document is housed at Oberlin College Archives.

[6]"William Watkins (b. circa 1803—d. circa 1858)," MSA SC 5496-002535, Maryland State Archives, https://msa.maryland.gov/megafile/msa/speccol/sc5400/sc5496/002500/002535/html/002535bio.html. See also Benjamin Quarles, *Black Abolitionists* (New York: Oxford University Press, 1969), 19. To read William Lloyd Garrison's own confession of a change of heart toward a radical abolitionist position from a supporter of the American Colonization Society, see William Lloyd Garrison, "To the Public," *Liberator*, January 1, 1831, in William E. Cain, ed., *William Lloyd Garrison and the Fight Against Slavery: Selections from The Liberator* (Boston: Bedford, 1995), 70–72, reprinted by PBS, Africans in America, www.pbs.org/wgbh/aia/part4/4h2928.html.

students who wanted to admit African Americans, indicating her early interest in racial equity.[7]

Among the trustees, there was no clear majority of support for the admission of Black students. Even Stewart, Shipherd's protégé and cofounder of the institute and colony, voted against the resolution, later resigning from the board in part due to his opposition. After several debates regarding the proposal, John Keep, the board chair, cast the deciding vote, making the total five votes in favor and four against Shipherd's resolution to admit students of any color. The die was cast for the new social, racial, and religious experiment called Oberlin. But the town was also divided on the issue. Some townspeople feared that the admission of Blacks would lead to the town being overrun by them. Tensions like these regarding racial equality, abolitionism, and how Christianity fits into the larger discussion were part of the landscape in early Oberlin, and they continue in American culture to the present.[8]

Disaffected trustees (two of whom resigned) were not the only ones to protest Oberlin's new admissions policy. The student poll made it clear that at least thirty-two White students opposed Oberlin's venture into racial inclusion. After his departure from Oberlin, Delazon Smith, the disgruntled young dropout we met in chapter five, decided that it was his duty to himself and "to the rest of mankind" to publish a scathing exposé of the institute. He revealed Oberlin's "treasonable" participation in the Underground Railroad that shuttled freedom seekers to Canada and decried the way that White students not only mingled freely with their Black classmates but intentionally cultivated relationships with them. "My heart sickens," Smith moaned, "and my hand becomes almost paralyzed in recalling and exposing these abominations." Students who remained at Oberlin and embraced its principles sustained contempt and abuse from many in the surrounding communities, receiving a "double portion" of the "bitterness and mean hatred which anti-slavery men encountered in many portions of Ohio."[9]

---

[7] John Jay Shipherd, "Letter to Oberlin Colony," January 27, 1835, in Robert Fletcher Papers, Oberlin College Archives.

[8] Fletcher, History, 196.

[9] Delazon Smith went on to become a short-lived senator in the new state of Oregon, failing to win reelection after one month in office. Upon his death in 1860, the Oberlin Evangelist published a scathing obituary titled "Misplaced Honors," which described Smith's Oberlin exposé as "scurrilous" and "fatuous" and concluded: "It is a somewhat painful comment on the distribution of

Figure 8.1. Oberlin College's racially integrated incoming class of 1855

Oberlin revivalists' radicalism went beyond the relatively modest ideas of other White abolitionists. Many White abolitionists in America at the time wanted to end slavery while maintaining White privilege and superiority. Some even supported the removal of free Blacks by the American Colonization Society. Oberlin abolitionists, however, were not satisfied with the minimalist goals articulated by abolitionists elsewhere and advocated instead for full racial equity.

STORIES FROM EARLY BLACK OBERLIN STUDENTS

It was that commitment among many Oberlin residents, to accept African Americans in the town and collegiate community and engage their education at all levels, that drew many free Blacks to Oberlin in the middle of the nineteenth century. By 1860, they would make up 20 percent of the town's total population, five times the proportion of Blacks in Philadelphia

public honors and trusts, that of more than ten thousand students who have been in attendance here, the least worthy has attained the highest distinction." *Oberlin Evangelist*, December 19, 1860, Oberlin Library Special Collections, http://dcollections.oberlin.edu/digital/collection/evangelist /id/5551; Delazon Smith, *A History of Oberlin, or New Lights of the West: Embracing the Conduct and Character of the Officers and Students of the Institution; Together with the Colonists, from the Founding of the Institution* (Cleveland: S. Underhill and Son, 1837), 3, 58; Fairchild, *Oberlin*, 26.

and ten times that of either New York City or Boston. The Black community grew in Oberlin as African Americans arrived there as free men and women or as freedom seekers, those escaping enslavement (often via the Underground Railroad). They came as students and as seekers of a new life and a good education for themselves and their families.[10]

Many Black Oberlinites had grown up in Black Methodist or Baptist church traditions and possessed fully developed faith practices and revivalist impulses. They came with commitments to radical abolitionism, equality, and Black self-determination that were nurtured by independent Black church life. Despite their background in Black church settings, quite a few newly arrived African Americans joined the largely White faith community at Oberlin's First Congregational Church. While it is true that First Church was the only option for worship in the early years of Oberlin's history, many Blacks nonetheless felt comfortable in its environment because of the church's commitment to inclusion.

Oberlin Collegiate Institute also became known as a place of permanent and temporary refuge for both enslaved and free Blacks. Between 1835 and 1840, twenty African Americans matriculated, fifteen males and five females. In September 1835, brothers Gideon and Charles Langston were the first African American students to enroll in Oberlin Institute's preparatory school. They would go on to become major public fixtures in the life of early Oberlin, especially Charles. The Langston men, together with their brother, John Mercer Langston, were the sons of a wealthy White Virginia slaveholder, Ralph Quarles, and his former slave, Lucy Jane Langston. Despite Virginia law, Quarles supported his sons by willing his land to his children upon his death. With money from the sale of the land, the brothers decided to move to Chillicothe, Ohio, and later to Cincinnati, to re-create life as men in a nominally free state. While living in Chillicothe, the Langston brothers were co-organizers of the Colored Anti-slavery Society and later became actively involved in Cincinnati's Black Christian community at Baker Street Baptist Church. Long before they arrived in Oberlin, then, the Langston men had already been steeped in Christian faith and antislavery radicalism. They all became active members of the Oberlin community, Charles distinguishing

---

[10]Gary J. Kornblith and Carol Lasser, *Elusive Utopia: The Struggle for Racial Equality in Oberlin, Ohio* (Baton Rouge, LA: LSU Press, 2018), 33.

himself as one of the first two individuals to stand trial for the famous Oberlin-Wellington rescue of an enslaved freedom seeker, John Price.[11]

Another early Black student, James Bradley, the only African American Lane Rebel, was admitted in 1836 to the Sheffield Manual Labor Institute, an affiliated preparatory school of Oberlin Collegiate Institute. Sheffield was one of four such preparatory schools that had been founded to meet the overflowing influx of students arriving at Oberlin. The institute at Sheffield admitted men and women, both Black and White, to its campus, including Gideon and Charles Langston. Unfortunately, the Ohio legislature refused to grant a charter to Sheffield unless it excluded Black students, and when the institute closed in 1837 rather than compromise Oberlin's egalitarian principles, Bradley did not return to the main Oberlin campus.[12]

In 1844, George B. Vashon became the first African American to graduate with a bachelor's degree from Oberlin. Arriving from Pittsburgh in 1840, the sixteen-year-old was already prepared for college-level education and was immediately admitted to the collegiate curriculum. He graduated four years later as valedictorian and had "the Master of Arts degree conferred on him by Oberlin, in recognition of his scholarly pursuits and accomplishments." Vashon became the first practicing Black lawyer in New York State and a professor at New York Central College, another revivalist abolitionist school.[13]

Vashon was heavily influenced by two men: his father, John Vashon, an entrepreneur and abolitionist who opened his home as a stop on the Underground Railroad; and George's pastor, mentor, and teacher, the Reverend Lewis Woodson, an African Methodist Episcopal Church minister and

---

[11]John Price was captured by slave hunters in Oberlin and taken to the neighboring town of Wellington where he was to be transported back south and re-enslaved. He was rescued by Black and White citizens of Oberlin and Wellington and swept off to Canada and freedom. Charles Langston gave an impassioned speech in Price's defense at his sentencing trial. Kornblith and Lasser, *Elusive Utopia*, 34, 37; John Mercer Langston, *From the Virginia Plantation to the National Capital: or The First and Only Negro Representative in Congress from the Old Dominion* (Hartford, CT: American, 1894); "Charles Langston's Speech at the Cuyahoga County Courthouse" (Cleveland, May 12, 1859), Electronic Oberlin Group, https://www2.oberlin.edu/external/EOG/Oberlin-Wellington_Rescue/c._langston_speech.htm.

[12]Charles E. Herdendorf, ed., "Sheffield Manual Labor Institute (1836–1837)," *Village Pioneer* 3, no. 1 (March 2008), Sheffield Village Historical Society and Cultural Center online, 9, https://sheffieldvillage.com/the-village-pioneer; Ron Gorman, "James Bradley—from Hopeless Bondage to Lane Rebel," *Oberlin Heritage Center Blog*, September 5, 2013, www.oberlinheritagecenter.org/blog/2013/09/james-bradley-from-hopeless-bondage-to-lane-rebel/.

[13]Paul N. D. Thornell, "The Absent Ones and the Providers: A Biography of the Vashons," *Journal of Negro History* 83, no. 4 (1998): 290.

educator whom some identified as the "father of Black nationalism." John was active in the spiritual and educational reform work of the church that Woodson pastored and consistently maintained that Black churches should preserve their independence, arguing that White churches might not be able to overcome their White supremacy. Woodson, for his part arguing for the right of Blacks to organize their own churches with their own leadership, called for Black self-determination for the moral elevation of the race.[14]

Following the lead of his father and Rev. Woodson, in 1838, at age fourteen, George Vashon joined and served as secretary of the Pittsburgh Juvenile Anti-slavery Society, which enrolled fifty young people within its first year. His student activism continued at Oberlin, where he organized a First of August celebration to commemorate emancipation from slavery in the British West Indies as an alternative to celebrating Independence Day on the Fourth of July. David Ingraham observed a similar First of August Emancipation Day celebration in Jamaica, which he recorded in his journal with strong approval, perhaps after having witnessed the commemorations that took place in Oberlin. During winter recess one year, Vashon went to Chillicothe to teach at a church school that had been organized by Black citizens there. (It was typical at the time for Oberlin students to go to communities without schools and serve as teachers in makeshift educational establishments.)[15]

John Mercer Langston, the brother of Gideon and Charles, was a student in Vashon's class in Chillicothe. Vashon encouraged Langston to apply to Oberlin Institute and escorted him to Oberlin to begin his education. By 1853 he had completed three degrees, including in the arts and theology. Following Vashon's example, Langston applied to law schools but was rejected because of his color. Nonetheless, in 1854, he read for and passed the Ohio bar exam under the tutelage of Judge Philemon Bliss of Elyria, Ohio. Langston was admitted to the bar, but only when Bliss pointed out to the court that because Langston's father was White, Langston was also deemed White by Ohio law and thus had to be admitted to practice. Langston

---

[14]Floyd J. Miller, "'The Father of Black Nationalism': Another Contender," *Civil War History* 17, no. 4 (1971): 310-19.

[15]In 1852, Frederick Douglass called the Fourth of July a "sham" celebration. See Kornblith and Lasser, *Elusive Utopia*, 46; Frederick Douglass, "What, to the Slave, Is the Fourth of July" (Rochester, NY, July 5, 1852), www.blackpast.org/african-american-history/speeches-african -american-history/1852-frederick-douglass-what-slave-fourth-july/; David Ingraham, manuscript journal, Adrian College Achives, 4-5.

married Caroline Matilda Wall, an Oberlin Institute senior, the same year he passed the bar, and they made their home in the Oberlin area until after the end of the Civil War.[16]

Figure 8.2. Daguerreotype of John Mercer Langston made in 1853, the year he received his master's degree from Oberlin's Graduate School of Theology

While the couple annually rented a pew at First Church, where John Langston's brothers were both members (seat reservation in a particular pew by rental was a common practice for regular attenders in many churches at

---

[16]John Mercer Langston, *Virginia Plantation*, 77, 124-25.

that time), they never became official members themselves. It is not clear what to make of this reticence. John certainly held a high view of Oberlin. He reflected on Oberlin's strong commitment to justice and faith in his autobiography, insisting that

> from the beginning in Oberlin, extreme radical views were held and maintained on all matters of reform, religion, education and anti-slavery. . . . The principles of religious faith and life, as inculcated in the severest teachings and philosophy of Jesus Christ and the Apostles, were accepted and pressed as indispensable to individual and popular obligation. Education, which meant the development of the whole human being in intellectual, moral and spiritual powers, with due consecration of all learning, genius, talent and influence to God and humanity, without distinction of sex or color, was recognized as the duty and privilege of every child of man. And upon all subjects of freedom—the unconstitutionality of slavery, its utter violation of the maxims of the Bible, and its outrage of all the fundamental doctrines of genuine democracy—its position was clear, comprehensive and decisive.[17]

But John Langston also continued to hold a special place in his heart for the historic African American church within which he had been raised and nurtured. That fact might explain why he and his wife never joined the predominantly White First Church in Oberlin. In 1876, in a speech commemorating the life and work of Bishop Richard Allen, the founder of the African Methodist Episcopal Church, Langston argued that the denomination's founding represented "the organized Christian protest of the colored American against unjust, inhuman, and cruel complexional discriminations," and provided the Black Christian the "opportunity to be himself, to think his own thoughts, express his own convictions, make his own utterances, test his own powers, cultivate self-reliance, and thus, in the exercise of the faculties of his own soul, trust and achieve."[18]

Another Black student at Oberlin, Fanny Jackson (later Coppin), was born into slavery in 1837 in Washington, DC. She was purchased at the age of twelve by her aunt and then sent north to be raised by another relative

---

[17]Langston, Virginia Plantation, 100-101.

[18]John Mercer Langston, *Freedom and Citizenship: Selected Lectures and Addresses* (Washington, DC: Rufus H. Darby, 1883; repr., Miami, FL: Mnemosyne, 1969), 134-35. See also William Cheek and Aimee Lee Cheek, *John Mercer Langston and the Fight for Black Freedom, 1829–65* (Urbana: University of Illinois Press, 1989), 70.

Figure 8.3. Fanny M. Jackson, Oberlin class of 1865

in New Bedford, Massachusetts. (Jackson's grandfather had saved enough money to purchase several of his children during his lifetime.) Arriving at Oberlin in 1861, Fanny Jackson applied for and was accepted into the "gentlemen's course," which was a rare feat for a woman. The course included Latin, Greek, and higher mathematics. She was supported financially by her several aunts and by African Methodist Episcopal Church Bishop Daniel A. Payne, who gave her a scholarship of "nine dollars a year upon entering Oberlin."[19]

Fanny Jackson so excelled that in her junior year she was asked to teach in the preparatory school. "I was to distinctly understand," she wrote, "that if the pupils rebelled against my teaching, they did not intend to force it. Fortunately for my training at the normal school, and my own dear love of teaching, tho [sic] there was a little surprise on the faces of some when they came into the class, and saw the teacher, there were no signs of rebellion." It is clear from Jackson's recounting that vestiges of prejudice remained both within the college and the town, as most of the children in the preparatory school were White. The college administration was not willing to stand its ground on racial equality if parents or students objected to having Fanny Jackson as a teacher. Yet even though Fanny Jackson encountered instances of prejudice, she still remembered her life in Oberlin fondly. After moving to Philadelphia, where she became the principal of the Institute for Colored Youth for twenty-eight years (until she married Bishop Levi J. Coppin of the AME Church), she reminisced that

> I had been so long in Oberlin that I had forgotten about my color, but I was sharply reminded of it when, in a storm of rain, a Philadelphia street car conductor forbid my entering a car that did not have on it "for colored people," so I had to wait in the storm until one came in which colored people could ride. This was my first unpleasant experience in Philadelphia. Visiting Oberlin not long after my work began in Philadelphia, President Finney asked me how I was growing in grace; I told him that I was growing as fast as the American people would let me. When told of some of the conditions which were meeting me, he seemed to think it unspeakable.[20]

---

[19]Fanny Jackson-Coppin, *Reminiscences of School Life, and Hints on Teaching* (Philadelphia: AME Book Concern, 1913), 10, 13.

[20]Fanny Jackson-Coppin, *Reminiscences of School Life*, 12, 14.

SEGREGATION AND SELF-DETERMINATION

Over the decades that followed, Black students and migrants came to Oberlin hoping (as Dr. King phrased it a century later) to "not be judged by the color of their skin but by the content of their character." They expected to benefit from the educational opportunities and social uplift that composed Oberlin's reputation as an abolitionist outpost. Yet Oberlin was becoming a stratified society, with unpleasant implications for how Black and White Oberlin residents lived together. While a few Black students enrolled at the Institute, many more within the Black population came to the town of Oberlin not to enroll but simply as freedom seekers or free people of color looking for a place to reside and make a new life. Some who came could be described as mixed race, with one parent, generally the father, being White and the mother usually Black or of mixed race herself. These people of mixed background typically had wealth or an inheritance to live on. The 1860 census indicates that eighty-six persons of color were heads of household, with ten of them accounting for 60 percent of the property owned by persons of color. Most of these brought their wealth with them to Oberlin.[21]

The majority of Blacks in Oberlin, however, were not landowners, merchants, or skilled craftsmen, but rather were day laborers, farmers, maids, or other unskilled workers, unlikely to own property. These poorer African American households accounted for less than 8 percent of the total number of property owners. Darker persons of color held less economic and social power than those whose skin was lighter. According to the 1860 census, Oberlin was geographically divided into four sections that generally fell along economic and racial lines, with the vast majority of Blacks living in the southeast quadrant of the town.[22]

E. H. Fairchild, the White principal of the preparatory department, described Oberlin and its race relationships in glowing terms. "Of our colored citizens," he wrote,

> who compose one-fifth of the population, it is a pleasure to say that, in general, they are peaceable, orderly, industrious, and rapidly improving in cultivation

---

[21]Martin Luther King Jr., "I Have a Dream" (Washington, DC, August 28, 1963), National Archives online, www.archives.gov/files/social-media/transcripts/transcript-march-pt3-of-3-2602934 .pdf, 3; Kornblith and Lasser, *Elusive Utopia*, 70.

[22]Kornblith and Lasser, *Elusive Utopia*, 70-71, 78-79.

and the comforts of life. They mingle freely with the white population in all the business relationships of life, without the least danger of a "war of races," or any other collision. It is found as easy and agreeable to sit in the Town Council or on the Board of School Directors with a negro, as in a barber's shop or a barouche [horse-drawn carriage].

Over time, however, lines of class, race, and caste emerged in Oberlin's public life.[23]

In the early years of the city, Charles Finney's First Church was the only one in town, and all were welcomed. Black students and townspeople were active members of the congregation, and in 1836, Gideon and Charles Langston became two of its first African American members. John Langston attended as a student and an adult. When its first building was constructed in 1844, Black carpenters, blacksmiths, and other laborers helped, and their families worshiped at the new church. These same Black craftsmen helped to build various other structures on campus and in the town.[24]

By 1860, as First Church grew, it decided to split, and Second Congregational Church was born. African Americans joined the new congregation as well, including the family of Wilson Bruce Evans, a carpenter, businessman, and abolitionist who served as a deacon.[25]

Even though Congregationalists continued to dominate the religious landscape of the early Oberlin community, by the late 1840s and early 1850s other communions had formed as well, gathering in homes or other facilities. Christ Episcopal Church had its first services in homes beginning in 1852. The Baptists emerged in the early 1860s as "it was said that there were enough people in the Oberlin Congregational Churches who were more Baptist than Congregationalist to make a fair sized Baptist Church." On one occasion, Charles Finney reportedly prayed, "O Lord, Thou knowest we don't need a Baptist Church in Oberlin, but, Lord if Thou seest it is best to have one, if Thou canst, we pray Thee to bless it." The prayer spoke to the broader dominance of Congregationalism in Oberlin and to potential

---

[23]E. H. Fairchild, *Historical Sketch of Oberlin College* (Springfield, OH: Republic, 1868), 25.

[24]Marlene Merrill, "First Church and Oberlin's Early African American Community," paper presented at Oberlin African American Genealogy and History Group, Oberlin, OH, December 6, 2003, Electronic Oberlin Group online, https://www2.oberlin.edu/external/EOG/FirstChurch/FirstChurch-Merrill.html.

[25]Merrill, "First Church."

opposition to other faith communities' emergence in Oberlin. Those dynamics may have held equally true toward Blacks who desired to develop churches of their own.[26]

Several Methodist denominations also made inroads into the Oberlin Congregational stronghold. The Wesleyan Methodists, a small holiness group that was organized in part as an antislavery denomination, made their foray into Oberlin through the efforts of a young White theological student named George Congdon Hicks, who organized a church on the east side of town in 1862. Though the racial membership of this church is uncertain, there were apparently some African Americans involved in the congregation. Hicks probably received assistance organizing the church from a Black Oberlin student, Marcus Dale, who was ordained in 1861 as an AME Church elder. Hicks "eventually . . . left the active pastorate in the Wesleyan Church, and finally joined the Congregationalists," an unsurprising transition given the close association in those days between Wesleyan Methodists and Congregationalists, both in terms of holiness theology and abolitionist social activism.[27]

Dale's attempt to organize a congregation in Oberlin was most likely a joint effort with Hicks, as the two were students in Oberlin institutions at the same time. Dale's work within the Black community gives clues as to why some Black people were reticent to worship at First Church and desired to establish their own worship sites. He described his work among Blacks in Oberlin in an April 1861 letter to George Whipple, the secretary of the American Missionary Association (and also a Lane Rebel and

---

[26]"A Brief Chronological Sketch of Oberlin Churches," 1, Oberlin Heritage Archives; Mary L. VanDyke, "Churches of Oberlin," prepared for the Oberlin Historical Improvement Organization (OHIO) for the conference of the Hymn Society in the United States and Canada, Oberlin, OH, July 1996, Electronic Oberlin Group website, https://www2.oberlin.edu/external/EOG/HousesofWorship/ChurchesOfOberlin.html; see esp. site B, Mrs. Chesbro, "First Baptist Church of Oberlin," accessible from the same URL.

[27]Dale, who was from Detroit, waived his plans to participate in the emergent emigration movement that aimed to see African Americans relocate to Liberia; he pursued formal education at Oberlin instead. Dale and Mary L. Williams, his wife, were each admitted to Oberlin's preparatory school, in 1859 and 1860, respectively. Dale pursued two years in the preparatory school while working to support himself, his wife, and their children. After withdrawing from the Institute, he continued working as a barrel maker in Oberlin. In 1864, Dale returned to Detroit and enlisted in the 102nd US Colored Regiment of Michigan, ultimately serving in Louisiana. Dale spent the remainder of his life as an AME Church pastor in New Orleans. See William J. Simmons, *Men of Mark: Eminent, Progressive and Rising* (Cleveland: Newell, 1887), 687; Leslie D. Wilcox, *Wesleyan Methodism in Ohio* (ca. 1940–1949), 58-59.

former theology student and faculty member at the Institute). Dale wrote that he had "but little" contact with White First Church members, save some fellowship with their class meeting. Rather, as a self-determined AME clergyman, Dale spent most of his time doing ministry within the Black community.[28]

Dale explained to Whipple that there were "two classes of colored people" in Oberlin: one was "made up of persons of good circumstances." The other class was "made of persons who are ignorant and poor and . . . said to be lazy and low. This latter class does not visit the larger church [First Church]." Two years earlier, on first arriving in Oberlin, Dale inquired among this class of Blacks as to why they did not attend First Church. "They were ignorant," he was told, "and could not understand the preaching of those that preached there." Though Dale countered that they might indeed understand Mr. Finney, even "though he was a very learned man," nonetheless Dale "could not persuade them to come out to the Oberlin Church." One is left to wonder: What caused the African Americans to be uncomfortable at First Church? Were there differences of class along with race?[29]

Responding to the spiritual concerns of the Black residents, Dale proposed to hold services for them. When they accepted, he "preached and held prayer meetings until they formed themselves into a Wesleyan church." Dale wrote in his letter that the Wesleyan conference "sends a minister to preach to them," most likely George Congdon Hicks. Despite having an African Methodist Episcopal affiliation, Dale didn't try to organize an AME congregation, choosing with other Oberlin Blacks to join the Wesleyan Methodist denomination instead, perhaps because of its strong emphasis on sanctification and abolition.[30]

The mainline Methodist (Methodist Episcopal) presence eventually divided along racial lines. Methodist circuit riders had founded a Methodist Episcopal society in Oberlin in the 1830s, but the formal First Methodist Church did not organize until 1869. As the congregation was forming, it

---

[28]Dale is likely referring to a Sunday School class; Marcus Dale to George Whipple, American Missionary Association, April 2, 1861, photocopy, Lawson-Merrill Papers, box 3, Oberlin College Archives.

[29]Marcus Dale to George Whipple.

[30]Marcus Dale to George Whipple. It is unclear what happened to the East Oberlin Wesleyan Methodist congregation after Hicks's 1864 Oberlin graduation and Dale's enlistment in the Union Army.

seems to have initially been biracial, but by 1872, a year before the church erected its first structure, a group of Blacks separated to form Second Methodist Church, which would come to be known as Rust Methodist Episcopal (later United Methodist) Church.[31]

The segmentation and segregation of both the college and the town intensified during the post-Reconstruction era. Once the abolitionist fires settled to ashes, so did the call for racial equity. Oberlin followed the national trend toward both de facto and de jure Jim Crow segregation. As Oberlin archivist W. E. Bigglestone wrote in 1971,

> working and fighting for freedom for a slave was not the same as defending him against widespread discriminatory practices. Perhaps Oberlin had exhausted its interest and enthusiasm for blacks during the anti-slavery struggle. In any event, black students were treated differently from white students at Oberlin College during the period between the end of the Civil War and the beginning of World War II.[32]

Black members of the First Baptist Church responded to the town's accelerating segregation by breaking with the White majority and meeting in various homes and halls throughout Oberlin, eventually establishing Mt. Zion Church in Oberlin in the 1880s. Mt. Zion Baptist and Rust Methodist Episcopal became the center of Black Oberlin's social and political life. They also became an important source of support for Black students who found themselves increasingly excluded from campus culture as their college followed in the segregationist footsteps of its community. "Evidence," writes Cally L. Waite, a scholar of the period, "indicates that the churches were the center of political activity as the college began to segregate. As Black students were excluded from campus life, they turned to Black churches in the town."[33]

As the town of Oberlin moved into the early twentieth century, it found itself in a quandary about race. Covenants, land restrictions, and housing

---

[31]VanDyke, "First United Methodist Church," site M in "Churches of Oberlin"; "A Brief Chronological Sketch of Oberlin Churches," 2.

[32]W. E. Bigglestone, "Oberlin College and the Negro Student, 1865–1940," *Journal of Negro History* 56, no. 3 (1971): 198.

[33]Lee Davis, Alison Dennis, and Satoko Kanahara, "Mount Zion Baptist Church," 2003, Oberlin College online, https://www2.oberlin.edu/external/EOG/AfAmChurches/MtZion.htm; Cally L. Waite, "The Segregation of Black Students at Oberlin College After Reconstruction," *History of Education Quarterly* 41, no. 3 (2001): 350.

segregation, all of them race-based, became the norm. The college also began to restrict student housing to White students, forced Black students to find off-campus housing, and segregated its dining facilities. Furthermore, Oberlin's Black alumni of the late 1800s and early twentieth century actively reminded the institution's leaders of who they were called to be, pointed out how the institution had strayed from the original Oberlin tradition, and encouraged student resistance and protest. They wrote letters, visited the campus, kept each other informed on the issues, and exerted financial pressure. Throughout the Jim Crow period, they succeeded in pressuring Oberlin to maintain "at least token integration," even in the face of White protest.[34]

This was all in stark contrast to the reputation that Oberlin College had developed as one of the earliest higher educational institutions to be consistently open to African Americans. In his 1903 study of Black higher education, W. E. B. Du Bois praised Oberlin for having graduated more than 40 percent of all Black alumni from predominantly White higher educational institutions and for being a great pioneer in "blotting out the color-line in college." Yet by the beginning of the twentieth century, Oberlin College had moved away from being a radical abolitionist and revivalist institution, and the town itself compromised with Jim Crow America. Oberlin lost its way as a school and a town that focused on revivalism, sanctification, and racial equality.[35]

CONCLUSION

As followers of Jesus, what can we learn about the grand experiment called Oberlin? Its story is complicated. Nineteenth-century Black and White

---

[34]Bigglestone, "Oberlin College and the Negro Student," 209; Waite, "Segregation of Black Students," 352; James Oliver Horton, "Black Education at Oberlin College: A Controversial Commitment," *Journal of Negro Education* 54, no. 4 (1985): 490, https://doi.org/10.2307/2294710.

[35]In his study, Du Bois surveyed both Black and predominately White higher educational institutions and published his findings. He separated his research into two categories: historically Black colleges and universities (HBCUs) and predominately White ones. Excluding the HBCUs, Du Bois found that the predominately White colleges and universities, both 9 "large universities" (Harvard, Yale, the University of Michigan, Cornell, Columbia, etc.) and 31 "colleges of second rank" (Oberlin, the University of Kansas, Bates, Colgate, etc.), graduated a total of 310 blacks. Of the predominately White "large" universities, Harvard topped the list with 11 Black graduated students. Oberlin graduated an incredible 128 students, far more than its "college of second rank" competitor, the University of Kansas, which only graduated 16. See W. E. Burghardt Du Bois, *The College-Bred Negro: Report of a Social Study Made Under the Direction of Atlanta University in 1900* (Atlanta: Atlanta University Press, 1900), 29.

revivalists and abolitionists went against the grain to carve out this small enclave of social and racial exploration, undergirded with a commitment to holiness and sanctification. This chapter has teased out the complex early history of the town of Oberlin, allowing some of the voices of the enslaved and free Black people who found refuge, safety, and livelihood in Oberlin to be heard. The history of Oberlin, both the town and the college, shows us how forces of cultural and structural racism can insidiously reshape a community even as its ideals of equality continue to be publicly and communally affirmed, as my wife and I found out as we were purchasing our property.

Oberlin's story suggests that spiritual, mental, and physical freedom is a work in progress. Each generation must be willing to ask critical questions of itself about how it is working toward a Christian vision "irrespective of color." This is especially true of those of us who carry the legacies of early Black and White revivalists and abolitionists, whether our congregations are predominantly White, predominantly Black, multiracial, or of other racial groups. Our task is to be continually self-reflective and critical regarding justice issues, always asking whether we are matching up to the Great Commandments of loving God and neighbor, watching for ways in which our commitments might be slipping.

In Oberlin and elsewhere, the world has made progress. Despite the held-over and, by then, illegal language that my wife and I found in the housing documents, such racial covenants prohibiting Blacks from purchasing land had been struck down across the United States by the Supreme Court in 1948. We now live on the latter side of the civil rights movement, the assassinations of both Malcolm X and Martin Luther King Jr., and the historic presidency and vice presidency of Barack Obama and Kamala Harris, respectively. But even as some feel that we have come close to declaring a postracial America, we now face a renewed rise of White Christian nationalism and persistent, systemic racism, perpetuating injustice that is structural and insidious.

Yet the prophetic call for Christians, even as we worship in our congregations in their ethnic and cultural diversity, is to find ways to reach across our divides and find common ground, collectively living out Jesus' mission of Luke 4:18-19:

The Spirit of the Lord is upon me,
    because he has anointed me
        to bring good news to the poor.
He has sent me to proclaim release to the captives
    and recovery of sight to the blind,
        to let the oppressed go free,
to proclaim the year of the Lord's favor.[36]

We must find ways to rise above those voices that would call us to believe that hate is right, that police brutality is justified, that abridging the exercise of one's democratic rights is tolerable, and that Jesus would approve of prejudice over justice and equality. We must find ways of dialoguing that call for critique, healing, and the building of a critically diverse unity throughout the body of Christ as a part of God's good creation. As we grapple with continuing vestiges of discrimination and other forms of oppression today, we should be guided by the voice of the prophet Isaiah: "I will make justice the measuring line and righteousness the plumb line" (Isaiah 28:17 NIV). We must also allow ourselves to be humbled, rebuked, and challenged by the stories and prophetic voices of the past as well as by the prophets of the present. May their collective witness help to restore us to our convictions, guiding us toward the difficult and courageous choices that will usher in justice and righteousness for all people.

---

[36]Cf. Isaiah 61:1-2.

A PROPHETIC PAST

Estrelda Y. Alexander

AT THE END OF EVERY SIGNIFICANT DISCUSSION, a question remains: "So what?" or more specifically, "What will we do with what we have learned?" Such questions inevitably arise as we encounter the poignant narratives of the lives and ministries of David Ingraham, a White nineteenth-century Christian abolitionist, and his associates—James Bradley, a formerly enslaved fellow seminarian, and Nancy Prince, a missionary coworker who was a free Black woman. What do their stories and those of other revivalist abolitionists tell us about our ethical commitments? What do they say about the ongoing attempts of contemporary Christians to engage the racial circumstances that surround us? Without looking deeper than the surface, some people might conclude that their lives unfolded in a different time and space and therefore have little applicability to our present context, even if they are interesting or compelling. But that would be an unfortunate assessment. To make that move would be to miss out on a legacy that has great relevance for today.

At least that's what the fourteen scholars and practitioners who convened as the Dialogue on Race and Faith have concluded. Coming from different parts of the United States as we do, we represent varying life experiences, varying academic disciplines and approaches, and varying Christian denominational traditions. This group of African American, African, Asian American, and White men and women traveled with one another, visited historical sites and contemporary venues, ate together, fellowshiped together, and heard one another's stories in addition to performing the work of analyzing primary documents.

It was hard for us not to be moved when we read Ingraham's gripping diary entries—his commitment to end slavery, his efforts to improve the lives of previously enslaved people, his zeal for helping others to grow as disciples of Jesus, his earnest prayers and fervent worship, his self-doubts, the debilitating effects of his tuberculosis. But we were even more moved by his depictions of the horrendous conditions of the transatlantic slave trade and the harsh post-emancipation plight of Blacks in Jamaica.

The young, ailing missionary cared enough about what he was witnessing to document with great care what he saw and experienced. He did not know that nearly two centuries later his journal would find its way to Christians who were interested in retelling his narrative to the world. He could not have imagined that it might fall into the hands of those who desired to further his unfulfilled hopes for a just society.

The journal, with its diagram of the repulsive slave ship *Ulysses*, paired with Ingraham's newspaper account of the brig's capture (see appendix D), evokes emotions similar to those elicited by graphic depictions of racist violence in today's media. Indeed, the timing of the journal's discovery underscores how important it is that Christians cooperate to seek real solutions and racial reconciliation.[1]

The 556 enslaved persons who landed in Jamaica on the *Ulysses* represented a tiny fraction of the millions of other men, women, youth, and children who suffered through the horrors of the transatlantic passage and more than two hundred years of chattel slavery that reduced them to less-than-human status in the eyes of those in power. Ingraham's description of the conditions aboard the brig makes the compassionate person cringe. Yet while the representations of the middle passage, slavery, and its aftermath rightly stir the emotions, we should be no less stirred by the toll that discrimination continues to take on African Americans and other communities. Generations of Black persons in the United States have continued to suffer racial injustice in its various forms. Neighborhoods continue to be segregated. Housing practices continue to be unfair. Economic disparities between racial groups persist, as do inadequate education, unequal access to healthcare, and targeted, dehumanized violence toward people of color. We would do something far worse than a grave disservice to Jesus' call to

---

[1] D. S. Ingraham, "Capture of the *Ulysses*—Sufferings of the Slaves," *The Colored American*, April 4, 1840.

justice if we were to miss the parallels between the world that Ingraham described and the one we inhabit now.

Ingraham's diary wasn't alone in firing those convictions for us. As we encountered the narratives of Bradley and Prince as well, we were further convinced that the life stories of the three activists and others like them spoke to common themes of human suffering and our responsibility as Christians to address racial injustice, and that the stories deserve (demand, really) to be shared with our Christian communities today. Ingraham's account of his labors to educate and support emancipated Jamaicans and Prince's reflections on post-slavery Jamaica, for example, confront us with the economic, social, and spiritual challenges that have remained long after slavery on these shores came to an end.

Sifting through the pages of these incredible narratives, one wonders whether the timing of the discovery of Ingraham's diary and the rediscovery of Bradley and Prince's writings are providential. That constellation of events has taken place at a moment when our nation has once again come face-to-face with the appalling nature of its sins, particularly racism and injustice, and plainly has no excuse for pretending that their ugliness has not continued to scar its society and the church. Nor can we ignore any longer the residual effects that such prejudice has had on historically marginalized communities, just as Ingraham and Prince saw the poor living conditions of recently freed Jamaican slaves.

But the parallels can also be catalysts for hope. Three ordinary people, Jesus followers who possessed a willingness to channel faith into action despite the risk, demonstrated extraordinary courage to address a seemingly intractable blight. There were other courageous activists too. Entries in Ingraham's journal, along with other historical records, provide us with an intimate look at an entire cadre of Christian abolitionists who defied cultural expectations, gave of their resources, and worked tirelessly for the cause of emancipation and racial equality. Some of the names of these abolitionists are relatively well-known, at least among Christian historians, with names like Theodore Weld, Angelina Grimké, Asa Mahan, John Langston, and Lewis Tappan. But this narrative also brings forward to public recognition previously unknown figures—men and women, Black and White, from all walks of life and various Christian traditions—all of whom worked for the common goal of ameliorating the conditions of others with whom they shared little but their common humanity.

Together, these Christians have bequeathed to the church and the world their prophetic witness, a priceless gift that can nurture and guide us today as we continue their work of establishing God's wholeness and justice. By examining what drove them and sustained their commitment, by identifying the myriad ways in which they opposed injustice and promoted human flourishing, and by acknowledging how their efforts sometimes fell short, we can find encouragement and wisdom as we continue the work they started. These nineteenth-century activists dare us to declare our theology and worship practices to be the foundation of our justice work, showing us what is involved in the long toil of forming and sustaining interracial community. They remind us that injustice is global, holistic, and multifaceted, and involves every member of our communities, and they inspire us to imagine responses that are equal to the task.

THEOLOGY MATTERS

"Our theology informs our anthropology," writes Brenda Salter McNeil, a twenty-first-century reconciler and activist, "which in turn informs our sociology. That is to say, what we believe about God will tell us what we believe about people; and what we believe about people will tell us what kinds of communities and societies we believe we should strive to create." The personal and public writings of nineteenth-century revivalist abolitionists testify to that cascade of influences. Their activism was the inevitable embodiment of their theological convictions, which were nourished and sustained by vital practices of worship and devotion. Those earlier Christians had a lived theology, not just sets of doctrinal commitments, and what they believed compelled them to care about those whom they held to be their brothers and sisters. Our theology should operate in the same way. The beliefs we profess about the brotherhood and sisterhood of humanity must drive us to think and act in ways that are consistent with justice, and not just as an idea but as a way of life rooted in the truth of Jesus' saving love.[2]

---

[2]Brenda Salter McNeil, *Roadmap to Reconciliation 2.0: Moving Communities into Unity, Wholeness, and Justice* (Downers Grove, IL: InterVarsity Press, 2020), 27.

The holiness revivalism and spirituality that revivalist abolitionists practiced allowed no dichotomous split between personal piety and social activism. They thought the two tied together so tightly that a person could not
claim to be sanctified without showing concern for those who were oppressed. The fight for abolition and the uplifting of those who had been
emancipated was a spiritual matter first, for one could not love the God they
had not seen while caring nothing for the welfare of their human brothers
and sisters. Ingraham depicted the *Ulysses* in his journal and in newspaper
articles because the evidence of such a clear violation of God's image demanded an active Christian response. For their frank statement of brutal
truth in the media available at the time, the slave ship diagrams in Ingraham's writings can be compared to video of George Floyd's murder in 2020.
They forbid us to forget the reality of racial injustice and call us to respond
with concrete action.[3]

If a solid theological grounding anchors us in mission, shared spiritual
practices uphold and propel our work. Authentic piety (spirituality) and
corporate worship are not just optional add-ons but indispensable components of our Christian justice advocacy. Ingraham and his abolitionist colleagues had experiences of conversion to Jesus (repentant redemption) that
fostered their biblical devotion, which in turn drove them to holy activism.
As we obediently participate in Christ's work, we are formed more and more
into his image and come to embody his presence with one another. Corporate worship, what we do when we gather as the body of Christ, shapes us
for the labor of justice while also serving as a vibrant witness to that work.
Liberative liturgies can bring honor to God, while simultaneously exhorting
us to resist fatigue or distraction and to persevere in the race toward liberation for all people, shaking us from the sleep of our insensitivity while
strengthening us to work for those who suffer. A focus on God's mission
today can cut across denominational boundaries and other humanly constructed barriers, bringing people together who might not otherwise think
they have much in common and strengthening the movement toward the
flourishing of the world.

The affective worship of the Christian revivals of the 1800s emphasized
the belief that a person's spiritual senses could be stirred by the grace of God

---

[3]See James 2:16; 1 John 4:20.

to the point of conviction. Worship for the revivalist abolitionist was not a
route of escape from the world and its troubles. It cannot be for us either.
More than anything, worship was an invitation *into* the brokenness of the
world and its systems in order that they might be injected with the healing
touch of Jesus in the same way that the converted sinner had experienced
Jesus' healing for her- or himself. In vital worship, we encounter a true and
living God who prepares our hearts to seek justice and strengthens us with
the fortitude and resolve we need for carrying out the work. Revivalist abolitionists did not hold these ideas simply as theories. They believed that an
encounter with Christ was necessarily life-changing and would set a person
toward becoming like Jesus in every area of life, including his or her relationship with the oppressed. Our worship should follow the same pattern. It
is well and good for worship to be an emotive experience, but it must also
be an authentic, transformative encounter with the God who shapes our
attitudes and behaviors. After all, when we worship, we come face-to-face
with the One whose very nature is just. We should not be surprised to find
in the proclamation of that One's Word the motivation for our struggle and
inspiration for going out to proclaim in words and deeds the good news we
have heard, living our lives "in a manner worthy of the gospel of Christ"
(Philippians 1:27).

SUSTAINING A MULTIRACIAL, JUSTICE-FOCUSED COMMUNITY

Abolitionists of the revivalist tradition did not separate their identity as
Christians from their identity as citizens in an unjust culture. They took seriously their responsibility to provide a Christlike answer to issues of inequality, defying what they saw as unchristian action and challenging social
norms. They formed intentional, interracial communities to reflect what the
social reformer Jonathan Blanchard called the sanctified "perfect state of
society" that God wanted to establish on earth as it is in heaven. Community
formation of that sort and on that scale was not easy work. It required
courage, vulnerability, and a willingness to be dislocated. But over time, as
individuals who were raised to be suspicious of each other began to talk and
listen to one another, conversation turned into trust, trust became respect,
and respect gave birth to friendship. Bradley's testimony that "prejudice

against color does not exist in Lane Seminary," Ingraham's reports of close fellowship with Jamaicans, and Prince's account of "kind friends," both Black and White, each attest to deep, interracial relationships of a sort that can only be forged through strenuous, love-fired effort, usually over long periods of time.[4]

Contemporary Christians can follow their example, moving beyond rhetoric about inclusivity to create genuine connections with one another across lines that have historically divided us. The work of helping people to cross racial and cultural barriers and build vital relationships with one another starts at the level of the human heart and hands as individuals reach out to others with whom they would not have otherwise been involved, remaining in close connection with them even when it becomes uncomfortable or disorienting.

When we live with that kind of love, we're in good company. Oberlin, both the town and the college, a backdrop for the lives of our three revivalist abolitionists, was the site of an unprecedented attempt to live out authentic racial equality while taking a public stance against an issue so volatile that it split the nation, including the Christian community. As frail humans, the Oberlinites did not always get things right. Their egalitarian communities at Oberlin and the Jamaica mission station were fragile, imperfect, and short-lived. Nevertheless, they represented a sincere effort to create interracial harmony, and it stayed the course for two whole generations, right up until being poisoned and sabotaged by the post-Reconstruction backlash of Jim Crow. Yet that short, beautiful period of equitable community was an outstanding accomplishment given the particularly venomous nature of America's racist culture at the time. The ideal worked as long as the members of the communities remained in proximate, embodied relationship with one another, knowing each other, working together, praying in unity, studying the Word, and sharing meals. Deep relationships prompted some Whites to resist the racism of the larger culture all around them and demonstrated to some Blacks that not all Whites were irredeemably beholden to racist ideas.

Revivalist abolitionists did not even agree with each other all the time, including about what tactics to use in the pursuit of justice. We shouldn't

---

[4]Jonathan Blanchard, *A Perfect State of Society: Address Before the "Society of Inquiry," in Oberlin Collegiate Institute: Delivered at Oberlin, Lorain Co. Ohio, at the Annual Commencement, Sep. 3, 1839* (Oberlin, OH: James Steele, 1839).

expect ourselves always to agree either. Disagreement on methods did not deter them from working toward the common goal of ending slavery and improving the well-being of ex-slaves. Neither should our differences deter us from seeking a more just society. Christians can use a variety of tools to achieve the desired end. By seeking God's wisdom together and keeping our shared vision in focus, we can discover places of mutuality and craft workable solutions.

The interracial, egalitarian communities that abolitionists created in Ohio and Jamaica existed in considerable tension with the world. Their members expected and received scorn and criticism from those around them as they pushed against the status quo. Over time, a healthy spirit of cultural defiance became part of their DNA, fueling their perseverance when the going did not get easier for long stretches. But after the abolitionists' immediate goals were achieved and slavery came to an end, second- and third-generation members showed themselves less likely to maintain their predecessors' level of cultural tension. As the urgency they felt toward their mission lessened, so did their will to stand in opposition to the world around them, especially when such a stance invited criticism or put them at a social disadvantage. Little by little, they began to mirror the surrounding culture, their subversive witness becoming dimmer and dimmer as the fire died down inside of them.

The mission enterprise pioneered in Jamaica in the late 1830s by David Ingraham, for example, was meant to embody Oberlin's theological commitment to living a holy life, siding with the oppressed, and cultivating vulnerable relationships in a diverse interracial community. Ingraham's journal and other writings make it clear that he and his wife Betsey strived to live out those ideals, and he consistently referred to Jamaican congregants and friends with expressions of respect and affection. However, when David and Betsey's daughter, Sarah Ingraham Penfield, returned to Jamaica in 1858 with her husband, Thornton Bigelow Penfield, to join the missionary work at Oberlin Station near Kingston, she experienced a very different reality. Sarah's story, told through her letters, generates important insights for Christian communities that seek to maintain their commitment to equity and justice in the long term.

As soon as they had a house of their own in Jamaica, Sarah and Bigelow began to board Black Jamaican children, teaching and mentoring them under their roof. Just as quickly, they ran into opposition from their fellow White missionaries because they treated the children as their own, inviting them to eat at their dinner table and share their food. In letter after letter, Sarah and Bigelow each referenced the deepening conflict with their colleagues and expressed disappointment and distress at the racist conduct they encountered, which Sarah described as "utterly adverse to our Oberlin training." On one occasion, a fellow missionary ambushed the couple in Sarah's sickroom as she recovered from childbirth. He "gave us such a talking to about our treating of the native children," she wrote. "He said we were losing the confidence of the rest of the mission, that we should find ourselves isolated from the rest of the mission if we persisted, that we had no right to set aside the experience of the other missionaries, we should ruin the children, & etc." Although Sarah and Bigelow initially expressed hope that they would resolve the "caste question" by spurring a "revolution" in thinking and renewing the "Oberlin spirit," even they eventually capitulated to social pressure and agreed to keep Black Jamaican children away from their table when other missionaries were present. Though the compromise troubled them, they were afraid that if they didn't give in, "a division in the mission would ensue which would very likely result in our being sent home." As it was, the young couple were in fact asked to leave Oberlin Station in 1861 and relocated away from those they had offended.[5]

What happened at Oberlin Station in Jamaica that made it so difficult to address and change a racist practice, one that had, in Sarah's words, "so entrenched itself among us"? Similar to what happened during the post-Reconstruction era in Oberlin, legalized slavery was firmly in the past by the time Sarah and Bigelow arrived in Jamaica. But just like the pullback from racial equality that occurred in the United States following Reconstruction, wealthy White planters in Jamaica desperately maneuvered to preserve their power and privilege. In 1865, the planters succeeded in establishing direct British rule in Jamaica, officially turning the island into a crown colony. The

---

[5]Sarah Ingraham Penfield to Elizabeth Ingraham, March 4, 1859, in Thornton Bigelow Penfield and Sarah Ingraham Penfield, *Letters from Jamaica: 1858–1866,* ed. Charles G. Gosselink (Silver Bay, NY: Boat House, 2005), 37, 38, Penfield Family Web Site, www.penfield.fm/jamaica/jamaica .pdf; Sarah Ingraham Penfield to Elizabeth Ingraham, March 3, 1860, in Penfield and Penfield, *Letters from Jamaica,* 68; Sarah Ingraham Penfield to Elizabeth Ingraham, November 8, 1859, in Penfield and Penfield, *Letters from Jamaica,* 61; Thornton Bigelow Penfield to Minerva Penfield Cowles, July 19, 1859, in Penfield and Penfield, *Letters from Jamaica,* 52.

arrangement ensured that "Jamaica's white or near-white propertied class continued to hold the dominant position in every respect" and that "the vast majority of the black population remained poor and unenfranchised." As Whites, the Oberlin missionaries, even though they were from American rather than British backgrounds, still shared a measure of the power, privilege, and social "respectability" of Jamaica's upper class. Without active and sustained recognition of subtle colonial practices and a willingness to resist them, the missionary community slowly merged with those practices and regressed in its commitment to justice. When Bigelow and Sarah challenged the colonial culture, their witness was perceived as a threat to the status quo and the cultural respectability that the community maintained, along with the power that the community's image afforded its members. Although Oberlin missionaries continued to support America's abolitionist cause throughout Sarah and Bigelow's sojourn in Jamaica (cheering on the Union as the Civil War began, for instance), most of the missionaries neglected to see abolitionism's implications on how they treated the Black Jamaicans who were part of their daily lives.[6]

Beverly Daniel Tatum, a psychologist and educator who focuses on racial development, compares cultural racism to smog in the air that we cannot avoid breathing in night and day, even when we don't see or notice or approve of it. The smog of racism is so pervasive and insidious that "most Americans have internalized the espoused cultural values of fairness and justice for all *at the same time* that they have been breathing the smog of racial biases and stereotypes." The stories of Oberlin, Ohio, and Oberlin Station, Jamaica, show how the insidious pollution of racism invades and infects communities, tainting their ideals even when they continue to be affirmed in public by the community.[7]

Yet these stories also show us that the bad air can be pierced and challenged by the cleansing influence of outsiders, those who call communities back to their original values and encourage them to reapply the cultural

---

[6]Thornton Bigelow Penfield and Sarah Ingraham Penfield to Minerva Penfield Cowles, April 26, 1860, in Penfield and Penfield, *Letters*, 79; Rex A. Hudson and Daniel J. Seyler, "Jamaica," chap. 2 in *Islands of the Commonwealth Caribbean: A Regional Study*, ed. Sandra W. Meditz and Dennis M. Hanratty (Washington, DC: Federal Research Division, Library of Congress, 1989), 51.
[7]Beverly Daniel Tatum, *Why Are All the Black Kids Sitting Together in the Cafeteria? and Other Conversations About Race* (New York: Basic, 2017), 86, 220, emphasis original.

tension that those values produce. For Oberlin Station in Jamaica, Sarah and Bigelow Penfield offered the gift of a prophetic perspective that challenged the community to return and reform. They appealed to the missionaries' "Oberlin training" and "Oberlin spirit" and pushed for actions consistent with the biblical values that had originally emboldened Oberlin's Christian activism. If we desire to sustain communities that are committed to justice and equity, it's imperative to admit that we breathe the smog of cultural racism. We have to seek and welcome the perspective of prophets from the outside, those who can hold us accountable to the ideals and values that we espouse, illuminating how the smog has polluted those ideals and pulled us to the dangerous comfort of conformity. It's particularly important that we empower the voices of individuals in the culture around us who are marginalized, even when their feedback feels accusatory and requires sacrifice on our part. Those voices can foster realignment if we let them. The process can be painful and force us onto the downward path of humility, but the historical record makes it clear that walking that road, and trusting the guides who know better than we do which way it points, is an indispensable discipline if we are to sustain communities of prophets who speak and act for justice.

INJUSTICE RUNS DEEP AND WIDE

While the protagonists of this book were all active in the American abolition movement, their ultimate goal was not just the end of slavery, nor was the United States their sole geographic focus. Their activity and concern had implications on events spanning from Jamaica and the United States to as far away as Britain, Portugal, Sierra Leone, the West African kingdom of Dahomey (in modern-day Benin), and Russia. These places were interconnected even then, and both the just and the unjust aspects of their cultures and institutions impacted the lives of nineteenth-century individuals, whether or not they were far away from their countries of origin. How much more is that true for us today! A pandemic might only take weeks to span the world; a war or natural disaster in one place on the planet can affect the economy of every nation. The unprecedented interdependence and interconnectivity means that our work toward justice cannot and will not be limited merely to the communities that we occupy in our small corners of the world. What we do on a small scale can reverberate around the globe.

David Ingraham must have sensed that idea, because he did not confine his work to American abolition. He understood, like Dr. Martin Luther King Jr., that "injustice anywhere is a threat to justice everywhere." It was not enough for Ingraham, Bradley, and Prince that slavery should legally end; they also sought to improve the quality of life of those who had been emancipated. Bradley used the model of the relatively nonracist student body at Lane Seminary as an anticipatory sign that pointed toward God's future reign in which people "of every color will meet at the feet of Jesus." Ingraham saw a relatively nonracist Oberlin and Prince saw a relatively nonracist Russia as archetypes of a more just future in Jamaica. Both Ingraham and Prince sought to use the empowerment of Blacks in Jamaica as a model for the potential uplift of African Americans in the United States once they were freed. And all three of our figures affirmed that Christian communities, when acting rightly, are places of spiritual nurture that show egalitarian models for society.[8]

Though Ingraham resolutely insisted that "slavery must fall and may the time come soon," he did not live to see slavery end. Instead, he joined the "cloud of witnesses" that Scripture tells us were faithful to the end of life but died still yet to "receive what was promised," since the end of slavery would not come for another quarter century (Hebrews 11:39; 12:1). Likewise, despite our most sincere efforts, we may not see all the change we desire in our lifetime. But can we be as resolute in adding our voices and efforts to declare that the time will soon come when racism will fall, and work toward that end in the sure hope that it will come about? By doing so, we continue the legacy of Ingraham, Bradley, Prince, and their abolitionist colleagues. Their witness exhorts us to continue the work of moving toward a more just society.[9]

What we can learn from this prophetic past is much grander than merely reconciling the historic animosities between Blacks and Whites in the United States, though that is essential on its own. While the enslavement of Africans became the most paradigmatic expression of oppression in

---

[8]While celebrating nineteenth-century Russia's lack of racism, Prince also noted the existence of a horrendous classism, as represented by serfdom; see chapter 3 in this book. Martin Luther King Jr., "Martin Luther King Jr.'s 'Letter from Birmingham Jail,'" *The Atlantic,* originally published August 1963 under the headline "The Negro Is Your Brother," republished online April 4, 2018, www.theatlantic.com/magazine/archive/2018/02/letter-from-a-birmingham-jail/552461; James Bradley, "Brief Account of an Emancipated Slave Written by Himself, at the Request of the Editor," in *The Oasis,* ed. Lydia Maria Child (Boston: Benjamin C. Bacon, 1834), 110.

[9]David Ingraham, manuscript journal, Adrian College Archives, 50.

American society, many other forms of injustice have also been evident in our cultures, both here in the United States and around the world. Hatred and bitterness continue to plague encounters between people of different classes, racial and ethnic backgrounds, and political persuasions. In the United States, Latinos and Latinas, Asian Americans, Native Americans, Jews, women, and members of the LGBTQ+ community have been targets of bigotry, and many Americans harbor resentment toward immigrants. There are also countless examples of ethnic tensions and hostilities practically everywhere around the globe. The work, words, and witness of early abolitionists challenge Christians the world over to rethink our actions and attitudes toward the injustices we encounter.

While we're cultivating interracial, person-to-person relationships, we must also work to tear down structural discrimination. Justice advocacy is sometimes categorized as a political issue and then dismissed as inappropriate for congregational conversation. But it is a spiritual issue as well. Members of local churches can choose to have honest conversations that identify the opportunities and obstacles that come to light in the struggle to construct a more inclusive society. Stories like the ones in this book can provide material and inspiration to help congregations envision a more racially just future, perhaps using education and discipleship programs to host such conversations. No longer can we shy away from hard questions about what is required of us to see genuine justice become a way of life in the world. We have to advance beyond gestures. We have to dismantle unjust systems.

AN ACTIVE, HOLISTIC, AND MULTIFACETED RESPONSE

Revivalist abolitionists did not simply know and care for one another as Christian brothers and sisters, modeling egalitarian community as they knew how in their day-to-day lives. They also involved themselves as activists. They confronted their contemporaries one-on-one, raising people's consciousness about racial justice issues and soliciting support from those who had previously been unconcerned. Some of the activists addressed racial justice publicly in their sermons, lectures, and essays, arguing on biblical and theological grounds. Abolitionist pastors kept the antislavery cause before their congregations and expected their hearers, confessors of the Christian faith, to live out its implications. Other abolitionists (both pastors and laypeople) served as conductors and agents along the Underground Railroad. Some entered the halls of politics and worked to change discriminatory laws through the arduous process of legislation. Whatever forms their various pursuits of justice took, revivalist abolitionists held fellow believers accountable and challenged each other not to settle for the status quo.

Abolitionists also refused to justify slavery as a pragmatic necessity. They saw and named it as the sinful practice that it was. For them, there was no acceptable justification for holding another human being as property. For us, there can be no justification for tolerating the kind of racial injustice that holds entire ethnic groups hostage to discrimination and the lack of opportunity. We must ask ourselves the same questions that nineteenth-century abolitionists asked each other, discerning what it means to be faithful followers of Jesus in an unjust world. David Ingraham said of his day that "it seems as if the church were asleep." The same could be said about us, the Christians of today's church, who watch silently over and over again as injustice unfolds before our eyes. Our forebears, abolitionists like Ingraham, Bradley, Prince, and others, refused to remain asleep. Their stories show us that every segment of the Christian community, whether it's in our churches, our schools, our fellowship groups, or the other ways we gather and serve, has something to contribute. As people of faith, we can lead in the work of reconciliation if only we will take the initiative![10]

That principle applies regardless of how old a person is. Ingraham and his fellow abolitionists demonstrated that age is not a disqualifier. Efforts to end slavery involved young students every bit as much as seasoned professors, pastors, and laypeople, all of whom sensed that they could play meaningful roles in changing an intolerable situation. Ingraham and Bradley were young men; Prince was older; but age did not stop any of them. You cannot be too young or too old to participate in God's project.

Concerns over sexism and racism resonate with one another, and attention to activism in one realm enhances the pursuit of justice in the other. As we have seen in this book, the treatment of enslaved and other Black women shows that injustice can be found in many forms, and the record implores us to confess that Christians are duty-bound to stand against such evils, all of them, wherever and however we encounter them. Nancy Prince

---

[10]Ingraham, journal, 24.

and Sarah Ingraham Penfield were examples of women who effectively combined faith in Christ, personal piety, and social activism to defy patriarchal attitudes and lodge a credible witness to the role of women as important partners in the search for a better world.

Because nineteenth-century activists recognized the holistic nature of justice, they involved themselves in a variety of ways, investing their time, talent, and material resources in a range of endeavors, from literacy training to land acquisition to gathering supplies in support of the newly emancipated. Those who had substantial means contributed their finances. Those who had little means but were talented in speaking or publishing contributed those skills. Those who had networks of contacts canvassed their colleagues. Whites, free Blacks, and freed persons alike—whatever loaves and fish each person had, they gave them to the Lord to be used in the struggle for a holier social order.

Sometimes a few loaves and fish seem to be all we have. Despite the strides we've made in the last two centuries, many advocates today observe that true racial equality is still elusive, the gains are often small and hard-won, and there appears to be little progress most of the time. The roots of social injustice run deep. Much of the dysfunction in today's African American communities, for example, is a fruit of the brokenness that the White power structure planted in the Black psyche through slavery and the regression in racial attitudes that occurred after Reconstruction. Laws and judicial decrees to remove systemic inequalities have been important and have sometimes brought redemption to historical injustices around the rights and possessions of the oppressed and their descendants. But true reconciliation is only possible when we share our lives across racial lines, and that work is much harder, runs much deeper, and requires immensely more perseverance than it takes even to move the levers of legislation. It is here that churches, whether or not they are multiracial, can create fellowship that models a new reality in our world, breaking down unholy attitudes that generate prejudice and lure us to accept injustice as normal. Our faith communities are positioned as incubators of such crosscultural engagement today.

Just as James Bradley was able to draw on his personal experience of slavery to entice listeners toward empathy with the stories of former slaves, Christians who hold power must be willing to listen to those who suffer injustice, paying close attention to their stories and coming to understand their hopes and dreams for the future. Their narratives usher our imaginations to picture a more just society, beckoning us to involve ourselves in the work it will take to bring it about. Cross-racial work is time-consuming and labor-intensive, but the rewards can be priceless glimpses of the new heaven and new earth even here, even now, and of the character of the Lord who gave us such incredible diversity in the way we were made. It is our identity as disciples of Jesus, not our racial or ethnic identities or denominational affiliations, that should determine how we witness revival to a broken social world. Our common faith in Christ Jesus binds us together as we share a vision of hope in the unfolding kingdom of God.

It would have been easy for Chris Momany to shelve David Ingraham's journal as just another item from the archive of history, an interesting document, perhaps, but relatively inconsequential. But he rightly sensed that what he had was something much more. He knew that the stories of revivalist abolitionists like Ingraham, Bradley, and Prince had an important message for today's generation of Christians, one that deserved to be proclaimed far and wide.

What is that message? James Bradley's hopeful exclamation rings as true today as it did in 1834. Bradley implored God to strengthen Christians in the sanctified work of "this holy cause, until the walls of prejudice are broken down, and chains burst in pieces, and men of every color meet at the feet of Jesus, speaking kind words, and looking upon each other in love willing to live together on earth, as they hope to live in Heaven!" May Bradley's words wake us up to our responsibility to live out the ethics, the justice, of Jesus. Let us name the sins of racism in our churches, in our academies, in our private conversations, in the public square, in our very homes. Bradley, Ingraham, and Prince knew that for those who were suffering, time was short. May we recognize that what our generation does in these few, short days we have on earth matters to Jesus and the human race he came to serve. May we prove faithful to the legacy we have inherited. May we stay strong in the struggle as we obey God's call. And may we so practice justice in our fractured world that future generations, to the glory of God, might say of us as we say of the abolitionist saints of this book, that theirs was a prophetic past.[11]

---

[11]Bradley, "Brief Account," 111-12.

TIMELINE OF SIGNIFICANT DATES

Names of key figures are **bolded** at first occurrence

1792

- **Charles G. Finney** born in Warren, CT

1799

- **Nancy Prince** (née Gardner) born in Newburyport, MA
- **Asa Mahan** born in Vernon, NY

1807

- The United Kingdom prohibits the slave trade in the British Empire, including Jamaica

1808

- The United States outlaws external slave trade, but illegal smuggling persists

1810

- **James Bradley** born in West Africa; abducted and enslaved at age two or three; forcibly shipped to Charleston, SC; sold to a slaveowner who eventually takes him to Arkansas Territory

1812

- **David S. Ingraham** born in western NY, probably near Rochester

1815

- **Elizabeth (Betsey) Harston** born

1819

- Prince converted and baptized

1824

- Prince (recently married) and her husband, Nero Prince, move to St. Petersburg, Russia

- Mahan graduates from Hamilton College, Clinton, NY

1825

- Finney's evangelistic revival ministry expands throughout central and western New York

1826

- **Theodore D. Weld** converted in Utica, NY, under Finney's ministry

1827

- Mahan graduates from Andover Theological Seminary, Andover, MA

1828

- Bradley has conversion experience in Arkansas Territory

1829

- Mahan begins serving as pastor of Second Congregational Church, Pittsford, NY

1830

- Ingraham joins Pittsford Second Congregational Church

1830

- Finney's Rochester, NY, revival begins, including preaching at Second Congregational Church in Pittsford

1831

- Ingraham attends Chester Academy in Chester, VT

- Mahan becomes pastor of Cincinnati's Sixth Presbyterian Church and a trustee of Lane Seminary

1832

- **Lyman Beecher** accepts the presidency of Lane Seminary, funded by **Lewis and Arthur Tappan** of New York City

- Ingraham moves to Cincinnati, joins Sixth Presbyterian Church, and enters Lane Seminary, at the same time as a number of students who had previously attended Oneida Institute in Whitesboro, NY, including Weld

1833

- Prince returns to the United States after living nine years in Russia and (now widowed) begins a seven-year stay with the family of Free-Will Baptist pastor **Jonas W. Holman** in Boston

- Bradley purchases his own freedom for $700 (approx. $26,500 in 2024) and travels from Arkansas Territory to Cincinnati

- Bradley admitted to Lane Seminary, as the school's only African American student

- Oberlin Collegiate Institute admits its first students (all White for the first two years)

- American Anti-slavery Society established by William Lloyd Garrison, Weld, the Tappan brothers, Frederick Douglass, and others

- Slavery Abolition Act passed in Parliament, commanding the immediate end of slavery in most parts of the British Empire on August 1, 1834. Emancipation in British territories, including Jamaica, but emancipation was accompanied by an "apprenticeship" system in which former enslavers became the (often unscrupulous) employers

1834

- *February*: Lane students, organized by Weld, hold series of "debates" (actually a protracted meeting of speeches and prayers) regarding the abolition of slavery; Bradley is one of the key speakers

- *June*: Bradley writes his "Brief Account," published in *The Oasis*, a book edited by Lydia Maria Child

- *July*: Anti-abolitionist riots in New York City stoke fear of violence by White mobs

- *Summer*: Lane students teach and live in Cincinnati's Black community

- *August 1*: End of slavery in Jamaica (Slavery Abolition Act of 1833 comes into force), but "apprenticeship" system continues to force formerly enslaved people to work uncompensated until 1838

- *October*: Lane trustees prohibit the discussion of abolition, after which a majority of students ("the Lane Rebels"), including Bradley, Ingraham, and Weld, leave the school

- *December*: Betsey Harston and twenty-five other Oberlin students sign statement that advocates "admitting students of color"

1835

- After Tappan brothers agree—under certain conditions—to help fund Oberlin Collegiate Institute, Oberlin trustees narrowly vote to allow the faculty to control most aspects of the school, knowing that this governance decision would result in a policy of no discrimination in student admission, thereby becoming the second institution in the country, after Oneida Institute, to admit Black students on a regular basis

- Lane Rebels enroll at Oberlin Collegiate Institute; Mahan is asked to become Oberlin's President

- Oberlin Anti-slavery Society established; the Society's agenda includes "the emancipation of the free colored man from the oppression of public sentiment, and the elevation of both [enslaved and free Blacks] to an intellectual, moral, and political equality with the Whites"

- Finney publishes *Lectures on Revivals of Religion*

1836

- *March*: Bradley and another Lane Rebel, Hiram Wilson, travel from Cincinnati to Oberlin; Bradley is confronted and threatened by a slaveowner on a steamboat on the Ohio River and by other White racists during the overland portion of their journey

- Along with other students, including African Americans **Gideon and Charles Langston,** Bradley enrolls at Sheffield Institute, a satellite preparatory campus of Oberlin Collegiate Institute, fifteen miles northeast

- *September*: Revival at Oberlin includes inquiry about the possibility of entire sanctification or Christian perfection. Mahan receives an experience of Christian perfection

1836

- Mahan and Finney begin preaching together in New York City
- Ingraham visits Mahan and Finney in New York City while on his way to Cuba, where he plans his mission to Jamaica

1837

- Finney joins Oberlin faculty; publishes *Lectures to Professing Christians* (including an address on "Sanctification by Faith" and two on "Christian Perfection")
- Lane Rebel C. Stewart Renshaw refers to Bradley as "our dear brother," the last known reference to Bradley
- Ingraham again takes classes in Oberlin and is ordained as a Congregationalist clergyman
- *August*: Ingraham marries Elizabeth (Betsey) Harston in Oberlin; Mahan officiates
- *December*: David and Betsey Ingraham arrive in Jamaica as the first Oberlin missionaries to work among emancipated Afro-Caribbean people, intending to establish an educational and evangelistic ministry for Jamaicans as an independent ("faith") mission—later (beginning on January 1, 1840) to be partially funded by the London Missionary Society
- Mahan begins preaching sermon series on Christian perfection at Boston's Marlboro Chapel

1838

- *April*: Holman preaches and publishes sermon on "The Glory of the Church," articulating holiness and antislavery themes
- David and Betsey Ingraham organize a church and school for Black Jamaicans at Cotton Tree (Shortwood estate), six miles north of Kingston

- *August*: Enslaved people in Jamaica receive full emancipation with the abolition of the apprenticeship system; Ingraham states it was "the happiest day of my life"
- *September*: Mahan lectures on Christian perfection at Oberlin; published in the inaugural issue of *The Oberlin Evangelist* in November

1839

- Mahan publishes *Scripture Doctrine of Christian Perfection*
- Finney gives series of lectures on sanctification and then publishes them (in early 1840) in *The Oberlin Evangelist*; Ingraham reads one of the lectures and comments on it
- Renshaw establishes Oberlin Mission Station at Grant Hill, St. Andrew, Jamaica, sixteen miles north of Kingston (current site of Oberlin Church and School)—in later years to be funded by the American Missionary Association (through the largesse of the Tappans)
- *March*: Ingraham writes letters to American papers extolling the work ethic of "free labor" Jamaicans and decrying the low salaries paid to Black laborers by White landowners
- *July*: Ingraham writes first entry in his journal
- *August*: Ingraham witnesses Jamaicans celebrating the anniversary of their emancipation by praising God
- *August*: The schooner *Amistad* is seized off Long Island, NY; all abducted Africans on board are brought to New London, CT. *The Oberlin Evangelist* and other abolitionists follow the saga of the captives closely. The legal defense of the Africans is funded by the Tappan brothers. Eventually, on March 31, 1841, *The Oberlin Evangelist* reports: "The oppressor is confounded. The Captive is free"
- *Fall*: Portuguese slave runners from the brig *Ulysses*, perhaps with the assistance of the notorious slave trader Francisco Félix de Souza, shackle 556 abducted Africans from the ports of Ouidah and Popo in Dahomey (now Benin); Badagry (now Nigeria); and the River Nunez (now Guinea). The slave runners forcibly transport these abducted people to the Caribbean; the slave brig is intercepted by the British navy warship *Skipjack*; brought to Port Royal, Jamaica; and (in November) the enslaved people are freed

- *December*: Ingraham examines the *Ulysses*, impounded by the British navy; he writes to American papers about the "nefarious traffic" of the slave trade and the inhumane conditions on the ship

1840

- *Spring*: Ingraham leaves Jamaica for a tour of the Northern United States to raise support, to recruit more missionaries, and to consult with physicians regarding his health; recuperates at the home of Weld and his family (**Angelina Grimké Weld** and **Sarah Grimké**)
- *Summer*: Ingraham visits New York City, Oneida Institute in Whitesboro, NY, Oberlin, OH, his prior home in Pittsford, NY, and his parents' home in Wayne, MI, among other places
- *Summer*: Emigrees from the *Ulysses* demand better working conditions and are supported by Black Jamaicans
- *October*: Prince is "bent upon going to Jamaica" as "a field of usefulness." Ingraham visits Boston and lectures at Marlboro Chapel; while in Boston, he calls on Prince and recruits her to be a missionary teacher in Jamaica
- *Late fall*: Ingraham and Prince travel to Jamaica on different boats

1841

- *Winter*: Prince teaches school at St. Ann (north shore of Jamaica); dismissed for criticizing loose church discipline regarding members' lax "moral conduct" and lack of conversion experiences
- *Summer*: Prince and Ingraham meet up at the Mico Institute in Kingston. Prince notes that Ingraham has had to give up his missionary post, probably due to poor health
- *Summer*: Ingraham's health deteriorates; he and his family leave Jamaica for the final time to return to the United States. Prince also leaves Jamaica for the United States, in order to raise money for establishing a school for destitute Jamaican girls
- *August*: Ingraham dies of consumption (tuberculosis) at the home of Weld and the Grimké sisters in Belleville, NJ, on the anniversary day of West Indian emancipation; prominent African American pastor Theodore S. Wright is asked to conduct the funeral service

1842

- *April*: After "collecting funds" in the United States, and staying three weeks with Ingraham's relative, Prince returns to Jamaica

- *September*: Prince experiences political and social instability in Jamaica (fomented by White landowners); she concludes that "it was not safe" to remain on the island and therefore "useless to spend my time there"; she leaves Jamaica for a final time to return to the United States

- *October*: In New York City, Prince's "kind friend" Lewis Tappan raises funds to assist Prince after she was swindled by a White ship captain

1844

- **John Mercer Langston** begins his studies at Oberlin

1845

- Betsey Harston Ingraham dies

1850

- Prince publishes first edition of her *Narrative*

- Fugitive Slave Act passed, requiring that escaped freedom seekers be returned even when they are captured in free states

1853

- Prince publishes second, revised edition of her *Narrative*

1857

- **Sarah Ingraham Penfield** and her husband, Thornton Bigelow Penfield, arrive in Jamaica as missionaries to the Oberlin School in St. Andrew, supported by the American Missionary Association

1859

- Prince dies and is buried in Woodlawn cemetery, Everett, MA

1863

- Emancipation Proclamation

1865

- Thirteenth Amendment to the Constitution abolishes slavery in the United States

James Bradley, "Brief Account of an Emancipated Slave Written by Himself, at the Request of the Editor," 1834

DEAR MADAM,—I will try to write a short account of my life, as nearly as I can remember; though it makes me sorrowful to think of my past days; for they have been very dark and full of tears. I always longed and prayed for liberty, and had at times hopes that I should obtain it. I would pray, and try to study out some way to earn money enough to buy myself, by working in the night-time. But then something would happen to disappoint my hopes, and it seemed as though I must live and die a slave, with none to pity me.

I will begin as far back as I can remember. I think I was between two and three years old when the soul-destroyers tore me from my mother's arms, somewhere in Africa, far back from the sea. They carried me a long distance to a ship; all the way I looked back, and cried. The ship was full of men and women loaded with chains; but I was so small, they let me run about on deck.

After many long days, they brought us into Charleston, South Carolina. A slave-holder bought me, and took me up into Pendleton County. I suppose that I staid with him about six months. He sold me to a Mr. Bradley, by whose name I have ever since been called. This man was considered a wonderfully kind master; and it is true that I was treated better than most of the slaves I knew. I never suffered for food, and never was flogged with the whip;

From *The Oasis,* ed. Lydia Maria Child (Boston: Benjamin C. Bacon, 1834), 106-12.

but, oh my soul! I was tormented with kicks and knocks more than I can tell. My master often knocked me down, when I was young. Once, when I was a boy, about nine years old, he struck me so hard that I fell down and lost my senses. I remained thus some time, and when I came to myself, he told he thought he had killed me. At another time he struck me with a curry comb, and sunk the knob into my head. I have said that I had food enough; I wish I could say as much concerning my clothing. But I let that subject alone; because I cannot think of any suitable words to use in telling you.

I used to work very hard. I was always obliged to be in the field by sunrise, and I labored till dark, stopping only at noon long enough to eat dinner. When I was about fifteen years old, I took what was called the cold plague, in consequence of being overworked, and I was sick a long time. My master came to me one day, and hearing me groan with pain, he said, "This fellow will never be of any more use to me—I would as soon knock him in the head, as if he were an opossum." His children sometimes came in, and shook axes and knives at me, as if they were about to knock me on the head. But I have said enough of this. The Lord at length raised me up from the bed of sickness, but I entirely lost the use of one of my ankles. Not long after this, my master moved to Arkansas Territory, and died. Then the family let me out, but after a while my mistress sent for me, to carry on the plantation, saying she could not do without me. My master had kept me ignorant of everything he could. I was never told anything about God, or my own soul. Yet from the time I was fourteen years old, I used to think a great deal about freedom. It was my heart's desire; I could not keep it out of my mind. Many a sleepless night I have spent in tears, because I was a slave. I looked back on all I had suffered—and when I looked ahead, all was dark and hopeless bondage. My heart ached to feel within me the life of liberty. After the death of my master, I began to contrive how I might buy myself. After toiling all day for my mistress, I used to sleep three or four hours, and then get up and work for myself the remainder of the night. I made collars for horses, out of plaited husks. I could weave one in about eight hours; and I generally took time enough from my sleep to make two collars in the course of a week. I sold them for fifty cents each. One summer, I tried to take two or three hours from my sleep every night; but found that I grew weak, and I was obliged to sleep more. With my first money I bought a pig. The next year I earned for myself about thirteen dollars; and the next about thirty. There was a good deal of wild land in the neighborhood, that belonged to Congress. I used to go out with my hoe, and dig up little patches, which I planted with corn, and got up in the night to tend it. My hogs were fattened with this corn, and I used to sell a number every year. Besides this, I used to raise small patches of tobacco, and sell it to buy more corn for my pigs. In this way I worked for five years; at the end of which time, after taking out my losses, I found that I had earned one hundred and sixty dollars. With this money I hired my own time for two years. During this period, I worked almost all the time, night and day. The hope of liberty stung my nerves, and braced up my soul so much, that I could do with very little sleep or rest. I could do a great deal more work than I was ever able to do before. At the end of the two years, I had earned three hundred dollars, besides feeding and clothing myself. I now bought my time for eighteen months longer, and went two hundred and fifty miles west, nearly into Texas, where I could make more money. Here I earned enough to buy myself; which I did in 1833, about one year ago. I paid for myself, including what I gave for my time, about seven hundred dollars.

As soon as I was free, I started for a free State. When I arrived in Cincinnati, I heard of Lane Seminary, about two miles out of the city. I had for years been praying to God that my dark mind might see the light of knowledge. I asked for admission into the Seminary. They pitied me, and granted my request, though I knew nothing of the studies which were required for admission. I am so ignorant, that I suppose it will take me two years to get up with the lowest class in the institution. But in all respects I am treated just as kindly, and as much like a brother by the students, as if my skin were as white, and my education as good as their own. Thanks to the Lord, prejudice against color does not exist in Lane Seminary! If my life is spared, I shall probably spend several years here, and prepare to preach the gospel.

I will now mention a few things, that I could not conveniently bring in, as I was going along with my story.

In the year 1828, I saw some Christians, who talked with me concerning my soul, and the sinfulness of my nature. They told me I must repent, and live to do good. This led me to the cross of Christ;—and then, oh, how I longed to be able to read the Bible! I made out to get an old spelling-book, which I carried in my hat for many months, until I could spell pretty well, and read easy words. When I got up in the night to work, I used to read for a few minutes, if I could manage to get a light. Indeed, every chance I could find, I worked away at my spelling-book. After I had learned to read a little, I wanted very much to learn to write; and I persuaded one of my young masters to teach me. But the second night, my mistress came in, bustled about, scolded her son, and called him out. I overheard her say to him, "You fool! What are you doing? If you teach him to write, he will write himself a pass and run away." That was the end of my instruction in writing; but I persevered, and made marks of all sorts and shapes that I could think of. By turning every way, I was, after a long time, able to write tolerably plain.

I have said a good deal about my desire for freedom. How strange it is that anybody should believe any human being *could* be a slave, and yet be contented! I do not believe there ever was a slave, who did not long for liberty. I know very well that slave-owners take a great deal of pains to make the people in the free states believe that the slaves are happy; but I know, likewise, that I was never acquainted with a slave, however well he was treated, who did not long to be free. There is one thing about this, that people in the free States do not understand. When they ask slaves whether they wish for their liberty, they answer, "No;" and very likely they will go as far as to say they would not leave their masters for the world. But, at the same time, they desire liberty more than anything else, and have, perhaps, all along been laying plans to get free. The truth is, if a slave shows any discontent, he is sure to be treated worse, and worked harder for it; and every slave knows this. This is why they are careful not to show any uneasiness when white men ask them about freedom. When they are alone by themselves, all their talk is about liberty—liberty! It is the great thought and feeling that fills the mind full all the time.

I could say much more; but as your letter requested a "short account" of my life, I am afraid I have written too much already. I will say but a few words more. My heart overflows when I hear what is doing for the poor broken-hearted slave, and free men of color. God will help those who take part with the oppressed. Yes, blessed be His holy name! He will surely do it. Dear Madam, I do hope I shall meet you at the resurrection of the just. God preserve you, and strengthen you in this holy cause, until the walls of

prejudice are broken down, the chains burst in pieces, and men of every color meet at the feet of Jesus, speaking kind words, and looking upon each other in love—willing to live together on earth, as they hope to live in Heaven!
JAMES BRADLEY.
Lane Seminary, June 1834*

---

*A letter from Theodore D. Weld, of the same institution, says: "We have established five day schools among the three thousand colored people of Cincinnati; a Lyceum with tri-weekly lectures; evening schools for teaching adults to read; Sabbath schools and Bible classes. We are also trying to establish a reading-room and library for them. I have never seen such eagerness to acquire knowledge, nor such rapidity of acquisition."

EXCERPTS FROM THE JOURNAL OF DAVID S. INGRAHAM, 1839-1841

Original journal in the Adrian College Archives, Adrian, Michigan

[PAGE 3]

July 14th, 1839 This has been one of my <u>best Sabbaths</u> O how unworthy am I of such blessed privileges. We have once more celebrated the Lord's death till he come[1] + our hearts were made glad by receiving new soldiers into our ranks.[2] <u>Twenty two</u> for the first time (most of them) publickly [*sic*] consecrated themselves to God + his cause. O what a glorious sight. I used to think that God would bless my labors in some degree, but I hardly expected to see such a sight—22 who had a little time since been in the very depths of sin— living in fornication drunkenness + "such like things" now "clothed + in their right minds"[3] + taking the vows of God upon themselves O that we may all be encouraged to walk nearer to God + do more for the salvation of the O.[oppressed] Our church now numbers 62 + most seem to be truly the disciples of Jesus. O for more and more of the Holy Spirit to enlighten, lead, strengthen, + <u>sanctify</u> us all, that we may be holy + without blemish before Christ in love. Our chapel is now getting <u>too small</u> + we hope to take away the partion [partition] + have the whole building in the chapel O for a heart

---

[1]Ingraham is referring to Communion or the Lord's Supper.
[2]Ingraham is referring to new members being received into his church at Cotton Tree (Short-wood), six miles north of Kingston, Jamaica.
[3]Mark 5:15//Luke 8:35.

to praise the Lord who alone has done great things for us. "It is the Lord's doing + marvelous in my eyes."[4]

[PAGE 4]

Aug. 1ˢᵗ [1839] At an early hour we were awoke by the song of "Jubilee" sung by several cheerful souls on their way to the house of prayer: the meeting commenced at daylight + was well attended. Several of the people prayed + really they seemed thankful for their freedom, + seemed much drawn out for their brethren yet in slavery.[5] May God <u>soon</u> hear + answer + the last <u>shackle</u> fall. At 10½ we met to form a Tee total Soc[iety][6] + blessed be God we had a good time. Several spoke who a year since united with the old pledge + all seemed to rejoice in what they had done + ready to take "a new step" we formed a Soc[iety] of nearly 100 members + hope great good will result. Not one as we know who united with the Soc[iety] a year since has violated their word. Bless the Lord for that.

In the PM preaching + collection of £ 12 we resolved also as soon a good chance shall occur to give a collection for those yet in slavery. O that the great + glorious changes which have taken place in this Isle [Jamaica] during the past year may take place in America, Cuba + wherever the sight of the oppressed is heard. O for the freedom of the <u>world</u> For this let me labor   for this let me pray

[PAGE 5]

Aug 5ᵗʰ [1839] This eve we attended the monthly concert [of prayer][7] for the first time + it was a truly good time. I laid the condition of the O[ppressed] + many were astonished + seemed much affected + all wished to <u>do</u> something for those more destitute than ourselves, + we formed a Soc[iety] to send the Gospel to the Isle of St. Lucia where there is not a single Minister of the Gospel. Several seemed ready + willing to go if they could do any

---

[4]Psalm 118:23.
[5]August 1 was the anniversary of universal emancipation in British colonial territories, which occurred on August 1, 1834—though full freedom from uncompensated labor was not enacted in Jamaica until August 1, 1838.
[6]Persons joining a Tee Total Society pledged to abstain from all alcoholic beverages.
[7]Abolitionists frequently held monthly "concerts of prayer"—group prayer meetings on behalf of the cause of antislavery.

good. We are to take a collection every month + as soon as we can send some one to that place.

"Fly abroad thou mighty Gospel
Win + conquer never cease"[8]

[August] 6th [1839] This PM I went down to Town [Kingston] + attended the formation of a Soc[iety] for the "Abolition of slavery + the slave trade throughout the world" + it went off well. When it commenced I feared we should not succeed as many were much opposed but thro' God we did valiantly + came off conquerors. O that the world may feel the influences of this Soc[iety] O that the giant {tread} of Liberty may shake every fabric of slavery till all shall fall to use no more

Capt Charles Stewart[9] attended the meeting. he is truly a holy, prudent, + persevering man. God speed him. He has been in all the W[est] I[ndian] Isles + America.

[PAGE 13]

[September] 16th [1839] I have lately had a meeting for such as wished to unite with the church + several came + a part seemed truly to have given their hearts to God + others seemed to be truly seeking after the Lord + what is quite encouraging nearly all of this class have been in the night school + can read I find it much easier to deal with such than those who cannot read.[10] O I feel to praise God that I see from time to time sinners giving up their hearts to God.

[PAGE 24]

Dec. 25th 1839 At Port Royal for health. As the Slave Brig "Ulysses" has been lately taken by the English Schooner of War Skip Jack + brot [sic] to this Port I have taken a part of the day to examine the Brig + measure the apartments where the slaves were stored + when told that 556 slaves occupied but about 800 square feet + that their rooms were but 2—[feet] 5 in[ches] in the clear it seemed almost impossible.[11] O where are the sympathies of christians for

---

[8]Hymn lyrics by Thomas Kelly
[9]Probably Charles Stuart (1783–1865), a Scottish abolitionist and friend of Theodore Weld who spent time in Jamaica during the 1830s.
[10]Ingraham connects spiritual growth with education and literacy.
[11]For a fuller account of Ingraham's inspection of the *Ulysses*, see Appendix D.

the slave + where are their exersians [*sic*] for their liberation. O it seems as if the church were asleep + Satan has the world following him. I took the rise, slope + the measurement of the 4 apartments where the slaves were confined + the following is a view of the same with the number + class confined in each room.

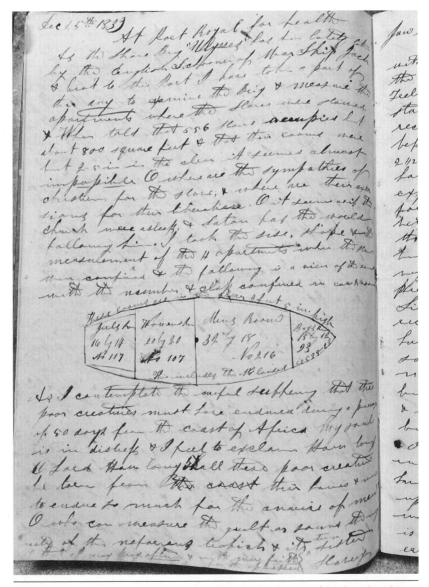

Figure A.1. Page from David Ingraham's journal showing his diagram of the slave ship Ulysses

Notations on sketch:

- *These rooms are in the clear 2 feet 5 in. high*
  - *Girls Room 16 by 14 No 117*
    - *Women's Room 20 y 20 No 107*
      - *Mens Room 32 by 18 No 216*
        - *Boys Room 15 by 12 No 93*
- *This includes the No. landed is 533-23*

As I contemplate the awful suffering that these poor creatures must have endured during a passage of 50 days from the coast of Africa my soul is in disbelief + I feel to exclaim How long O Lord How long[12] shall these poor creatures be torn from ~~their coast~~ their homes + made to endure so much for the avarice of men? O who can measure the guilt or sound the iniquity of this nefarious trafick [*sic*] + its twin sister slavery O that I may pray <u>often</u> + with more <u>faith</u> for the oppressed

[PAGE 30]

Eve [February] 14th [1840] Our A'n [American] Brethren [Julius] Beardslee,[13] [Amos] Dresser,[14] [Ralph] Tyler,[15] + [C. Stewart] Renshaw[16] met at our house + had a meeting for our mutual improvement. it was a precious season. Nearly all seemed to be discouraged about my health. But not thus with me.

[PAGE 31]

[Feb] 20th [1840] In looking back upon my past life it seems to have been one of toil, care responsibility + hurry—+ I feel that I need a little time for calm + sober reflection + to wash the feet of that blessed Savior[17] whose goodness has been so great to me + whose love has been so boundless. Surely

---

[12] Allusion to Psalm 94:3.
[13] Julius O. Beardslee (1814–1879).
[14] Amos Dresser (1812–1904), who attended the Oneida Institute, Lane Seminary (one of the Lane Rebels), and was graduated from the seminary at Oberlin in 1839.
[15] Ralph Tyler (1808–1885), who studied in the seminary at Oberlin, 1837–1838.
[16] Charles Stewart Renshaw (1811–1860) was one of the Lane Rebels who then studied at Oberlin, 1834–1836 and was graduated from the seminary in 1838.
[17] Allusion to Luke 7.

+ truly I can say "Thus far the <u>Lord</u> hath led me on"[18] I had a wearisome night (last) but enjoyed something of God's pleasure. The Savior seemed near.

[PAGE 34]

March 7th 1840 It is now more than a week since I left home + came to Kingston to consult Doct[or] Furguson[19] as to the propriety of a sea voyage for my health. He was quite surprised at my state + my pulse being then over 100. + my health in all respects much worse than when I last saw him. He advised me to stop in the city [Kingston] so that he could see me often + try to get me clear of this fever, which was in consequence of the inflammation of the air tubes +c leading to the lungs. I at once stopped at the Wooldridges[20] where I have been since that time Mrs. I[ngraham] came down the morning after I did + we have our home here for the present. I was never so sick before or so much reduced. This morn. I went out of doors for the first time in more than a week. I am still very weak tho' I have great reason to bless God that I am still in the land of the living. Many of my friends have considered my work done + that I should never recover, but O the mercy of God in rebuking my disease. During my sickness my mind has been in great peace + I have felt most of the time to cast all my care on Jesus. O how sweet to feel <u>perfectly</u> submissive to all God <u>says</u> or <u>does</u>. I am advised to take a voyage to A'[merica] in a few weeks + O that it may result in the glory of God. if it

[PAGE 35]

be his will that I go. I love my <u>work</u> more than I love friends—kindred or country. + had I the ability I should prefer to remain to labor for my Master, but as I now am + have been for nearly a month I am little or no service here + I do hope + pray + it is the opinion of my physician that a tour to A[merica] of a few months will enable me to go on with my work. The Lord knoweth in in [sic] his hands I leave <u>all</u>. My dear church feel a deep interest for me + are incessant in prayer for my recovery. Before I came here they brought loads of <u>herbs</u> +c to cure my cough + since I came down here they still come +

---

[18]Hymn lyrics by Isaac Watts.
[19]Probably John Ferguson (d. 1857), a Scottish doctor (MD, Edinburgh, 1815) who lived in Kingston, Jamaica, and served as President of the College of Physicians and Surgeons, Jamaica, and of the Board of Health.
[20]Husband was John Wooldrige (d. 1840), who worked for London Missionary Society in Jamaica, 1834–1840.

bring fowls, eggs, +c +c 7 have {been} to-day + most brot [sic] a presant [sic] + *all* seemed to feel the greatest anxiety for my recovery some wept while they spoke of this desire that I should recover + once more tell them the good word poor people I now leave them in the hands of a merciful shepherd who never slumbers or sleeps. May God build them up + lead them on to holiness + heaven. I must leave them at least for the present. + since I was taken sick there has been a meeting of the Miss.[ionaries] + Bro Wooldridge is to be [. . .] to [. . .] + Bro Howell[21] is to occupy my place for the present

[PAGE 36]

[March] 11th [1840] By the blessing of God I am a little on the gain as to health. I have had a severe temptation to-day in regard to the state of my worldly affairs + as to my future hope of returning to my dear people. At "Cotton Tree" I thot I had cast all my care on Jesus but alas! Satan would have me take it back again, but I hope I see + feel that He alone can bare [sic] my burden. As I let my mind run upon my cares, the Lord let me feel their weight + my pulse increased to full 100 per minute I at first thot it a return of fever but perspiration soon showed me that it was not that + when I saw what it was I felt guilty + ashamed that I should doubt the word of God—"He calleth for you"[22] "All things shall work together +c"[23] O when will my dull heart learn to rest in God + leave all my trouble with him. O for entire submission + perfect love + confidence in God.

Several of the dear people from Cotn [Cotton Tree] have been down to-day + manifest the strongest love + attachment towards me + seem to be earnest in prayer that I should recover to tell them the "good word" + lead them on to God + heaven

[PAGE 38]

March 25th [1840] I have great reason to thank God for the health that I this day enjoy. Have not felt so well for several weeks + while I adore the goodness of God in thus far restoring my health—I would not forget that I know not what a day may bring forth"[24] O that I may live at the feet of Jesus + ever have

---

[21]James Howell (1810–1881) worked for the London Missionary Society in Jamaica, 1836–1840.
[22]1 Thessalonians 5:24.
[23]Romans 8:28.
[24]Proverbs 27:1.

my lamp trimmed + burning.[25] I have been looking over the state of the church at "Cotton Tree" + reviewing what has been done there since I commenced my labors there. I feel to praise God for what has been done but regret that I have had no more faith in God + consequently have seen no more of his salvation.

The church numbers	73	Day school	75
Class of Inquirers	96	Sab[bath] [school]	80
No. in Tem[perance] Society	85		
Tee total [society]	96		
Marriages [at Cotton Tree] + at Out station	59		
Adults baptized	22		
Children [baptized]	19		
Candidates for Com'n [Communion]	10		

I know not that I shall ever be able to go there again at least to say anything to them + my prayer to God for them is that they may run well + adorn the doctrine of God in all things. O that Christ may be formed in them + in me fully the hope of Glory.[26]

[PAGE 41]

[April] 15th [1840] Last Sab.[bath] I was able to go to Cotton Tree + attend service there during the day. In the PM I spoke to the dear people[27] for a short time + I do trust some good was done. They all seemed to sympathise with me + were deeply affected that I was about to leave them. I suffered in my health considerably for the effort but hope I did not sin. As I have engaged my passage for America I met the dear people on Mon. night to bid them farewell for the present + to receive a token of their regard for me to assist in paying my passage. The meeting was full + full of interest. There was much {feeling} among the people + all seemed anxious for my recovery + speedy return. Some wept aloud at parting at the close of the meeting they gave me about £ 15. + voted me £ 8. 9 we have in a Miss[ionary] Sox [Society] making in all about 70 or 75 dollars. They also brot [sic] me fruit, presents, cakes +c +c for my journey + expressed the strongest desire for my welfare. My business is now all settled + I am about

---

[25]Matthew 25; Luke 12:35.
[26]Allusion to Colossians 1:27.
[27]"Dear people": the Jamaican congregants of Ingraham's church at Cotton Tree.

ready to sail. I feel at the thought of leaving my dear wife + child for so long a time but as this seemed duty I hope we shall be able to do so cheerfully. I feel to bless God that we are all in so good health at the time of parting Mrs I.[ngraham] goes to Bro [Julius] Beardslee's to reside while I am absent + I do hope + trust that she will be protected from sickness + her soul dwell in perfect peace. She expects to be confined during my absence. The Lord protect her + us all.

[PAGE 44]

May 21 [1840] New York [City] at Mrs Nicholsons[28]

Since I came to this city I have been permitted to see several of my old friends + associates + all seem to sympathise with me in the loss of my health. I have seen Bro A Smith,[29] May O. G. Smith[30] S. Wells,[31] + Southard,[32] AM Miller, Jn J. Judd,[33] Fayer

[PAGE 45]

J Lewis,[34] + Bro Frasier These dear brethren I never expected to see when I left America but God has once more brot [*sic*] us together + I hope not in vain. O for more entire consecration that my entire influence might be for God. O that I might breathe nothing but love.

I find that my account of the slave ship has been very extensively circulated by many different papers[35] + I hope it may do much good as now I am unable to preach or talk much.

I think much about the dear bond of love[36] in Jamaica + long as soon as God is willing to return. My dear wife + child are ever before me, but I feel

---

[28]Asenath Nicholson operated a boarding house in New York City that served vegetarian meals based on the recommendations of the dietary reformer and temperance advocate, Sylvester Graham—the inventor of the graham cracker. Oberlin Collegiate Institute also served meals inspired by Graham.

[29]Possibly Alfred Smith, who was enrolled in Oberlin 1834–1835 and was from New York City.

[30]Possibly Gerrit Smith.

[31]Possibly the Samuel Wells who signed the "Defense of the Students" at Lane Seminary, 1834–1835.

[32]Probably Nathaniel Southard, editor of the *American Anti-slavery Almanac*.

[33]Possibly Russell J. Judd, who also signed the "Defense of the Students" at Lane.

[34]Possibly John S. Lewis, who enrolled at Oberlin 1835–1838 and at the seminary 1839–1843, earning a seminary degree in 1843.

[35]*Niles Weekly Register; The Colored American*, etc.

[36]The "bond of love" may be an allusion to a popular 1830s camp meeting hymn written by John Blair: "My dearest friends in bonds of love, whose hearts the sweetest union prove. How sweet

no anxiety about them for I feel confident that God will provide + take care of them. O that my dear companion may grow in grace + daily experience more + more of the fullness of the blessed Savior. I hope that the Lord has yet some work for me to do in Jam.[aica] + will give me health to do it. His will be done, + not mine. I want no will but His I have reason to thank God that I am so very comfortably situated + have so good care taken of me, It seems if the Lord ever goes before me + provides friends + all that I need + O how cruel + wicked to distrust or sin against such love + kindness. <u>Lord help me</u>.

[PAGE 46]

Sab.[bath] 23rd of May [1840] By the mercy of God I am still alive, during the past week I have recovered much, yesterday I felt better than I have for 6 months past, but this morn. I felt rather unwell + took a little medicine, which acted very powerfully as an emetic—owing to this + the damp state of the weather I have not been out to-day. But have had some joy in reading + meditating on the word of God, Have also read one of Prof Finneys lectures on Sanctification.[37] I see the subject plainer + plainer + see that nothing, but unbelief hinders me from the enjoyment of this great + glorious privilege. O this cruel unbelief, may God give me the victory over this + every sin.

I have had the privilege of seeing dear Bro Harman Kingsbury,[38] who was one of the first to give me some means + encouragement in [sic] for my mission to Jamaica. He is still full of love + rejoises [sic] in what God has done thro' me for the poor in Jam.[aica]

O that God would carry forward his work there + help the efforts of all the dear bond of love there. O that there might be a great revival among the missionaries there, + salvation like a wave roll over the whole Isle. I think much + try to pray for my dear <u>family</u> + church—will God keep them in <u>perfect peace</u> + <u>safety</u> + bring us together once more to rejoice in the goodness + mercy of our Redeemer.

---

the hours have passed away, where we have met to sing and pray." See also Ingraham's references to the dear "bond of love" on pages 46 and 77.

[37]Charles Finney published a nine-part lecture series on the topic of sanctification in multiple issues of *The Oberlin Evangelist* from January through April 1840.

[38]Harmon Kingsbury (1793–1868), a large land owner and benefactor in northern Ohio who endowed a biblical and law professorship at Oberlin under the direction of Henry Cowles.

[PAGE 50]

Bell[e]ville [N.J.] June 19th [1840] I have at last the joy of hearing from my dear family + the dear brethren in Jam.[aica] Several letters + papers have just arrived which were started about 3 weeks after I left. I rejoice that all were well + prosperous at that date. I had felt much concern for my dear wife as I left her in a delicate condition[39] + the Lord has finally relieved me for the present. O that God would still be with them, + temper the wind to the shorn lamb.[40]

My letter on the effects of freedom in the W[est] Indies has just been finished + it thought it will do much good The Lord grant that it may. I feel to rejoice if I can serve the cause of my master in any way, tho' I am not able to preach or talk much. I have also been writing a little for the AS [Anti-slavery] Almanack which Bro Weld is compiling.[41] I rejoice to hear of several cases of recent emancipation The leven [*sic*] is at work + God grant it may go on till the whole lump is levened [*sic*].[42] Salvrey [*sic*] <u>must</u> fall + may the time soon come. "The Lord executeth judgment for all that are oppressed"[43] + blessed be his name. O that the oppressor may see + repent ere it be too late.

[PAGE 58]

Wayne Michigan. Home[44] July 27th 1840 I left my friends in Ohio on the 24th + arrived in safety at Detroit on the 25th but about 2 hours too late to get a conveyance home, it being Sat. I of course concluded to remain till Mon, tho' I should have been glad to have seen my dear parents from whom I have been separated 3 years. I called on Bro Bingham + spent the Sab[bath] very pleasantly + this morn I left at 6 o clock with a prayerful heart for home. During my passage up the lake [Erie] I was much affected by reading the feelings + dealings of God with his ancient people, when they had time + again gone away from God + were sorely oppressed in consequence— they cried to God + often at {first} refusing to hear them, when He saw them put away their idols + sins—His feelings are beautifully + {meltingly} expressed in the following language "His soul was <u>grieved</u> for the <u>misery</u>

---

[39]"Delicate condition" is most likely a reference to pregnancy.
[40]Quote from Laurence Sterne.
[41]Ingraham is probably referring to *The American Anti-slavery Almanac for 1840* (New York: American Anti-slavery Society, 1840).
[42]Galatians 5:9.
[43]Psalm 103:6.
[44]At that time, Ingraham's parents lived in Wayne, MI.

of Israel."[45] O what compassion!! O what love¡¡ I can't express what I feel as I look at this trait of His character. I can only weep wonder + admire. O what God is the Christian God¡¡ God forbid that I should ever offend such a being. O Bind me to the cross by love.[46]

[PAGE 65]

Sept [1840] Wednesday at Oberlin O. I have been prospered thus far + am in comfortable health tho' the weather is quite damp. This afternoon I heard several very interesting addresses from the graduating class[47]—they seem to breathe the spirit of heaven. Several are to be ordained + they seem indeed prepared to preach the Gospel from experience O that Ministers every where may be baptized with the spirit of their master + speak what they do know. O for more + more of this spirit to rest on me.

Saturday, at Elyria [Ohio]

This morn. I met my old friends in O[berlin] who took so much interest in us at the time we went out + gave them a short statement of what God had done in Jam.[aica] + the season seemed precious They seemed to rejoice that their + our labor had not been in vain in the Lord.[48] + to be encouraged + to continue their efforts. They had just assisted Bro Everts[49] + I did not ask or expect anything but their hearts were too full of sympathy to do nothing + they gave me in all about $25. All seemed full of sympathy for us in our low state of health I am rather discouraged about further attempts to speak as I have raised blood during the day + feel my throte [*sic*] very sore.

[PAGE 77]

New York [City] Oct 13th [18]40 I feel that all that I have or am or ever hope to be is in dedication to my Precious Master + his cause. I feel that I have no interests of my own to seek—all these I have left with Christ + O for grace so to trust in him as never again to have or appear to have a selfish feeling. I feel that the best offering I can make as a poor + miserable one but I feel

---

[45]Judges 10:16.
[46]It's possible that Ingraham is echoing a Charles Wesley hymn: "To the cross, thine altar, bind me with the chords of love."
[47]"Graduating class": from Oberlin Collegiate Institute.
[48]Allusion to 1 Corinthians 15:58.
[49]Probably William A. Evarts (d. 1853), who graduated from Oberlin in 1838 and from the seminary in 1841, and served in Jamaica as a missionary.

as if I wanted to go back to Ja[maica] + before all the dear "bond of love" to lay myself on the alter [*sic*] of that Mission + do all that I can for it + in whatever way I can, O I feel that it is a high + glorious + blessed privilege to "hew wood + draw water"[50] or anything even to "tarry by the stuff"[51] + pray for my brethren while they fight the Lords battles. O for more + more of the spirit of consecration till my whole being is lost in God + his cause.

I have just heard an indirect word from the dear brethren of Ja[maica] + my dear dear family: all are well Bless the Lord for this word of quietude + encouragement + Blessed be God that some are longing for a perfect knowledge + love of Christ + his Gospel in Ja[maica]—I am requested to bring a large no. of Oberlin Ꝋ Papers[52] + books[53] wherein these doctrines[54] are taught O has not God great things in store for Ja[maica] blessed be his name for the distant view. "The work O Lord is thine"

[PAGE 78]

Oct 14th [1840] Eve At half past 12 oclock all were on board + we shoved off to encounter the dangers of the deep. The weather was very pleasant + warm for this season of the year + as we have a fine breeze (to begin with) fine weather, a fine vessel an experienced captain + above all a kind, watchful + all powerful Creator to watch over us + protect us we hope for a good time. The crew are all colored or black + from what I have seen are first rate fellows. We have 18 passengers about ½ Americans + ½ English or Jamaicans. The former are all total abstinence men + women + I believe all professors of religion, while the latter are all "wine bibbers" + lovers of pleasure + I fear are taking their "good things in this life, but they are miserable "good things" + O how great their loss May the Lord be in our midst + enable us to set such an example as will cause all to take knowledge of us that we have been with Jesus[55]

Farewell America—You've many things to love + many things to hate, + while I would rejoice in all that's good + praise God as the Author I would mourn that there are so many + great sins about that God must ere long pour out his fury unless they repent + reform.

---

[50]Joshua 9:21.
[51]1 Samuel 30:24.
[52]Ingraham is referring to copies of *The Oberlin Evangelist*.
[53]Ingraham may be referring to Charles Finney's *Lectures to Professing Christians* (1837) and Asa Mahan's *Scripture Doctrine of Christian Perfection* (1839).
[54]"These doctrines": Christian holiness, entire sanctification, perfection in love.
[55]Allusion to Acts 4:13.

[PAGE 79]

Oct 22nd 1840. 8 days at sea in sight of St. Domingo + Cuba Thus far we have on the whole had a pleasant + prosperous passage for which the Lord be praised. I am sorry + feel greatly pained to say that the poor sailors—sons [of] Africa have been severely treated 3 of them have been severely beaten with large ropes for what I should call a very small offence—if offence at all. My heart yearned for them, + I felt to my very soul every stroke laid upon them or rough word spoken to them. They seem to suffer because they are black rather than for any other reason O when will men learn that God is on the side of the poor friendless, + oppressed—All will learn it at the judgment if not before O that men would learn + repent while it is called to-day When I shall cease to be a passenger here I shall feel at liberty to open my mouth for the dumb now the laws are such[56] +c that I do not feel it my duty to "interfere" directly. God give me grace to do my whole duty in this + all other subjects. My health is as good as could possibly be expected

[PAGE 94]

Kingston [Jamaica] Dec—[18]40. My dear church were much overjoyed to see me + received me as life from the dead but sorrow seemed to fill their hearts when I told them I could not preach to them any more at present. May the Lord provide for them a Pastor after His own heart I have lately been much encouraged to find such a sense of gratitude + affection among them for us. They heard of our poverty + almost went + at once expressed the strongest sympathy + requested to have us come + live near them + all would unite + see that we wanted for nothing + as I determined to go to Chapelton they offered to higher [sic] a house for Mrs I.[ngraham] + pay all her expenses + this without the least invitation on my part. O I feel to bless God for the unceasing evidence I have that they are dissiples [sic] indeed + that He in mercy seems to perpetuate the work He did by poor unworthy me. O may that be a true light in the D.[arkness] + some laughed—some wept some prayed—some kissed my hand + some embraced me ~~with a a~~ in their arms. + all seemed to bless God for my return

---

[56]Ingraham may be referring to the so-called Law of the Sea, under which national laws did not apply on ships, and only the ship's captain had jurisdiction.

[PAGE 95]

For the first time since I left the Isle [Jamaica] I have had the privilege to-day of sitting at the table of my Master to commemorate his dying love[57] + O may it be a permanent blessing to me. I need the assistance of all grace + every help that Christ has left for his Church to keep me in his Son + from being buried in the world. "Let thy grace Lord like a <u>fetter</u>
Bind my wandering heart to thee[58]

[PAGE 101]

March 14th [1841] Sabbath. This is a pleasant day for many reasons 1st It is the resurrection day of the Blessed Savior, which is a warrant that all true believers shall rise + live with him. Because I live ye shall live also.[59] + 2 Because it is the time when the christian world assemble to honor Christ. + revive their spiritual strength + gain new converts to their Master + 3 Because it is a day of rest to the Body + mind from the labors + cares of life which mankind so much need.—these with many other reasons make every Sab[bath] pleasant, but to day the atmosphere is clear, the climate delightful—the sun glorious riding in his strength + added to this my bodily health is better than it has been for some time past, + I do hope I feel some of the "Spirit" my health for a month past has been [v]ery poor indeed + my future prospects rather dark + I need much grace to keep my mind <u>stayed on God</u>. I have felt of late that it would be our duty to return to A[merica] this spring as we are doing no good here or <u>very little</u> + as there is no prospect of my recovery at present so as to teach or preach, + in fact my recovery seems almost impossible in my present situation of care + responsibility, + in my precarious state I feel it duty to place if possible my family among

[PAGE 102]

their kindred + friends so that in case I leave them they will not be alone or friendless. Several things of late seem to favor this movement + I hope + pray that the Lord will direct in the whole + direct for His glory

---

[57]Ingraham was referring to Communion or the Lord's Supper.
[58]Lines from the hymn "Come Thou Fount of Every Blessing," lyrics by Robert Robinson.
[59]John 14:19.

DAVID INGRAHAM, "CAPTURE OF THE ULYSSES—SUFFERINGS OF THE SLAVES," 1840

From the Youth's Cabinet
CAPTURE OF THE ULYSSES—SUFFERINGS OF THE SLAVES
Kingston, Jamaica
January 15, 1840
DEAR BROTHER SOUTHARD,—A Slaver having been taken near this Isle, and brought into the port, I have thought that some account of it might be interesting, instructive and useful to the dear children and youth who read the Cabinet; and should you think the facts worthy a place in your paper, they are at your disposal. I have taken some pains to ascertain the facts in the case, by visiting both the man of war and the slaver two or three times each.

The name of the slaver was "*Ulysses*"—a Portuguese brig, but said to have been built in America. She was taken by the British schooner of war Skipjack. Mr. Evans, a marine of the Skipjack, gave me the following account of the capture.

On the 30th of November, 1839, soon after daylight, the man at the mast-head discovered a vessel at some distance behind us, not having a sail up—thus thinking to hide from us. We at once gave her chase, and she as soon made sail, and fled from us. During the morning we gained but little on her, but in the afternoon the breeze increased, and we gained on her fast. At this time we could

Printed on page 2 of *The Colored American* (April 4, 1840). Charles B. Ray, Editor & Proprietor (New York: New Series Vol. 1, No. 5).

see them busily engaged in throwing overboard their arms, shackles, &c. We were now in sight of the Isle of Pine,[1] and as she saw we came up to her so fast, she made for land under Spanish colors, *pretending* to want a pilot. She ran aground about one-eighth of a mile from land under full sail, and immediately two captains, under which she sailed and two others who had been captains of slavers, and had been taken, took to the boat, and went ashore with $8000 in cash. We fired our big gun at them, which so frightened the slaves, (who had just been let out of their confinement) that great numbers leaped into the sea, and fifteen were either drowned or swam ashore, and were taken away by the Spaniards.

When we boarded the slaver, her deck and rooms where the slaves had been confined, were nearly ankle deep in filth, and so dreadful was the smell, that it could scarcely be endured for a moment. But the poor slaves seemed to forget this, and all their past sufferings—for all appeared to know that they were now *free.* Joy beamed in every countenance. They laughed—they wept—they leaped in ecstasy, and filled the air with acclamations, and, prostrating themselves, they even *kissed our feet,* to show their love and gratitude for having been rescued from the cruel oppressor, and from the wailings of hopeless bondage.

We made prisoners of the crew, 16 in number, and 16 others calling themselves passengers. Fourteen of these had been captains of slavers, and had been taken. We soon put things to rights so as to make the captives as comfortable as possible, and sailed for Jamaica, the land of the free.

From the Captain, Mr.——, the mate, Mr. R. Lurridge, and other officers of the Skipjack, I have been kindly furnished with some additional facts. The Ulysses was on her 8th voyage, and has often been chased by men-of-war, and once by a steamer, but has ever, till now, escaped. She took her cargo of 556 slaves from the river Nuna,[2] from Popo,[3] Sargos, Whydar, and Bodgerry. From the time they left Africa, till the slaves were landed in Montego Bay, Jamaica, it was just 50 days, during which time, but 8 died, besides the 15 lost at the time of the capture. The allowance of the slaves was a pint of ferenny, (a sample of which I send you) and a pint of water per day, with an occasional morsel of pork or beef. They were not allowed on deck at all, except to eat their allowance,

---

[1]Pine, or Pinos—an Island of the South side of Cuba, 25 miles long and 15 broad, mountainous and covered with pines. *[This footnote, and all subsequent footnotes, are original to the 1840 article by Ingraham.]*

[2]Nuna, or Nunez, a river in West Africa, 10 deg. N. Lat.

[3]Popo—a part of the slave coast about 6 deg. N. Lat. The inhabitants have scarcely any houses, except the king's village, which is on an island in a river.

and then but a small number at once. The slaves had no clothing whatever, except a *few* men who were made "overseers" over the rest, each of whom was furnished with a "cat," and flogged those who did not please the Spaniards. When the slaver was boarded, the slaves reached down her sides as far as possible, to help the men up; and, as the captain remarked, they could scarcely work the ship, so many were clinging around their legs; and, as the mate said, nothing could exceed the joy of the slaves when we took possession.

One of the first inquiries, after reading the above account, would be, *where* did they stow away such an immense number as 556 slaves, besides the crew, &c. numbering 36! *Especially* would this inquiry be made, it is generally known that slavers are, for the most part, quite *small* vessels. I went on board the slaver two or three times, and took the dimensions of her as accurately as I could, and also a drawing of the rooms where the slaves were confined, which I will now give.

The height of these rooms, including the beams on which the deck rests, is 2 feet 10 inches. The beams are very near each other, and 5 inches thick, so that except a little space between the beams, they had 2 feet 6 inches as the height of their dismal den, where they were literally wedged together, during a voyage of fifty days. Then let us consider the suffocation they must have endured from the little air they could get, and their consequent burning thirst, and small allowance of water; and who can but weep at the thought! And who can *think* of this and not *see* and *feel* through all his soul, the abomination and horror of that *foul* system which is commenced and generally continued at such an expense of human woe and cruelty?

Also, let us think of the awful suffering occasioned in enslaving so many; the fathers robbed of their wives and children—children torn from the embrace of their mothers, and every relation and feeling dear to the human heart, severed and mangled—who that has a heart to pray, can refrain from exclaiming, "How long, O Lord, how long" shall this nefarious traffic continue? And what Christian can cease to pray that every slaver may fall into the hands of the British cruisers, and that slavery, that *curse of curses*, may soon come to an end?

My God! I feel the mournful scene–
My bowels yearn for Africa's slain,
And *fain* my pity would regain,
And snatch the captive from the chain.

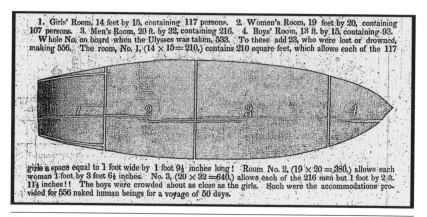

Figure A.2. Diagram of the slave ship *Ulysses*

I have still many things to say, but must stop for want of room. My prayer is that the facts I have stated, may make a deep and lasting impression upon all who may read them, and that many youthful hearts will thus be engaged to pray, and many hands be opened for the relief of the oppressed. Children and youth, as well as others, ought to *"remember those in bonds, as BOUND with them."* Though a stranger to most who may read this, I would ask the dear youth, as they enjoy so bountifully the comforts of life, to often think of the *scanty allowance* of the 93 boys and 117 girls, who were crammed into the small rooms in the ends of the Ulysses; and when they *think,* may they *feel;* and when they *feel,* may they *act;* and when they *act,* may God's blessing attend their efforts; and may the time soon come, when *slavery,* and all its attendant evils, shall curse our world no more.

I remain yours in labor for the oppressed,

D. S. INGRAHAM

P.S. I am sorry to tell you that my health has failed very much for some months past, in consequence of a severe cold on my lungs. I have not preached in more than a month, and probably shall not for some time to come. My physician says I must go to America as soon as April, but I hope I shall not have to leave my work for so long a time; but I can say, *"Thy will be done."*

EXCERPTS FROM *THE NARRATIVE OF NANCY PRINCE*, 1853

AFTER PRINCE'S STEPFATHER DIED, "my mother was again left a widow, with an infant six weeks old, and seven other children. When she heard of her husband's death, she exclaimed, 'I thought it; what shall I do with these children?' She was young, inexperienced, with no hope in God, and without the knowledge of her Saviour. Her grief, poverty, and responsibilities, were too much for her; she never again was the mother that she had been before." (7-8)

As a child, "I . . . thought myself fortunate to be with religious people, as I had enjoyed the happy privilege of religious instruction. My dear grandfather was a member of a Congregational Church, and a good man; he always attended meeting in the morning, and took his children with him. In the afternoon he took care of the smaller children, while my mother attended with her little group. He thought it was wrong for us to go to school where the teacher was not devoted to God. Thus I early knew the difference between right and wrong." (10-11)

As a teenager, "Hard labor and unkindness was too much for me; in three months [of employment], my health and strength were gone. I often looked at my [White] employers, and thought to myself, is this your religion? . . . They had family prayers, morning and evening. Oh! yes, they were sanctimonious! I was a poor stranger, but fourteen years of age, imposed upon by these good people; but I must leave them." (11-12)

"I was young and inexperienced, but God knew that my object was good. 'In wisdom he chooses the weak things of the earth.' Without his aid, how could I ever have rescued my lost sister [from a brothel]?" (13)

Second Edition: Boston, 1853, published by the author

"My brother George and myself were very desirous to make our mother comfortable: he went to sea for that purpose; the next April, I came to Boston to get a higher price for my labor; for we had agreed to support my mother, and hoped she would take home our little brother and take care of him, who was supported by the town." (16)

"I thought it a needy time, for I had not yielded my heart to the will of God, though I had many impressions, and formed many resolutions; but the situations that I had been placed in, (having left my mother's house at the age of eight,) had not permitted me to do as I wished, although the kind counsels of my dear grandfather and pious teachers followed me wherever I went. Care after care oppressed me—my mother wandered about like a Jew—the young children who were in families were dissatisfied; all hope but in God was lost. I resolved, in my mind, to seek an interest in my Savior, and put my trust in Him; and never shall I forget the place or time when God spake to my troubled conscience. Justified by faith I found peace with God, the forgiveness of sin through Jesus Christ my Lord. After living sixteen years without hope, and without a guide, May 6th, 1819, the Rev. Thomas Paul, baptized myself and seven others in obedience to the great command.

> We, on him our anchor cast—
> Poor and needy, lean on him,
> He will bring us through at last." (17)

"I could not see my mother suffer, therefore I left my place and went to Salem to watch over her and Samuel, and lived in the Rev. Dr. Bolle's family. In the Spring, I returned to Boston, and took my brother Samuel with me; soon after, my sister Lucy left her place and went to her mother, but was not permitted to stay; my mother wrote to me, requesting me to take care of her. I then determined, in my mind, to bring her to Boston, and if possible, procure a place for her; I then had Samuel and John on my hands; Lucy was not nine, and very small of her age, I could not easily get her a place, but fortunately obtained board for her and Samuel for one dollar a week. My brother John, whom I had boarded, at last got a place where he had wages. Soon the Lord opened the way for little Samuel; Dr. Phelps took him to bring up: so that I was left with one only to sustain; soon my hopes were blasted. John left his place, and was several months on my hands again." (19)

"My sister Silvia, was one of my greatest trials. Knowing she was in Boston, my mother, in one of her spells of insanity, got away from her home and travelled to Boston after her; she came where I lived, my employers were very kind to her, she tarried a few days, when I hired a horse and chaise and took them both back to Salem, and returned to my place in 1822, with a determination to do something for myself; I left my place after three months, and went to learn a trade; and after seven years of anxiety and toil, I made up my mind to leave my country. September 1st, 1823, Mr. Prince arrived from Russia. February 15th, 1824, we were married. April 14th, we embarked on board the Romulus, captain Epes Sargent commander, bound for Russia." (20-21)

In the Russian court, "They presented me with a watch, &c. It was customary in those days, when any one married, belonging to the court, to present them with gifts, according to their standard; there was no prejudice against color; there were there all casts, and the people of all nations, each in their place." (23)

"I am indebted to God for his great goodness is guiding my youthful steps; my mind was directed to my fellow brethren whose circumstances were similar to my own. [After returning from nine years in Russia and the death of her husband,] I found many a poor little orphan destitute and afflicted [in Boston], and on account of color shut out from all the asylums for poor children. At this my heart was moved, and I proposed to my friends the necessity of a home for such, where they might be sheltered from the contaminating evils that beset their path. For this purpose I called a meeting of the people and laid before them my plan: as I had had the privilege of assisting in forming an Asylum for such a purpose in St. Petersburg, I thought it would be well to establish one on the same principles, not knowing that any person had had a thought of anything of the kind. We commenced with eight children." (41-42)

"I made my home at the Rev. J.[onas] W. Holman's, a Free Will Baptist, until I sailed for Jamaica." (42) [Prince lived with the Holman family for seven years. Freewill Baptists were theologically similar to, and had close connections with, Oberlin.]

"Possibly I may not see so clearly as some, for the weight of prejudice has again oppressed me, and were it not for the promises of God, one's heart would fail, for *He* made man in his own image, in the image of God, created he him, male and female, that they should have dominion over the fish of the sea, the fowl of the air, and the beast of the field, &c. This power did God give man, that thus far should he go and no farther; but man has disobeyed his Maker, and become vain in his imagination, and their foolish hearts are darkened. We gather from this, that God has in all ages of the world punished every nation and people for their sins. The sins of my beloved country are not hid from his notice." (42-43)

"My mind, after the emancipation in the West Indies [1838], was bent upon going to Jamaica. A field of usefulness seemed spread out before me. While I was thinking about it, the Rev. Mr. Ingraham, who had spent seven [actually, three] years there, arrived [October 1840] in the city [Boston]. He lectured in the city at the Marlboro Chapel, on the results arising from the emancipation at the British Islands. He knew much about them, he had a station at a mountain near Kingston, and was very desirous to have persons go there to labor. He wished some one to go with him to his station. He called on me with the Rev. Mr. William Collier, to persuade me to go. I told him it was my intention to go if I could make myself useful, but that I was sensible that I was very limited in education. He told me that the moral condition of the people was very bad, and needed labor aside from any thing else. I left America, November 16th, 1840." (43-44)

"I will mention my object in visiting Jamaica. I hoped that I might aid, in some small degree, to raise up and encourage the emancipated inhabitants, and teach the young children to read and work, to fear God, and put their trust in the Savior." (45)

"As I lodged in the house of one of the [Jamaican Baptist] class-leaders I attended her class a few times, and when I learned the method, I stopped . . . I spoke to her of the necessity of being born of the spirit of God before we become members of the church of Christ, and told her I was sorry to see the people blinded in such a way. She was very angry with me and soon accomplished her end by complaining of me to the minister; and I soon found I was to be dismissed, unless I would yield to this class-leader. I told the minister that I did not come there to be guided by a poor foolish woman. He then told me that I had spoken something about the necessity of moral conduct in church members. I told him I had, and in my opinion, I was sorry to see it so much neglected. He replied, that he hoped I would not express myself so except to him; they have the gospel, he continued, and let them into the church. I [the minister] do not approve of women's societies; they destroy the world's [antislavery] convention; the American women have too many of them." (46-47)

"On May the 18ᵗʰ [1841], I attended the [English] Baptist Missionary meeting. . . . There was but one colored minister on the platform. It is generally the policy of these [White English] missionaries to have the sanction of colored ministers, to all their assessments and taxes. The colored people give more readily, and are less suspicious of imposition, if one from themselves recommends the measure; this the missionaries understand very well, and know how to take advantage of it." (48-49)

"[Jamaicans] are not the stupid set of beings they have been called; here [in Jamaica] *surely we see industry*; they are enterprising and quick in their perceptions, determined to possess themselves, and to possess property besides, and quite able to take care of themselves. They wished to know why I was so inquisitive about them. I told them we had heard in America that you are lazy, and that emancipation has been of no benefit to you; I wish to inform myself of the truth respecting you, and give a true account on my return. Am I right? More than two hundred people were around me listening to what I said. They thanked me heartily. I gave them some tracts, and told them if it so pleased God I would come back to them and bring them some more books, and try what could be done with some of the poor children to make them better." (50-51)

"Most of the people of Jamaica are emancipated slaves, many of them are old, worn out and degraded. Those who are able to work, have yet many obstacles to contend with, and very little to encourage them; every advantage is taken of their ignorance; the same spirit of cruelty is opposed to them that held them for centuries in bondage; even religious teaching is bartered for their hard earnings, while they are allowed but thirty-three cents a day, and are told if they will not work for that they shall not work at all; an extraordinary price is asked of them for every thing they may wish to purchase, even the Bibles are sold to them at a large advance on the first purchase. Where are their apologists, if they are found wanting in the strict morals that Christians ought to practice? Who kindly says, forgive them when they err. 'Forgive them, this is the bitter fruit of slavery.' Who has integrity sufficient to hold the balance when these poor people are to be weighed? Yet their present state is blissful, compared with slavery." (52-53)

[In speaking with a Jamaican man,] "I told him I was sent for by one of the missionaries [David Ingraham] to help him in his school. Indeed, said he, our color need the instruction." (54)

"I returned [to Kingston] with my mind fully made up what to do. Spent three weeks at the Mico establishment [a private school] and three with my colored friends from America. We [Prince and her friends] thought something ought to be done for the poor girls that were destitute; they consulted with their friends, called a meeting, and formed a society of forty; each agreed to pay three dollars a year and collect, and provide a house, while I came back to America to raise the money for all needful articles for the school. Here [in summer 1841] I met Mr. Ingraham for the first time [since Prince's arrival in Jamaica]; he had come from the mountains, and his health had rapidly declined. Wishing to get his family home before the Lord took him away, he embarked for Baltimore in the Orb [name of the ship], and I sailed for Philadelphia, July 20th, 1841. . . . [After landing in Philadelphia,] I started for New York; arrived safely, and staid with an old friend; ascertained that Mr. Ingraham's family were at Newark, at Theodore Wells' [sic, Weld's]. He [Ingraham] died four days after his arrival. I was invited to Mrs. Ingraham's, (his cousin's widow) to spend a week. There I met with much encouragement to labor in the cause. Missionaries were coming and going, and all seemed to be interested in my object [of establishing a girls' school in Jamaica]." (54-56)

"In the year 1838, general freedom throughout the British Islands gave the death blow to the power of the master, and mothers received with joy their emancipated children; they no longer looked the picture of despair, fearing to see their mulatto son or daughter beating or abusing their younger brothers and sisters of a darker skin. On this occasion there was an outrage committed by those who were in power. What little the poor colored people had gathered during their four years of freedom, was destroyed by violence; their fences were broken down, and their houses and hogs were taken from them." (58)

[After spending time in America raising money for her school and then returning to Jamaica in May 1842,] "it seemed useless to attempt to establish a Manual Labor School [for Jamaican girls], as the government was so unsettled that I could not be protected. Some of my former friends were gone as teachers to Africa, and some to other parts of the island. I called on the American Consul to consult with him, he said that although such a school was much wanted, yet every thing seemed so unsettled that I had no courage to proceed. I told him there was so much excitement that I wished to leave the island as soon as he could find me a passage, it seemed useless to spend my time there." (60)

While waiting for passage back to America, some of the Jamaicans "started to plunder me; but I detected their design, and was on my guard. . . . A more skillful plan than this, Satan never designed, but the power of God was above it. It is not surprising that this [Jamaican] people are full of deceit and lies, this is the fruits of slavery, it makes master and slaves knaves. It is the rule where slavery exists to swell the church with numbers, and hold out such doctrines as, *obedience to tyrants*, is a duty to God." (62)

An old Jamaican woman spoke to Prince, saying: "'in the time of slavery; then God spoke very loud to *Bucker* (the white people,) to let us go. Thank God, ever since that they give us up, we go pray, and we have it not so bad like as before.' I would recommend this poor woman's remark to the fair sons and daughters of America, the land of the pilgrims. 'Then God spoke very loud.' May these words be engraved on the post of every door in this land of New England. God speaks very loud, and while his judgments are on the earth, may the inhabitants learn righteousness!" (66-67)

"There are many places of worship of various denominations, namely, Church of England, and of Scotland, Wesleyan, the Baptist, and Roman Catholics, besides a Jewish Synagogue. These all differ from what I have seen in New England, and from those I have seen elsewhere. The Baptist hold what they call class-meetings. They have men and women deacons and deaconesses in these churches; these hold separate class-meetings; some of these can read, and some cannot. Such are the persons who hold the office of judges, and go round and urge the people to come to the class, and after they come in twice or three times, they are considered candidates for baptism. Some pay fifty cents, and some more, for being baptized; they receive a ticket as a passport into the church, paying one mark a quarter, or more, and some less, but nothing short of ten pence, that is, two English shillings a year. They must attend their class once a week, and pay three pence a week, total twelve

English shillings a year, besides the sums they pay once a month at communion, after service in the morning. On these occasions the minister retires, and the deacons examine the people, to ascertain if each one has bought a ticket; if not, they cannot commune; after this the minister returns, and performs the ceremony, then they give their money and depart. The churches are very large, holding from four to six thousand; many bring wood and other presents to their class-leaders, as a token of their attachment; where there are so many communicants, these presents and the money exacted, greatly enrich these establishments. Communicants are so ignorant of the ordinance, that they join the church merely to have a decent burial; for if they are not members, none will follow them to the grave, and no prayers will be said over them; these are borne through the streets by four men, the coffin a rough box; not so if they are church members; as soon as the news is spread that one is dying, all the class, with their leader, will assemble at the place, and join in singing hymns; this, they say, is to help the spirit up to glory; this exercise sometimes continues all night, in so loud a strain, that it is seldom that any of the people in the neighborhood are lost in sleep." (72-74)

While the ship that Prince was taking back to America was docked near New Orleans, she saw a group of enslaved people on the shore, and Prince "asked them [a group of White sailors] who made them Lord over God's inheritance. . . . Soon the [Black] washer-woman came with my [clean] clothes; they [the White sailors] spoke to her as if she had been a dog. I looked at them with as much astonishment as if I had never heard of such a thing. I asked them if they believed there was a God. 'Of course we do,' they replied. 'Then why not obey him?' 'We do.' 'You do not; permit me to say there is a God, and a just one, that will bring you all to account.' . . . 'I should think you would be concerned about yourself.' 'I am sure,' I replied, 'the Lord will take of me; you cannot harm me.'" (77-78)

"October 19th, 1842, arrived at New York, and thankful was I to set my feet on land. . . . I went at once to those who professed to be friends, but found myself mistaken. I hardly knew what was best. I had put up at Mrs. Rawes'; she did all she could to raise the twenty-five dollars that I must pay before I could take my baggage from the vessel. This seemed hard to obtain . . . at last I called at the Second Advent office; Mr. Nath'l Southard left his business at once, and took me to Mr. Lewis Tappan, and others; he raised the money, and went with me to the ship after my baggage. . . . At 8 o'clock on Saturday evening, I made out to have my things landed on the wharf; it was very dark, as it rained hard. My kind friend did not leave me until they [Prince's goods] were all safely lodged at my residence." (81-82)

"August 1ˢᵗ, 1843, arrived [back in Boston], poor in health, and poor in purse, having sacrificed both, hoping to benefit my fellow creatures. I trust it was acceptable to God, who in his providence preserved me in perils by land, and perils by sea.

> 'God moves in a mysterious way
> His wonders to perform . . .'" [William Cowper]   (82-83)

"The Lord is my defence, the Holy one of Israel is my Saviour. I'll trust him for strength and defence. What things were gain to me, I counted loss for Christ, for whom I have suffered all things; and do count them nothing, that I may win Christ, and be found in him, not having mine own righteousness, which is of the law, but that which is through the faith of Christ, that which is of God by faith, that I may know him, and the power of his resurrection, and the fellowship of his sufferings, being made conformable unto his death, strengthened with all might, according to his glorious power, unto all patience and long-suffering, with joyfulness, thinking it not strange concerning the fiery trials, as though some strange thing happened; for saith the apostle, it is better if the will of God so be that ye suffer for well doing, than for evil; they think it strange that ye run not with them to the same excess of riot, speaking evil of you. If they do these things in a green tree, what shall be done in a dry!

> 'I hate to walk, I hate to sit
>   With men of vanity and lies;
> The scoffer and the hypocrite
>   Are the abhorrence of my eyes.
> God knows their impious thoughts are vain,
>   And they shall feel his power;
> His wrath shall pierce their souls with pain,
>   In some surprising hour.'" [Isaac Watts] (83-84)

After working with other African Americans, Prince "shared in common the disadvantages and stigma that is heaped upon us, in this our professed

Christian land. . . . In the midst of my afflictions, sometimes I have thought my case like that of Paul's, when cast among wild beats [sic]. 'Had not the Lord been on my side, they would have swallowed me up; but blessed be the Lord who hath not given me a prey to their teeth.'" (84-85)

"God has preserved me through much suffering this past winter. I have passed through another furnace of affliction, and may God's dispensations be sanctified to me." (85)

"Truly the promises of God are given for our encouragement; they are yea and amen, in Christ Jesus; they are a covert from the storm, a shelter from the heat, a sure retreat for the weary and way worn traveller. Many are the trials and temptations to which we are exposed in this vale of tears, but in heaven we shall be free from the bondage of sin. Nothing can enter there to annoy or molest the redeemed ones: the Captain of our salvation was made perfect through suffering . . . and that he might sanctify the people with his own blood, suffered without the gate." (86)

"I have much to be thankful to God for; for the comforts of this life, and the kind friends who have so kindly bestowed their favors upon me, and while they in this life have an abundance, may they have the presence of God; and when the King shall come, may they have their lamps trimmed and burning: then shall he say, 'Come ye blessed of my Father, inherit the kingdom prepared for you from the foundation of the world: for I was an hungered, and ye gave me meat.' (86-87)

"The poorest can do something for the cause of Christ; even a cup of cold water, given with a desire to benefit a fellow creature, will be acceptable to God. May the power of God, and the spirit of Christ rule and reign in all hearts." (87)

"I am a wonder unto many, but the Lord is my strong refuge, and in him will I trust. I shall fear no evil, for thou, O Lord, art ever near to shield and protect thy dependent children. Underneath him is the everlasting arm of mercy; misfortune is never mournful for the soul that accepts it, for such do always see that every cloud is an angel's face; sorrow connects the soul with the invisible.

"O Father, fearful indeed is this world's pilgrimage, when the soul has learned that all its sounds are echoes, all its sights shadows. But lo! a cloud opens, a face serene and hopeful looks forth and saith, 'Be thou as a little child, and thus shalt thou become a seraph, and bow thyself in silent humility and pray, not that afflictions might not visit, but be willing to be purified through fire, and accept it meekly.'" (87-88)

"The Hiding Place"
Amid this world's tumultuous noise
For peace my soul to Jesus flies;
If I've an interest in his grace,
I want no other hiding place.

The world with all its charms is vain,
Its wealth and honors I disdain:
All its extensive aims embrace,
Can ne'er afford a hiding place.

A guilty, sinful heart is mine,
Jesus, unbounded love is thine!
When I behold thy smiling face,
'Tis then I see my hiding place.

To save, if once my Lord engage,
The world may laugh, and Satan rage:
The powers of hell can ne'er erase
My name from God's own hiding place.

I'm in a wilderness below,
Lord, guide me all my journey through
Plainly let me thy footsteps trace,
Which lead to heaven, my hiding place.

Should dangers thick impede my course,
O let my soul sustain no loss;
Help me to run the Christian race,
And enter safe my hiding place.

Then with enlarged powers,
I'll triumph in redeeming love,
Eternal ages will I praise
My Lord for such a hiding place. (89)

LIST OF AUTHORS

Estrelda Y. Alexander, PhD, president of William Joseph Seymour Foundation and Church of God pastor

Esther Chung-Kim, PhD, professor of religious studies at Claremont McKenna College; president, American Society of Church History; ordained in the United Methodist Church

David D. Daniels III, PhD, Henry Winters Luce Professor of Global Christianity at McCormick Theological Seminary, bishop in the Church of God in Christ

Sègbégnon Mathieu Gnonhossou, DMin, PhD, assistant professor of theological studies at Seattle Pacific University; adjunct professor in Benin; ordained in the Free Methodist Church

Diane Leclerc, PhD, professor of historical theology at Northwest Nazarene University and Theological Seminary, ordained in the Church of the Nazarene

Albert G. Miller, PhD, Associate Professor of Religion and African American Studies Emeritus in the department of Religion at Oberlin College and pastor of the House of the Lord Pentecostal Church

Christopher P. Momany, DMin, scholar, author, and researcher who identified David Ingraham's abolitionist journal; United Methodist Pastor

R. Matthew Sigler, PhD, assistant professor of Wesleyan studies and Worship studies at Seattle Pacific University and Seminary; ordained in the United Methodist Church

Douglas M. Strong, PhD, Paul T. Walls Professor of Wesleyan Studies and the History of Christianity at Seattle Pacific University and founding

Dean of Seattle Pacific Seminary; ordained in the United Methodist Church; Director, Dialogue on Race and Faith

Jemar Tisby, PhD, professor of history and public theology and founding director of the Center for Racial Justice, Simmons College

IMAGE CREDITS

Figure 3.2.	Courtesy of Constance Sanders Photography
Figure 4.1.	Dialogue on Race and Faith; photo by Erin Morrow
Figure 4.2.	John Wesley, *A Collection of Hymns, for the Use of the People Called Methodists* (London: John Mason, 1779), cover and 184 / Internet Archive
Figure 5.1.	Dialogue on Race and Faith; map created by Heather McDaniel
Figure 5.2.	Oberlin College Archives
Figure 5.3.	Oberlin College Archives
Figure 6.1.	*The Second Report of the Female Society for Birmingham, West-Bromwich . . . for the Relief of British Negro Slaves* (Birmingham, 1826) / Slavery Images: A Visual Record of the African Slave Trade and Slave Life in the Early African Diaspora
Figure 6.2.	Oberlin College Archives
Figure 7.1.	Dialogue on Race and Faith; map created by Heather McDaniel
Figure 7.2.	Schomburg Center for Research in Black Culture, Manuscripts, Archives and Rare Books Division / The New York Public Library Digital Collections
Figure 8.1.	Oberlin College Archives
Figure 8.2.	Oberlin College Archives
Figure 8.3.	Oberlin College Archives
Figure A.1.	Dialogue on Race and Faith; Adrian College; photo by Erin Morrow
Figure A.2.	David Ingraham, "Capture of the Ulysses—Sufferings of the Slaves," printed on p. 2 of *The Colored American* (April 4, 1840), Charles B. Ray, Editor & Proprietor (New York: New Series Vol. 1, No. 5)

INDEX

Additional resources, primary source materials, and an accompanying documentary film, *Awakening to Justice*, are available on the website: www.awakeningtojustice.com